EDUCATION 3-5

Marion Dowling was formerly Senior Primary Adviser for Dorset, and has contributed to early childhood education in-service courses in many parts of Britain and overseas. In the course of her career she has been a primary teacher, a nursery headteacher, and an advisory headteacher in Suffolk. As well as publishing articles in professional journals, she is the author of *The Modern Nursery* (1974, Longman) and *Early Projects* (1978, Longman), and is co-author of *Teaching 3–9 Year Olds* (1984, Ward Lock) and *Talking Together Language Materials* (1986, Nottingham Education Supplies).

EDUCATION 3–5
SECOND EDITION

MARION DOWLING

P·C·P
Paul Chapman
Publishing Ltd

To Charlotte, in admiration for the way she survived and succeeded in that first year of teaching.

Copyright © 1992 Marion Dowling

First published 1992

Paul Chapman Publishing Ltd
144 Liverpool Road
London
N1 1LA

British Library Cataloguing in Publication Data

Dowling, Marion
    Education 3-5. – 2nd ed
    I. Title
    372.21

    ISBN 1 85396 166 3

Typeset by Best-set Typesetter Ltd., Hong Kong
Printed in Great Britain by St Edmundsbury Press, and
bound by W. H. Ware, Clevedon

CONTENTS

PREFACE AND ACKNOWLEDGEMENTS

I have enjoyed revising this book, a task I also found both worrying and reassuring. The pleasure is gained in writing for people engaged in the job of educating and caring for young children: as ever it is written in the acknowledgement of all their hard work. I hope the additional information, such as that offered on provision for 4-year-olds and children with special educational needs, is helpful.

The pressures and anxieties experienced by nursery and reception teachers as a result of recent changes do cause concern. No really sound curriculum development can materialize unless the right emotional climate is created. Some teachers of young children have felt constrained to alter their practice, although not legally required to do so; others in nurseries have felt their future existence threatened.

Some uncertainties about the future remain but other anxieties are, it is hoped, subsiding, as practitioners begin to see some benefits of the new era. I hope they will share my conviction that the principles supporting young children learning remain constant. Although I have devised new curriculum headings and suggested more systematic planning and assessment, the essential messages about children learning are unaltered. The effect of these messages on action with children is as ever dependent on the quality of the adults working with them.

Marion Dowling
Dorset, 1991

INTRODUCTION

The last two decades have been a choppy voyage for the development of early-years education. The Seventies was a time of great promise that never came to fruition. The white paper of 1972, *A Framework for Expansion*,[1] promised the availability of nursery education for all those children whose parents wished them to benefit from it. This never materialized, and it was quickly followed by a period of contraction in which provision for the non-statutory sector proved to be particularly vulnerable. Some LEAs closed down their nurseries while others built units but were unable to equip and staff them. In 1976 capital expenditure for nursery education stood at £46 million; by 1982 it had fallen to less than £35 million. In 1989, part-time nursery places in England were available to a mere 24 per cent of the population – a stark contrast to the Plowden committee's estimation in 1967 that provision would be required for 90 per cent of 4-year-old and 50 per cent of 3-year-old children.[2]

However, this gloomy picture must be set in perspective. Some expansion did take place and is continuing, and some aspects of work with young children were introduced in the Seventies and (in gathering momentum) have made the Eighties and early Nineties a time when many more people are aware of the work involved with the under-5s.

Planned expansion had stimulated an interest in research related to pre-school education, and a range of work was supported by grants. Earlier studies were short term, specific and planned towards informing policy. They included some consideration of parental involvement, and a study of how children learn through play.[3,4] As the economic climate changed, some research focused on what could be achieved in different types of pre-school setting, including some low-cost provision.[5,6]

The promise of pre-school expansion had been in a context of unrealistic expectation. There was the belief that this non-statutory provision could prevent educational failure, particularly for the most disadvantaged groups. While it is not surprising that research failed to confirm this, some studies have provided powerful support for the essential nature of early-years intervention. John Brierley's work on the development of the brain in the young child is particularly impressive in stressing the importance of an early favourable environment.[7]

Two long-term studies revealed further that early education and care offer children identifiable long-term benefits. The High Scope pre-school curriculum was started in Ypsilanti, Michigan, in 1960, when people in the USA were beginning to think seriously about how to help 'disadvantaged children'. David Weikart, the main instigator, in a long-term study of this project, claims that the High Scope methodology is sound in terms of it offering pre-school gains. He argues that money invested in a child's earliest education can show returns for society in terms of less expenditure on late remedial education, less expense in containing delinquent behaviour and increased employment prospects for the participants.[8]

This US study is supported by more modest claims from the Bristol longitudinal study of a cohort of 1,400 children born in one week in April 1970. Seventy per cent of the children (from a range of social backgrounds) experienced at least three months in a playgroup, nursery school or day nursery. At the age of 5, and again at 10, the children's performance in reading, maths and general intelligence tests compared favourably with the 30 per cent of the group who had not been involved in certain pre-school experiences.[9]

A series of research during the past twenty years now reveals the young child as being much more intellectually able than was previously thought. Chris Athey's work (1990) is particularly helpful in demonstrating children's ways of thinking and showing how this affects what they absorb from curriculum content.[10]

Finally, research studies have highlighted how much young children learn from other people in a social context, rather than through their own self-initiated activity. The adult is seen as a powerful aid to this learning, through Bruner's description of his or her role as 'scaffolder'. This involves providing necessary support to enable the child to take on new learning and become confident, at which point the support is reduced and withdrawn.[11]

Central government has also played its part in highlighting early-years issues, through the production of two major parliamentary select committee reports on primary education and the under-5s[12,13] – one initiating a parliamentary working party to consider specific recommendations[13] – and two statutes: the Education Reform Act and the Children Act[14,15] (these initiatives will be referred to later in the book). These reports contain some clear messages for LEAs about the provision and curriculum for under-5s, and the Education Reform Act 1988 (ERA), while not legislating for this age-group, directs attention to the precursors of learning and programmes of study necessary for later National Curriculum work. The Children Act has only recently been implemented; its implications for practice are still unclear and there is wide scope for discretion in interpretation. However, the aim has been to produce one legal and consistent statement about the care and protection of children, with emphasis on the child's needs. It places a particular responsibility on voluntary and statutory agencies to rethink their practices and to co-ordinate initiatives.

Partly as a response to some of these developments, many LEAs have produced documents reflecting their philosophies and practices for under-5s. There are now many publications that describe curriculum and organization arrangements, and methods of assessing learning, for young children. Fifteen years ago such documents were rare, but there is now a good archive of experience that, if disseminated, can provide a foundation for reflection and further debate.

The current picture of provision, though patchy, is one of growth. Supported by research findings and responding to recommendations from major reports, LEAs are cautiously developing some early-education programmes through the help they offer to the voluntary sector as well as by means of State provision. Exploratory courses have developed, with the emphasis on multi-professional co-ordination and training for those working with under-5s. In some areas the High Scope approach is being piloted and evaluated; other authorities are supporting low-cost provision using a combination of professional and parental skills. Some initiatives have developed largely for pragmatic reasons. The NFER survey of admission procedures[16] reported a growing number of LEAs admitting children to school once a year rather than termly. This involves accommodating children as young as 4 years and 1 month – in a reception class often not adequately equipped or staffed for this age-group. This pattern of admission has arisen partly because of falling roles in the 1980s, the consequent availability of infant classrooms and parents' positive responses to having a full-time placement for their child. Despite the select committee enquiry recommending that such policies should be curtailed unless properly resourced,[13] some schools will be tempted to maintain or even introduce early admission in the competitive climate of local financial management. The most recent expansion of provision has been through the growth of workplace nurseries. Some of these are being established according to rigorous criteria and as a result of collaboration between industry and education authorities. Despite this, workplace nurseries are being established because of the demand by women to return to employment rather than as part of a concerted effort to provide the best-quality care and education for the child.

Thus the quality of nursery provision varies, and certainly much of it is thinly resourced. In the main the developments described reflect a heightening awareness of the value of early care and education and increased expertise in child development and ways of learning, rather than adequate funding to support what is urgently required.

Although more children are now offered a pre-school placement, the type of place offered varies widely. At 4, a child may attend a reception class in a main school, a nursery school or class, or a combined family or nursery centre. The child may have a place in an industrial, private, day nursery, or he or she may go to a playgroup or a private school, or be placed with a childminder. These provisions have their own distinct purposes and functions, and are financed, staffed and organized differently. Premises vary tremendously from a community-hall playgroup to institutions (ancient and modern) built and maintained by education and social-services departments. Purpose-built, well-equipped buildings are helpful, but they are not the heart of nursery education. The essential resources are skilful and sensitive adults working to provide for the children. It is not productive to put forward a polarized view for either voluntary or State provision. At present we need to maintain all we have, and to ensure that it is as good as possible.

This book aims to make a statement about quality education and care for children ages 3–5. The justification for any educational resources being offered to a child under 5 is to facilitate the child's cognitive development. This can be effective only if intellectual growth is considered together with the total development of the child and the very close links each child has with his or her family. Many types of provision pay attention to the child's learning processes, but this may be in a context where priority is placed more on adult education and the quality of parenting, as in many playgroups; or on offering the child from a less favoured home a stable daily environment, as in day nurseries. In an educational establishment, whether nursery class, school or family centre, the ideologies and training of staff focus on the child learning. This demands a sound knowledge of child development and early childhood curriculum on the part of the adult, with acknowledgement of the inter-dependence of any learning and development at this stage. In educational provision for young children, the professional nursery teacher is essential. He or she is even more important if we consider the young child with special needs. For these children, a measure of early and appropriate intervention can assist in preventing educational failure and avoiding the need for expensive and less effective remedies at a later stage.

However, although state nursery classes and schools are in a good position to meet the needs of young children, other settings do have a very important contribution to make.

The Rumbold Report[17] urged all adults working with young children to recognize the significance of their educational role. This can be strengthened by sharing understandings of quality education and the practices that nurture development.

In this book I hope to clarify and support the best of these educational practices. What I describe as nursery practice and provision will, I hope, be relevant in other settings for young children. I refer also to the 'nursery teacher' in the knowledge that many other adults, particularly nursery assistants, are involved in these practices. However, the particular challenge of accommodating 4-year-olds in reception classes is acknowledged and some of the issues particular to this group are discussed separately (see Chapter 5).

The term 'pre-school child' is convenient but negative, and not in any way descriptive of the exciting stages of development that occur during these years. References to 'rising-5' and 'under-5' are similarly unhelpful and can be positively insulting if we seriously consider the capabilities and needs of a 3- or 4-year-old. Accepting a need for shorthand, however, the child from 3 to 5 is referred to from now on as 'the young child' and those under 3 are termed 'toddlers'.

This book is being revised at a critical time. Nursery education is being affected by ERA in a particular way. Because it is non-statutory it is vulnerable and in some cases marginalized. Conjecture about the effects of local financial management is adding to insecurities. Conversely, the National Curriculum must also be regarded as a strong ally in promoting a good nursery foundation to allow children access to the statutory programmes of study. In so doing it supports continuity of experience when young children transfer to mainstream infant classes. In the best possible circumstances nurseries, while not being constrained by the requirements of the National Curriculum, could use the statutory framework as a guide to developing their own programmes of study.

Given what is known about child development and early education, there is an overriding case for quality provision for young children. The teacher's job is complex and demanding. Teachers need help in clarifying their ideologies, and support with the practicalities of the work. Consideration of nursery practice includes the care and pedagogy we offer to young children, how we offer them and how we can check that we are being successful in our practices.

REFERENCES

1. DES (1972) *Education: A Framework for Expansion*, HMSO, London.
2. Central Advisory Committee for Education (1967) *Children and Their Primary Schools* (the Plowden Report), HMSO, London.
3. DES (1975) *Preschool Education and Care: Some Topics Requiring Research or Development Projects*, HMSO, London.
4. DES (1975) op. cit. (note 3).
5. E. Ferri, D. Birchell, V. Gingell and C. Gipps (1981) *Combined Nursery Centres: A New Approach to Education and Day Care* (NCB series), Macmillan, London.
6. J. Bruner (1980) *Under Five in Britain* (Oxford Preschool Research Project), Grant McIntyre, London.
7. J. Brierley (1984) *A Human Birthright: Giving the Young Brain a Chance*, British Association for Early Childhood Education, London.
8. C. Breedlove and J. Schweinhart (1982) *The Cost Effectiveness of High-Quality Early Childhood Programs*, High Scope Educational Research Foundation, Ypsilanti, Mich. (report prepared for the 1982 US Southern Governors' Conference).
9. A. F. Osborn and J. E. Milbank (1985) *The Association of Preschool Educational Experiences with Subsequent Ability, Attainment and Behaviour*, University of Bristol Department of Child Health, Bristol (report to the DES).
10. C. Athey (1990) *Extending Thought in Young Children: A Parent–Teacher Partnership*, Paul Chapman Publishing, London.
11. J. Bruner (1983) *Child's Talk: Learning to Use Language*, Oxford University Press.
12. House of Commons Education, Science and Arts Committee (1986) *Achievement in Primary Schools: Third Report, Vol. 1*, HMSO, London.
13. House of Commons Education, Science and Arts Committee (1988) *Educational Provision for the Under Fives*, HMSO, London.
14. DES (1989) *Education Reform Act*, HMSO, London.
15. Department of Health (1989) *The Children Act*, HMSO, London.
16. C. Sharp (1986) Local education authority admission policies and practices, in *Four Year Olds in School; Policy and Practice*, NFER, Slough.
17. DES (1990) *Starting with Quality*. The report of the committee of inquiry into the quality of educational experience offered to 3 and 4 year olds, para 5, HMSO, London.

1

THE CONTEXT OF NURSERY WORK

Throughout this book, constant reference is made to different aspects of children's development, together with suggestions as to how best to foster this development. The danger of such an approach is that, by separating these aspects, the interrelationship of growth, development and learning tends to be forgotten. Let us therefore start with a pen portrait of the whole child.

Sean is 4 years old. He can play sociably with other children on most occasions, although sometimes he finds it difficult to share and take his turn in play activities. He relates well to other adults but at times of stress or uncertainty clings to his mum. Sean is able to feed, wash and dress himself but has difficulty doing up his shirt buttons and cannot yet tie his shoelaces. He is now able to run, skip and hop and is starting to keep time to music. Sean particularly enjoys playing outside and engaging in lively pretend play with others. He also likes to paint and make models; however, although these activities are often tackled with vigour initially, Sean soon tires of them. His paintings are becoming recognizable but mainly consist of an enclosed core with various radials sticking out to represent himself or his mum. Sean finds life full and interesting. He laughs and talks a lot both to himself and to his friends. His use of language includes suggesting ideas for play, describing his past experiences and giving a running commentary on his own activities. When talking Sean often pauses as if searching for a word to describe his feelings or thoughts. When things go wrong and friends cross him, Sean's language deserts him and he is likely to punch and kick to maintain his rights.

Sean or his equivalent is familiar to every nursery teacher. The teacher's task is to ensure that Sean's time in the nursery is worth while. What is worth while is in itself open to debate, but the statement of the aims of education found in the Warnock Report is surely very acceptable, namely 'first, to enlarge a child's knowledge, experiences and imaginative under-standing, and thus his awareness of moral values and capacity for enjoy-ment; and secondly, to enable him to enter the world after formal education is over as an active participant in society and a responsible contributor to it'.[1]

To start to achieve these aims for Sean and other children in the nursery, the teacher must plan a curriculum. Sean's curriculum needs to take account of his abilities, interests and weaknesses. Any offered curriculum includes the environmental setting – the experiences and messages children receive in school. Yet what the teacher believes he or she is offering may not be what is being received by the child. The received curriculum depends entirely on what children take up and this in turn depends on how the curriculum is offered.

Effective curriculum planning involves (1) a knowledge of how young children develop and learn most effectively; (2) familiarity with the materials, activities and methods that promote different types of devel-opment and learning; and (3) the resources available in terms of time, staff numbers, and expertise, accommodation and equipment. Although this planning will affect what happens in the nursery, the child's learning has already started in the home and will continue after nursery hours. The power of home influences and the way in which parents can be a key resource for their children deserve careful study. National Curriculum prescripts will also partly determine what the child will be learning at 5 years onwards, and any nursery curriculum should acknowledge this.

These aspects are considered in subsequent chapters. However, apart from the immediate factors to consider, such as the children's needs and the resources available to support learning, there are more general influences in today's society. We need to consider these to gain some picture of the complex environment in which many young families are living.

YOUNG FAMILIES

The younger the child, the more inextricably he or she is involved with his or her family. Thus some consideration of current family structures is relevant. The conventional family unit consisting of a married man who is working with a wife at home and two dependent children accounts for a mere 5 per cent of households in Britain today. The range of family patterns varies tremendously. While marriage remains popular, the divorce rate is well known. The 1985 reported rate of divorce was double that reported in 1971.[2] Over 60 per cent of divorces involve children under 16. Teenage marriages are particularly vulnerable. Young couples in late adolescence enter into a partnership with unrealistic expectations, and the problems of sharing a life together can be greatly aggravated by the arrival of a baby; often there are not the resources to deal with a demanding young child.

Young children may also come from single-parent families, from a partnership where parents are cohabiting or from step-families where one parent has remarried. Although most children under 4 years still live with two natural parents, it may be assumed that marital disharmony exists in many of these households before the break-up of the partnership.[3]

The position of women is seen to have changed. Widening educational, social and work opportunities have encouraged them to expect the same things in life as men. Potentially they have a bewildering number of choices. Some groups urge them to gain satisfaction from child rearing and the home; others urge them to take up the opportunities offered by the demand for an increased female workforce and to expect shared parenting from their partners. However, despite some successful examples of role reversal and shared upbringing of children, this last expectation is still not common practice. Studies indicate that, although fathers' involvement with their families has increased, the majority still place their work first and families second.[4] Even women who work full time still see their families as their first responsibility.

Unemployment figures continue to fluctuate in different parts of the country but it remains widespread with the current recession. Workers in low-paid, unskilled manual jobs are in particular danger of losing their jobs and remaining unemployed for long periods. Children of all ages are likely to be affected by their parents' loss of income and self-esteem. The youngest children, being at home more of the time, will be especially exposed to some of the associated effects, such as an increase in family violence.

Even without unemployment, there is a vast inequality between standards of living. There is still no minimum wage. In 1982 the relative earnings of the lowest-paid men were lower than at any time during the 1970s.[5] Child poverty has also increased. In 1971, 22 per cent of the poorest households contained children. In 1985 this proportion had risen to 30 per cent.[6]

Many young families in both urban and rural areas live in inadequate, overcrowded housing with little play space. The National Children's Bureau Child Development Study[7] found that by the age of 16 one in five children had lived in a home that lacked the basic amenities of bathroom, hot-water supply and indoor lavatory. That report was in 1976. Today the urgent problem for many is lack of a home. The numbers of homeless people to be recorded for 1991 is expected to exceed 480,000.[8] By law, councils have to find accommodation for families with children but much of this is bed-and-breakfast provision in cheap hotels.

Some young families faced with a combination of these problems are clearly under stress and less well placed to be caring and responsible parents. One indicator of stress comes from the Samaritans. The number of new clients registered with the Samaritans rose from 90,000 in 1971 to just under 400,000 in 1985. The largest single group of clients were women aged 25–39.[9]

One issue of particular concern that can affect any family is that of child abuse. This problem is not new but, increasingly, adults have been willing to talk about childhood experiences and there is now greater awareness of the damage and distress that can be caused to young children. The NSPCC records for 1990 show a 35-per-cent increase in the number of children added to child protection registers.[10] Some children will be referred for nursery placements already having their names on this register. Nursery teachers not only have the responsibility to monitor children in this category but also to be alert for any signs indicating emotional, physical or sexual abuse in all children. They should be aware of significant factors relating to the problem. Sexual offenders, for instance, are likely to move into positions and professions that put them into contact with children. They may also be in a more immediate relationship, as the majority of offences are committed by someone known to the child within the circle of family and friends. Second, because child molesters are good at hiding their behaviour and can persuade children to keep silent, the pattern of abuse can be long term. Finally, even after detection and treatment, the majority of offenders will repeat their behaviour.[11]

Teachers do have an important role to play in preventing child abuse because of their regular contact with children over a period of time. Through sensitive and trusting relationships they can help children to be open and confident from the earliest age in preventing unwanted approaches. The decision about when and how to take action is inevitably difficult and stressful, particularly when bound up with intimate family relationships. Links with other agencies are a very necessary support in this area of work.

The way in which young children spend their time at home will have a powerful effect on their learning and development. Tizard and Hughes see the environment of very ordinary homes as a rich source of stimulus. They point out that children can be interested and involved in all aspects of home life irrespective of social class.[12] The television is dominant in many young children's lives. An NFER study in 1986 reported that it was the one single activity on which children under 5 spent the most time.[13] Gammage reports that Canadian and British children observed in his studies watched television for between 20 and 25 hours a week.[14] As with other experiences, children will actively process their viewing in order to make sense of it. Winick and Winick comment that a 'young viewer can relate only to what his/her development has made it possible to under-stand'.[15] However, we also know that the young brain is very impression-able and there are concerns about the effects of viewing sex and violence on young children's behaviour. One study indicates that stylistic aggression can have some positive effects on children's imaginative play. However, it also stresses that many young children have difficulty in distinguishing between fact and fantasy.[16] Television is an effective tool for learning and should be acknowledged in the nursery. However, teachers witness anxious and frightened behaviour from children who are exposed to indiscriminate viewing.

PARENTAL INVOLVEMENT

A major issue continuing to affect teachers, parents and children is the notion of parental involvement. Parents now have increased represen-tation on governing bodies and their choice of mainstream school is now facilitated through open enrolment. The National Curriculum prescripts also require that parents receive more information about their child's learning and progress. All these developments will impinge indirectly or directly on the nursery sector. For instance, HMI state clearly that the assessment legislation may make demands on the nursery curriculum and the way in which it is communicated to parents:

> Given that parents will be informed of the progress expected of children within the levels and attainment targets of the National Curriculum, it is understand-able that they will wish to see their children make a good start, particularly with aspects of reading, writing and mathematics. Parents will certainly not

wish to see their children held back if they think them capable of tackling more challenging work than the teaching and provision for under-fives allows.[17]

Although the parents' role in education has received only partial recognition over the years, it was considered an integral part of nursery provision as viewed by Margaret McMillan when she opened her nursery school in Deptford in 1911. She claimed that the nursery school, although available to all children, should be the special right of working-class parents:

> And the working class mother, what of her nursery? To begin with it would seem much more important to make her sovereign, if not ruler of this new domain, rather than to assume at once that she can never be anything but an outsider. . . . The existing nursery schools are not yet controlled by the mothers of the children who attend them. But already parents' committees are being formed.
> Already, too, it is clear to many that the nurseries must be built as an annexe to homes and that as far as possible the homes should open on to these child gardens so as to make the frequent visits and constant oversight of mothers a possibility.[18]

Margaret McMillan speaking today would be at the forefront of current thinking. Many of her plans were at the time too advanced to be considered, and even today parental involvement is variously interpreted and practised. Later in this book we examine the findings of recent research studies, with suggestions as to how a nursery can develop profitable relationships with parents that will be beneficial to all concerned.

The nursery teacher today works in a climate that encourages parents to become more informed about and active in their child's education. The media provide a range of books, magazines and radio and television programmes specifically for young parents. The pre-school playgroup movement must be admired for its energy and enthusiasm. Many parents concerned with this movement have learnt a great deal about their young child's development and how they can promote it. Other parents may have read widely and taken every opportunity to make the task of parenting enjoyable and positive. These parents will assist their child's confidence and provide an interested and enriched home environment, which every teacher knows is the right background to enable children to take advantage of a nursery experience.

Other parents are interested in their child's early education but may be misinformed. Tizard's two-year intervention study, which tried out different ways of involving parents in nursery classes and schools, revealed that there are large gaps in some parents' understanding. Despite intensive efforts from nursery teachers, many parents remained unclear about the purposes of nursery education.[19]

A further group of parents may not see the relevance of their role to their child's development. Van der Eyken's study of Home Start in Leicester revealed an approach to working with isolated, depressed and hard-to-reach families.[20] The criteria for the success of this scheme are the increased confidence of the parent, reduction in family stress and reduction in children at risk, rather than any consideration of early childhood education programmes. Admittedly these three groupings are crude – parents are individual and any programme of involvement must consider individual needs and attitudes. However, it is a good starting-point to consider the concluding comments in the DES study of children's home lives:

> We cannot emphasize strongly enough the love, pride and interest that all the parents in the sample showed towards their children. Nursery staff have a unique opportunity to establish relations with parents at the initial stages of a child's school career, to capitalize on this goodwill and boost the parents' own sense of responsibility and confidence in their ability to contribute to their own children's education.[21]

DIFFERENT GROUPS

Although the nursery has always accommodated a wide range of children, the need for sensitive awareness of differences and appropriate action has been a strong and recurring theme in recent years.

The increasing concern over early identification and support for children with special educational needs (SEN) was heightened with the Warnock Committee's recommendations[22] and subsquently the Education Act 1981. The concept of SEN was introduced that embraced those children with mild learning difficulties or with minor emotional or behavioural disorders, as well as those with more obvious handicaps. Emphasis was given to integrating these children rather than providing special schooling. Many nurseries have traditionally accommodated children with both learning and physical disability. However, the broader view of disability has alerted teachers to the need for early assessment and carefully devised learning programmes to meet particular needs.

Attention to gender issues has also meant a careful appraisal of the nursery curriculum. If we believe that early learning experiences can and do affect subsequent achievement and the development of attitudes in later life, it is essential that all children are offered – as far as possible – equal learning opportunities, and that former rigid role expectations are reassessed more broadly. The nursery teacher has a special responsibility to ensure that these learning experiences are not affected by difference. The Equal Opportunities Commission suggests that 'stereotyping can blind a teacher or a parent to the individual talent and potential of a girl or boy, and by restricting the expectations of the adult, stereotyping can severely restrict the aspirations of children to their detriment in adult life'.[23]

Children from ethnic-minority backgrounds constitute a further vulnerable group. There are over three million immigrants and their descendants in Britain today. While some of these people have been assimilated, others have remained culturally distinct. The Swann Report on minority groups made a strong bid for a pluralistic approach to society – for all to acknowledge the diversity of race, colour and creed that exists in many parts of the country but to appreciate the contributions each distinct group can offer.[24] Racial tensions nevertheless exist, and young children who live with prejudice will learn through imitation. Studies have indicated that attitudes are forming by the age of 3. Thus, the onus is on any educator of young children to provide a model of tolerance based on interest in and understanding of differences in people. In areas that are not yet multi-ethnic in composition, the need is perhaps even greater to prepare children in our nurseries for future living in a pluralistic society.

Special educational needs, gender and race are considered in more detail later. They are central matters any nursery teacher must address when planning a child's education and, as such, they have implications for whole-staff professional development.

A COHERENT AND CO-ORDINATED SERVICE

Because there has been no statutory obligation on local authorities to provide pre-school services, provision for under-5s has developed in a piecemeal and uncoordinated way. Parents with a young child have traditionally had to find their way through a system in which different departments offer different services and benefits according to the part of the country in which they live. In a review of these services by the Under Fives Unit of the National Children's Bureau in 1986, four main strands of provision were identified:

[One] concerned with the developmental needs of children and based on principles of free and universally available service; one more interventionist in nature, based on a rigorous selection process, and concerned with the ability of parents to cope with the upbringing of their children; one responding to parents' requirements for day care; and one emanating from the voluntary sector and based on principles of self-help and parent involvement.[25]

As previously indicated, provision in local authorities varies greatly both in quantity and quality. Developments have generally occurred in response to political and economic trends rather than a carefully considered policy for young children. However, the under-5s survey revealed a number of interesting local initiatives that could be considered as models of practice. The Mosborough Townships Under Fives Service in Sheffield is one example. This is jointly run by the education department and social services. Children aged 3 and over have nursery provision with extended hours in units attached to infant schools, while those under 3 have home-based care with salaried childminders recruited and trained by social services.[26] Other examples of extended and co-ordinated work are discussed in Chapter 2.

Co-ordination of services for under-5s is not considered to be a substitute for increased provision, but common sense dictates that the best use should be made of the resources available. In a report resulting from a two-year research project on co-ordination jointly commissioned by the DES and DHSS, Bradley viewed it as 'involving a reappraisal of the attitudes of personnel towards one another, seeking jointly to perceive the goals of service in relation to the needs of children and their families while accepting the existence of each type of provision as a separate entity'.[27]

The 1986 survey reflected clear interest and some action from local authorities in rethinking their provision for young families, but Pugh considered that developments would be limited while departments held on to vested interests and lacked a shared sense of purpose. She suggested that 'the challenge now is for central government to provide an overall framework within which services can be developed flexibly at local level. For this to carry any weight it may require the establishment of a senior policy-making body'.[28] This challenge has been reinforced by recent legislation and a report of the committee of inquiry considering the quality of education for the under-5s.

The law about caring for and protecting children has been piecemeal and inconsistent. The Children Act, implemented in full in 1991, is a comprehensive piece of legislation, designed to strike a new balance between family autonomy and child protection.[29] The Act requires education and social services departments to work closely together regarding young children, particularly in the following ways:

- *Identification and provision for children in need*   Local authorities are required to identify children who are physically disabled – unlikely to achieve or maintain a reasonable standard of health or development. They must provide day care for these children and support links with their families.
- *Review of provision for children in need*   Local authorities must work with their education departments to review this provision within one year, together with a review of all training provided for those who offer day care. These reviews should have representation from health authorities and voluntary bodies and the subsequent report should be published widely. A triennial review must take place with a published report.
- *Registration and monitoring of all provision*   Social services departments are required to register and approve all provision for young children including playgroups and childminders. Thereafter providers must be inspected annually and social services may call on the assistance of local education advisers or inspectors with regard to the educational aspect of this work.

The Act is based on the principle that children are best looked after within the family, and it introduces the notion of 'parental responsibility'. This stresses the duties of the person or authority who also assumes the rights of a parent. Unnecessary intervention into family life is to be discouraged. However, the above requirements indicate that, when the local authority does become involved, there is an expectation that departments work closely together at all levels, have shared aims and open access to each other's information.

The Report of the Committee of Inquiry on the Under Fives[30] embraces the tenets of the Children Act, describing it as a 'major landmark in the development of services for children'. Although the report makes a bid for more provision for young children, it focuses on its terms of reference: namely, to consider the quality of educational experiences for 3- and 4-year-olds. Within this brief the need for co-ordination features strongly. The report highlights factors that will facilitate a more coherent approach and these strengthen the points made in the under-5s unit's discussion paper. Factors include the need for a clear, agreed policy and departmental structures that support provision, delegated policy-making and executive powers for under-5s committees, clarity of roles and responsibilites, clear means of involving health authorities and voluntary bodies and support from elected members and chief officers. The report also makes the important point that

Better co-ordination does not necessarily require unified services: the purpose may be served by a network of facilities linked through common admissions or close working relationships. What is important – and what the provisions of the [Children] Act should help to secure – is that the pattern of co-ordination should take full account of local needs and opportunities and should be supported by local policies and management structures.[31]

Both the Children Act and the committee of inquiry report are important milestones in the move towards interdisciplinary approaches for young children. However the issue is a longstanding one and practitioners will doubtless be cautious in expecting positive outcomes in terms of policy. Both the Act and the report have resource implications, and the report argues for a national framework from central government to provide the setting for local developments. In the meantime the recommendations for local action are sound. Practitioners are urged to consider

- how to establish or improve links between the practitioner's own organisation and other local services for the under fives.
- whether there is scope for co-ordinating with other services aspects such as admissions policies, liaison with families, assessment and record-keeping arrangements.
- suggesting new approaches to those responsible for existing arrangements which impede collaboration.[32]

THE EDUCATIONAL CLIMATE

Despite the initiatives listed in the introduction that have served to bring nursery education into a more central position, most have not supported the sector in a practical or financial sense. Moreover, current educational measures, in applying to the statutory sector, place the nursery phase in an ambivalent position.

Nursery teachers are not bound by the National Curriculum but are rightly aware that their work with young children must be linked in to the statutory prescripts in the interests of continuity. Some nursery teachers, however, have not been included in LEA National Curriculum INSET programmes. Others feel ill equipped to provide a comprehensive programme that will offer appropriate experiences for 3- and 4-year-olds in all core and foundation subjects, which will hold them in good stead for statutory schooling. All nursery staff, although not required to respond to the Education Reform Act 1988 (ERA) have been aware of the need to keep abreast of new developments and have felt the pressures of the pace of change.

Where nurseries have their own governing bodies they share the same

challenges as mainstream schools in working with governors in partnership – empowering them to take on their central role in the school and
then duly respecting the powers and responsibilities held. This is an
onerous task for any headteacher but a successful outcome should mean
the armoury of a well-informed and supportive governing body. However, some nurseries do not have their own governing bodies and this lack
of support is in itself a concern.

As the attendant effects of open enrolment come about, nurseries may
feel an increased pressure to offer a similar programme to that being
offered in a mainstream school. In those LEAs where nurseries exist
alongside provision for 4-year-olds in reception classes, there is concern
that parents will increasingly opt for mainstream school provision in the
belief that these children will embark more quickly and progress more
rapidly through National Curriculum programmes of study in Key Stage
One (KSI). It seems that a parallel is being established to that existing
in 1862 when the system of 'payment by results' was introduced and
extended down to children of 5 years of age. Part of the rationale for
early admission at that time was that children were more likely to reach
the required Standard 1 if they had been introduced to the classroom
from an early age.[33]

Teacher shortages have affected the nursery sector heavily, and there
is a particular lack of trained nursery practitioners available to teach
the youngest children in infant schools. Surveys have shown as few as
10 per cent of primary teachers with nursery/infant training.[34] Where
authorities are facing great difficulty in recruiting primary teachers, there
is a fear that priority will go to staffing the statutory sector, once
more leaving the youngest children in the most vulnerable position. New
nursery units and classes planned by LEAs have not materialized because
of staffing difficulties. Other nursery classes have been reconstituted as
'pre-school groups' and are run by nursery nurses as a temporary measure
but, in fact, they constitute a change in the character of the school within
the terms of section 12 (d) of the Education Act 1980.[35]

Given these present or potential difficulties with numbers and resources, some nurseries may want to move towards greater autonomy
by managing their own budgets. However, although the government is
allowing for small schools to assume financial control by 1994, the difficulties of small units managing very limited amounts of money without
some protection from the education authority is in itself a concern. It may
be that, where it is geographically viable, clusters of nurseries will seek
ways of sharing finances and benefiting from collaborative purchasing –
as is beginning to happen with clusters of primary schools.

Some primary schools view grant-maintained status as a natural extension of financial control. This option is, of course, open to primary schools with attached nursery units but not to separate nursery schools. Because local authorities are not legally required to provide education for children under 5, so nursery schools were not included in legislation that allowed primary schools with fewer than 300 children to opt out.

These developments provide a backcloth for any nursery establishment in the country. If the job of educating and caring for young children is to be properly tackled, all these influences are relevant to planning, and some of the practical implications are discussed later in the book. The nursery teacher is working in a period of political sensitivity where increased information about the benefits of early education for all children are balanced against a market force economy and moves to push more provision into the private sector. Despite these tensions, as Chris Athey states, the teacher's role is to improve children through education: 'Teachers must believe that all children can flourish irrespective of initial IQ, of the effects of social class on entry to school and of future job opportunities. Bringing about improvement in individual learners is at the heart of teaching'.[36]

Suggested action

Overview

- Consider the issues mentioned in the chapter and note down the context in which you work with young children.
- Reflect on how each aspect affects your work and what resources you have to deal with it.

The child in the family

- Consider how much useful and relevant information you have about the home background of each child in the nursery. What additional information do you need?
- Review the procedures you have for acquiring background information about children. How can these be improved? For example, through contact with parents; through formal and informal links with other agencies.
- Select those children whom you consider to be adversely affected by family circumstances. List the ways in which these adverse effects are manifested in behaviour.
- List the ways in which your provision is helping to meet these

children's needs: (1) through curriculum provision; (2) at specific times of the day through procedures and routines; and (3) through particular attention from an adult.

Effects of abuse

- Be aware of changes in behaviour. Timidity, over-anxiety and inappropriate sexual approaches by the child to adults may possibly be caused by abuse. Take considered action; if you have real concern on the basis of close observation and objective evidence you should discuss the matter with your headteacher, the family health visitor or social worker. Your concern regarding the child's behaviour needs to be shared with the parent at an early stage.
- Be aware of the sensitivity of this topic in the nursery. Meet with small groups of parents to raise the issue of helping children to protect themselves from an early age, and discuss any approaches before you use them.
- Use stories to demonstrate that, if something distressing happens, a teacher needs to know in order to help to put it right.
- Help children to recognize what is a wrong touch or embrace. Use dolls or puppets to role play and demonstrate private parts of their bodies.

Effects of the media

- Consider how much you know about the teievision programmes available for young children.
- Note the number of comments from children arising from their viewing television programmes and how their viewing is reflected in their play.
- Consider how often you use these occasions to develop active learning, e.g. to create a familiar television puppet character and use this for developing conversation with children. Make a relief map layout of a scene in a favourite programme, with pipe-cleaner figures, for miniature role play.
- Design a simple, illustrated guide for parents, offering advice on the most constructive use of television programmes with their children at home.
- Invite parents to the nursery for an informal meeting to share their views on children's television programmes and offer them this guide.

Different groups

- Recognize your power as a model of communication. Avoid communicating undesirable messages to children. Check your attitudes and behaviour for signs of patronization and sentimentality. Ensure that a child's independence and self-respect is maintained.
- Use every means of communication to link with a child, e.g. sign language, a child's first language and special words used.
- Use classroom relationships to promote harmonious living together.
- Foster self-esteem: within a whole group each child can state his or her name in turn. This can be developed with name-giving accompanied by some positive personal statement about him or herself.
- Help children to appreciate commonalities and differences: play games that link children together through preferences and clothing. For example, all those who like apples to eat go to the book corner. Or collect four photographs of children from different ethnic groups. Cut each photograph in half and ask small groups of children to reassemble the pictures. This activity will be of more value if an adult is present to discuss different and common features. Cut photographs into more complex shapes according to the ability of the group.

The educational climate

- How has ERA positively affected work in your nursery?
- How clear are your governing body about the principles and practices of work with young children? List the ways in which you have informed them and consider if there are any additional methods to use. How might their increased awareness be used to support you?
- Develop close links with local infant schools that admit 4-year-olds in order to work towards (1) an agreed statement of needs for this age-group (see Chapter 5); (2) consideration of how these needs can best be met in nursery and infant classes; and (3) an agreed admissions policy in which parents are encouraged to make an informed decision about the placement for their child, based on first-hand knowledge of what is available in the area.

REFERENCES

1. DES (1978) *Special Educational Needs; Report of the Committee of Enquiry into the Education of Handicapped Children and Young People, under the Chairmanship of Mrs H. M. Warnock*, HMSO, London.
2. *Social Trends* (1988) no. 18, Central Statistical Office, HMSO, London.
3. J. Haskey (1983) Marital status before marriage and age at marriage: their influence on the chance of divorce, *Population Trends*, Vol. 32, pp. 4–14.
4. N. Beail (1982) The role of the father during pregnancy and birth, in N. Beail and J. Mcguire (eds.) *Fathers; Psychological Perspectives*, Junction Books, London; L. Mckee (1982) Fathers' participation in infant care: a critique, in L. McKee and M. O'Brien (eds.) *The Father Figure*, Tavistock, London.
5. Department of Employment (1982) *New Earnings Survey*, HMSO, London.
6. *Social Trends* (1988) op. cit. (note 2).
7. M. Fogelman (ed.) (1976) *Britain's Sixteen Year Olds*, National Children's Bureau, London.
8. *Guardian* (1991) The homeless are always with us, 8 January.
9. *Social Trends* (1988) op. cit. (note 2).
10. NSPCC (1990) Sad indication. *Children's Friend*, no. 28. Autumn, p. 14.
11. M. Elliott (1986) *Keeping Safe. A Practical Guide to Talking with Children*, Bedford Square Press, London.
12. B. Tizard and M. Hughes (1984) *Young Children Learning*, Fontana, London.
13. C. E. Davie, S. J. Hutt, E. Vincent and M. Mason (1984) *The Young Child at Home*, NFER/Nelson, Slough.
14. P. Gammage (1990) The social world of the young child, in C. Desforges (ed.) *Early Childhood Education* (*British Journal of Educational Psychology* Monograph Series no. 4), Scottish Academic Press, Edinburgh, p. 90.
15. M. P. Winick and C. Winick (1979) *The Television Experience; What Children See*, Sage, Beverly Hills, Calif.
16. G. Noble (1973) Effects of different forms of filmed aggression on children's constructive and destructive play, *British Journal of Social and Clinical Psychology*, Vol. 9; no. 1, pp. 1–7.
17. HMI (1989) *Aspects of Primary Education; The Education of Children Under Five*, HMSO, London, p. 33.
18. M. McMillan (1919) *The Nursery School*, Dent, London.
19. B. Tizard, J. Mortimore and B. Burchell (1981) *Involving Parents in Nursery and Infant Schools*, Grant McIntyre, London.
20. W. van der Eyken (1982) *Home Start; A Four Year Evaluation*, Leicester Home Start Consultancy, Leicester.
21. C. E. Davie, S. J. Hutt, E. Vincent and M. Mason (1982) *The Young Child at Home*, NFER/Nelson, Slough.
22. DES (1978) op. cit. (note 1).
23. Equal Opportunities Commission (1982) *An Equal Start*, Manchester.
24. DES (1985) *Education for All; Report of the Committee of Enquiry into the Education of Children from Ethnic Minority Groups, under the Chairmanship of Lord Swann*, HMSO, London.
25. G. Pugh (1988) *Services for Under Fives. Developing a Co-ordinated Approach*, National Children's Bureau, London.

26. Sheffield City Council Working Group on Daytime Child Care (1986) *It's their Future, Report of the Working Group*, Sheffield.

27. M. Bradley (1982) *The Coordination of Services for Children Under Five*, NFER/Nelson, Slough.

28. G. Pugh (1988) op. cit. (note 25).

29. DHSS (1989) *The Children Act*, HMSO, London.

30. DES (1990) *Starting with Quality. The Report of the Committee of Inquiry into the Quality of the Educational Experience Offered to 3- and 4-year-olds*, HMSO, London.

31. DES (1990) op. cit., para. 220 (note 30).

32. *Ibid.* para. 227.

33. R. Szreter (1964) The origins of full-time compulsory education at five, *British Journal of Educational Studies*, no. 12, pp. 16–28.

34. *The Times Educational Supplement* (1988) DES shows disturbing survey in primary staffing, 9 September, p. 23.

35. DES (1990) op. cit., para. 152 (note 30).

36. C. Athey (1990) *Extending Thought in Young Children*, Paul Chapman Publishing, London, p. 4.

2

PLANNING WITH AND FOR THE FAMILY

The arguments for securing links with the young child's family are well rehearsed and reinforced through research projects and the statements in major reports. Lazar and Darlington (1982) concluded in their analysis of the American consortium studies that the involvement of parents in intervention programmes was an important element in the children's subsequent improved performance, and also that the provision of services for the whole family resulted in even more gains for the children.[1] In Osborn and Millbank's study, the authors found that parental involvement was significant in affecting children's cognitive development but only if the child's own parents were involved. This finding was sufficiently strong to be independent of the different pre-school settings studied, and was irrespective of social class or the amount of interest shown by the parents in the child's education.[2]

HMI support endeavours to work with families and stress that both parties will gain: 'A successful partnership between the home and the school enables parents to understand how they can best contribute to their children's education; . . . But the teachers also benefit from sharing the parents' greater knowledge of the child as an individual and from learning something of the child's home background'.[3] This work is further reinforced in the report of the 1990 Committee of Inquiry into Under Fives, where the involvement of parents is stated to be a key issue for practitioners to address.[4]

In this chapter we expand on these findings and recommendations. We shall argue that consideration of the child within the family is essential for any nursery that acknowledges the importance of the child's past experiences, the need for continuity of learning and the nursery teacher's responsibility towards families in the community. The term 'parental involvement' is used in a variety of contexts and to cover a variety of purposes. A brief look at nurseries that claim to work with parents still discloses a range of practices. Some establishments cautiously acknowledge that parents have a right of access but little more. Others are proud of the daily presence of a number of parents tackling different tasks with children during the nursery day. When one looks more closely, though, it is often difficult to see any planning or purpose to this involvement, other than the principle that 'we can always use an extra pair of hands'. Yet other nurseries may have a detailed written policy for parents – a stack of paperwork may be generated to keep parents informed, but the spirit of working together is not present.

If working to promote parental involvement is to be more than just an educational fashion, the nursery teacher must be clear about his or her intentions and methods. Below we consider some broad approaches to working with parents. Some nurseries will feel able to develop work in only one or two areas, but teachers should keep themselves informed and be open-minded about other possibilities.

INITIAL EXCHANGE OF INFORMATION

Looking at the role of parents and governing bodies, the Taylor Report emphasized that 'Every parent has a right to expect a school's teachers to recognize his status in the education of his child by the practical arrangements they make to communicate with him and the spirit in which they accept his interest'.[5] At that time recognition of that status was very varied in nurseries and schools. Fourteen years later, the Education Reform Act 1988 (ERA) has made explicit and compulsory requirements for parents to have access to certain information. However, no legislation is likely to identify with sensitivity the questions that concern parents before they send their child to a nursery or reception class. These may include the worry of how their child will adapt to a new regime and environment; what will be expected of the child; how he or she will get on with other children; and what he or she will learn that will be of assistance to the child in his or her future schooling. The nursery teacher must always be aware of the starting-point of the parents, especially the parent of a first child who will need to learn so much about this next step in his or her life. It may be necessary to stress that all provision for under-5s is voluntary.

This is obvious to the professional but not always recognized by the new parents, who may feel under pressure to school their child when their own preference is to have him or her at home a little longer.

If parents are to make an informed choice about sending their child to a nursery, they must know what is available. Attendance at baby groups or mother-and-toddler groups may have allowed some mothers to share their knowledge about local provision, although the NFER study on transition to pre-school found that mother-and-toddler groups were not necessarily very popular with parents. The report suggests that friends and relatives were the greatest source of information, and only 14 per cent of parents had heard of nurseries through visits to clinics, doctors and libraries.[6]

While in some areas there is very little provision for families with under-5s in others the range of opportunities can itself be confusing and offputting for parents. LEAs appear to be acknowledging this. Pugh's study in 1986 found that 60 local authorities had produced written information for parents on the availability of services for under-5s in their area and 22 more documents were in preparation.[7] Although the common intention was to explain to parents the different provisions available, the format and detail of the information varied, with some making provision for families who have English as a second language. However, as Pugh points out, the provision of documents does not ensure the details necessarily reach the families who require it. Personal contacts are clearly very important in spreading information.

Once parents are aware of what is available they need to be encouraged to view these provisions for themselves to see what is most appropriate for their child. In some areas, however, parents may have little choice, and a nursery class or school may be limited to receive only children from a clearly defined catchment area.

From the time the child is registered, there should be opportunities for parents to gain more specific information about the nursery. Two thirds of the parents interviewed in the transition study indicated that they wanted to meet the nursery staff.[8] Parents are also likely to be eager to see the facilities their children will be using, and some will want information about the nursery curriculum. The period before the child starts at the nursery can be important for getting to know about all these aspects of provision, and some informal parent groups can provide a useful forum for meeting staff in a relaxed atmosphere and generally becoming familiar with the nursery setting. A school brochure will enable parents to read information at home and to show it to their friends and neighbours. Tizard suggests that the best way of finding out what to put in a school brochure is to ask established parents what they would have liked to see included.[9] In the main, written information is probably most useful when it deals with factual matters such as names and roles of staff and governors, and information about routines such as daily dinner arrangements and provision for health inspection. It would be a mistake to rely on a brochure as a totally effective way of communication; at best it is helpful to have a written statement of what has already been discussed in a small group meeting with parents.

Staffing and the nursery environment and routines are relatively easy to communicate, but the nursery curriculum poses a greater challenge. This curriculum is not easy to explain to parents, who tend to think in terms of the subject-based, examination-oriented school work they last remember.

The way the nursery expresses its purposes and practices depends on the catchment area and on the understanding of parents. There is a range of educational material for parents through books, articles, Open University study units and television and radio programmes; some parents will have taken every opportunity to use this information and will arrive at the nursery with their child, conversant with many aspects of child development and learning. Other parents, equally aspiring for their children, may not be so aware or may hold different views. Tizard suggested that in most middle-class schools the parents were familiar with many educational terms and thus could more quickly grasp the reasons for specific activities: 'Parents with less previous exposure to these concepts and unfamiliar with modern theories of development and learning were at best likely to gather that the teacher believed that children in some way learned through playing with sand'.[10]

Further communication complications can arise if the nursery serves families from different cultures. Asian and Afro-Carribean families can have very different ideas about their children's upbringing and the place of play and toys in their children's education. If teachers are unaware of these views they may be in danger of enthusiastically promoting children's activities that make no sense at all to some parents. Tizard reports that 'it is not surprising that the teachers in our project from schools with a large proportion of non-indigenous parents became discouraged by failures of communication and generally abandoned attempts to run evening meetings, toy libraries or even book libraries'.[11]

There is thus a need to be very clear about the size of the communication gap before offering parents information. The better informed teachers are about the beliefs and styles of parenting from different cultures, the more sensitively they can move toward explaining how a nursery can help children.

A good example of this is the work of home–school liaison teachers involved in a Parents in Partnership Project in the north. In making videos to enhance home–school dialogue, a 'pyramid approach' was used: 'that is, a situation familiar to (or aspired to by) most parents was to be used as a starting-point (for example, a child successfully reading a text). The video would then move back in time, showing the sequence of steps which lead up to the child's success.'[12]

There is a general view that the more parents know about the methods and content of education, the better they are able to support their child's learning. However, it appears that there is still a great deal of work to do in this area. Recent studies reveal that most parents see nursery education as primarily fostering social development.[13] Although social development is important, this view implies a need for nursery staff to be more explicit about other aspects of their work and to couch their explanations in terms parents can understand. The pyramid approach seems an effective way of linking nursery activity to parents' long-term aspirations for their children.

Much emphasis has been placed on how schools can help and support parents. Much less attention has been given to how the parent can assist the professional. Yet the amount of information every parent has about his or her child is likely to be unmatched. Whatever the home circumstances or quality of relationship that exists, parents know about their child as an individual – his or her fears and excitements, favourite playthings, stamina and emotional strengths and weaknesses. They will also be aware of how their young child spends his or her time at home.

Young and McGeeney have described the work they tackled post-Plowden to encourage meetings, discussions with parents and home visits. Teachers commented on their increased awareness of their children's home lives: 'When I look at them now I think of all the things I know about them and realize just what some of them have to put up with'.[14] Such a comment suggests that teachers saw the benefits of acquiring information about their children's home lives in helping to sensitize them to the difficulties children and parents experience, thus making the teachers more sympathetic in their school provision. More recently, however, studies have revealed more positive reasons for teachers becoming better informed, by stressing the wealth of learning that takes place in the home. Wells's study, which represented all social groups, reported on the rich use of language at home by all children.[15]

Tizard and Hughes's study was less representative but supported this view.[16] The authors outlined why they considered the child's learning at home to be so productive, suggesting that a wide range of activities takes place in or around the home that provides the young child with a range of information, particularly about the roles of adults. Tizard and Hughes also indicate that small family size means the likelihood of a small number of children sharing the adults' time, and the time shared is linked to common past and present experiences. Furthermore, any learning for the child is likely to be within the context of an everyday experience involving household routines of washing-up, bedmaking and laying the table. The study argues that the close relationship between mother and child can be a positive factor in promoting the child's learning, more particularly the parent's personal aspirations for her child.

The study by Tizard and Hughes admittedly has a suggestion of the idealized home setting. Many readers will question how far this setting was affected by the presence of the researcher and whether the findings would have been the same had the study been across a wider social stratum or included boys. Despite this, the factors mentioned are very persuasive in fostering early learning. The implications are also a healthy antidote to the more usual picture of inadequate homes that are learning deserts. If we are persuaded of the learning that takes place at home, the next question is how the nursery practitioner can learn more about what happens to draw on this experience.

Whatever the level of working with parents, a welcoming atmosphere in the nursery and a friendly and open manner during home visiting will make for good, trusting relationships. However, as Tizard points out,

> although friendly relationships may make it easier to work with parents, they won't in themselves achieve the aims of parental involvement programmes. For the teacher who wants parents to understand what she is trying to achieve, to provide her with the kind of back-up she wants and to exchange views and information with her, informal contacts are not enough.[17]

Even at the level of offering and receiving information from parents, difficulties emerge through lack of resources. Teachers can tackle only what is possible. One sensible approach may be for each member of the nursery team to be allowed a 'case-load' of families. It is then the particular responsibility of that member of staff to relate to those parents and to develop a home profile which can then be used as a basis for developing further conversation and learning in the nursery. If parents are aware they have a particular adult as a first point of contact, this can make it easier to share information about their child.

Suggested action

Inform parents of available local facilities

- Find out about the range of statutory and voluntary provision for young families in the locality; keep a list of these to offer nursery parents with younger babies and toddlers, and ensure that these groups have information about the nursery to offer to their parents.
- Familiarize yourself with local playgroups; it helps if you can refer a parent to a local group if your nursery admission limit has been reached.
- Plan a weekend presentation when the nursery and other under-5s agencies publicize the range of facilities available for young families. This event needs to be publicized in the local press and on local radio.
- Arrange for nursery brochures, posters and displays of nursery work to be seen in local libraries, doctors' surgeries and supermarkets.

Plan a positive reception for parents at registration

The first impression of the nursery parents and child receive is crucial.

- Make it nursery policy that all prospective parents and children are warmly received and, if at all possible, shown around the nursery at that time. If this proves difficult, a convenient time should be arranged for the parents and child to return. Overcome a language problem by inviting a parent who speaks the language to accompany you with the new parents.
- Offer tangible evidence to the child that he or she will be coming to the nursery; e.g. provide a simple certificate to confirm the child's proposed date of entry to the nursery. The certificate can have a suitable nursery motif, a space for the child's name and attractive lettering stating that 'We look forward to you coming to our nursery'. Offer a nursery badge or sticker.
- Make the first visit brief but assure the parents it will be one of many.
- Aim to offer some written information before the parents leave. This may be the nursery brochure or a paper showing the proposed sequence of events leading up to the child's admission

to the nursery: e.g. availability of weekly parent/toddler group; details of an introductory home visit to be paid by the teacher; details and dates of admission procedures for new children.

Plan the nursery brochure

- Make the nursery brochure attractive and concise, using clear print and relevant illustrations.
- Make the information directly applicable to new parents; it may be preferable to have a series of brief documents rather than try to include too much information in one booklet.
- If there is more than one document, make it clear to parents just what is available, e.g. booklets on the value of various aspects of play, on ways in which parents can help children at home.
- Include a plan of the nursery in the brochure, showing the location of various activities, the parents' room and toilets.
- Provide the information in different languages where necessary. Local community leaders or parents could help with translations and offer advice on suitable format and illustrations.

Make personal contact with parents

- Arrange some weekly gatherings of new parents and children before they start at the nursery. The children may play alongside their parents or occasionally play in an adjoining nursery room. Parents can be given a range of information about the nursery and child management; they can see the nursery in session and can share information with other parents. Childminders should be invited to these daytime meetings if both parents are working; where most families are out all day it may be preferable to hold the meetings in the evening, having enlisted the support of established nursery parents to volunteer as baby-minders. The use of a video in the evening can be a good way of showing a nursery session.
- Arrange at least one semi-social gathering for new parents and teachers to meet over coffee, tea and cake after school or cheese and wine. This should provide an opportunity for the teachers to be seen as people; volunteer parents or nursery-assistant students could supervise children in an adjoining crèche.
- Some parents may feel more relaxed making initial contact on their home territory. The teacher might notify his or her intention to visit by sending the child a special nursery postcard. The aim of the visit should be to confirm arrangements for the child to

start at the nursery and to reassure the parents and child if
they have particular anxieties. A volunteer interpreter should
accompany the teacher where there may be a language barrier.

Explain the nursery curriculum

- Offer nursery pamphlets that help to explain the educational
  value of different activities. These are more likely to be read if
  they are given to parents after an informal meeting or discussion
  on that particular activity.
- Develop a parents' library with a range of books on child development and early childhood curriculum; these might be purchased from a parents' fund parents could organize themselves.
  Multi-ethnic centres can advise on literature available for parents
  of different cultures.
- Invite the local infant headteacher (or heads, in the case of a
  nursery school feeding a number of infant schools) to meetings
  with parents. In an informal setting the infant staff can help
  parents to be aware that activity learning continues in the main
  school.

Learn from parents

- Create opportunities to listen. Before starting at the nursery,
  parents should be asked to share what they know about their
  child with a positive emphasis. Tailor this opportunity to the
  particular catchment area. It may take place in the home or the
  nursery and may involve parents responding to a questionnaire or
  informally chatting to the teacher.
- Note home events. Offer a specific invitation for parents regularly
  to share any items of family interest that may have affected their
  child, e.g. death of a pet, dad getting a new job. This information
  may be conveyed casually, or there may be a regular time when
  each member of staff may be available to his or her small group
  of parents. A cup of tea after school with a volunteer older mum
  keeping an eye on the children will enable a more leisurely
  discussion between teacher and parents.
- Ask parents about their aspirations for their child: what do
  they expect the nursery to offer to support these aspirations?
  What part do they, as parents, expect to play in this stage of
  development?

WORKING TOGETHER

The child's entry to the nursery and subsequent pattern of relationships with parents has potential for establishing sound parental attitudes towards education, a growing appreciation of how their young child learns and the opportunity to keep in touch with this learning. Parents' understanding and support should in turn help nursery teachers in their professional role. Any moves towards parents and teachers working as partners requires regular close communication, which in itself needs a commitment from both parties. Initially there seems to be a need for the nursery team to have considered how the new child can be helped to adjust to the nursery and the respective roles teacher and parents will play in this process. The picture that emerges from studies, however, is that the settling in is often an uncertain time. Tizard found that 'the teacher might feel the mother should be left to settle her child on her own, yet the mother might not know how to do this and feel embarrassed or distressed because her child was clinging and unhappy'.[18] The mothers interviewed in the transition study were all invited to stay with their children initially, but generally felt this might not be seriously meant. One mother said: 'I didn't stay. I think [a member of staff] prefers you out of the way so she can get on with things'. It seems that most new children settled within a few weeks, but this might be less left to chance. Any policy regarding transition must of course be left open to interpret individual needs, but parents might feel happier if they had a clearer role to play.[19]

Opportunities for keeping in touch with parents are perhaps greater in the nursery than at any other time in a child's school life. Parents are required to come into the school at least twice a day to deliver and collect their children. A staggered daily entry often provides the chance to have a word with the member of staff, and the children's own insistence that parents see any new school pet or look at their painting when displayed makes it easier for the more reticent parent to enter the nursery. When parents work and employ childminders, contact is more difficult. Parents of under-5s are in any case often under pressure, and the daily contact with the nursery may be in the company of a toddler and a baby, both requiring supervision. Early parenthood, as we saw in Chapter 1, is likely to be a time of life for young adults when relationships are relatively new and money is short. Whatever their circumstances, many nursery parents will be quite new to their role *vis-à-vis* the school and so may be not sure what to expect. For all these reasons parents may not have the time, energy or courage to ask questions or to take the initiative in becoming more actively informed about nursery developments. This points to the need for nursery staff to plan ways of keeping their parents in touch. To succeed in this, they must be sensitive to what parents want. One nursery invited parents to an open evening shortly after the children had started school. Only 50 per cent responded, and those who went indicated they did so to be supportive to the staff rather than because they saw the occasion as useful.[20]

Bearing in mind the busy lives most parents lead, it is sensible to provide them with as much helpful information as possible without requiring them to attend a special occasion. Attractive noticeboards and handouts have their place, while an informal weekly briefing about certain activities can take place with parents towards the end of the nursery session during the children's story-time. As Atkin points out, parents are individual and will have their own preferred ways of seeking information, making judgements about their child's schooling and deciding what part they are going to play in it. She concludes that 'it is only by careful reflections and by seeking the views of parents that the appropriate range of contacts can be decided upon at a particular school'.[21]

Apart from gaining information about the nursery regime, every parent has a right to know how his or her child is succeeding. This right is now mandatory for parents of statutory-age children but traditionally parents of younger children have not always recognized or acted upon their entitlement as consumers. Studies show that parents are usually anxious to be reassured that their child is happy and physically cared for, but they rarely ask additional questions. However, when asked specifically whether they had sufficient information, one group of parents emphasized they would have liked to know more about their child's progress.[22] Teachers have tended to respond to requests for information rather than volunteer it. Understandably, because of the problems of time, priority is given to reassuring expressed anxieties. However, if parents are to appreciate the significance of nursery education and have the opportunity of sharing an informed view of the progress of their child, there is a need for more specific information. Sylva and Moore's study on record-keeping in nurseries in 1983 revealed that individual children's records were rarely used as an aid to discussion with parents: 'It seems safe to conclude that records are used more for "working" purposes than for communication, perhaps missing out on a valuable means of working in partnership with parents'.[23] Although no subsequent study has been undertaken, observations of nursery practice today suggest that evidence of children's development and progress is being more systematically recorded and shared (see Chapter 7).

Suggested action

Settling the child

- Provide a simple illustrated booklet for parents, outlining common forms of behaviour expected from new entrants with guidance for parent/teacher action.
- Take every opportunity to relate to the new parent and child and help them to manage the initial separation. You may do this by

  - joining them at the child's chosen activity and working with them (during this time the teacher can listen to and take part in the shared experiences of parent and child and use them with the child after the parent has left);
  - encouraging the parent to stay if the child still needs him or her;
  - involving the parent in some activity as a step towards separation, e.g. simple tasks such as cutting paper or mixing paints will allow the parent to observe how the child copes with other children and becomes involved without the parent;
  - suggesting when you think it is appropriate for the parent to leave if the parent is reluctant to take the decision;
  - giving the parent a detailed account of how his or her child has spent the time since the parent left him or her for the session.

Share information through notices and displays

- The noticeboard should be conveniently placed for parents to see when waiting for their children. Regular spaces for particular information and clear graphics will help parents to skim quickly for information: e.g. a space for social and fund-raising events; routine information on times and dates of opening and names and photographs of staff; and details of community facilities for young families. This information should look attractive and be changed regularly to encourage parents to make use of it.
- The school brochure will give a flavour of the nursery. More detailed information can be gained by parents receiving half-termly curriculum plans from the teacher. These can include details of proposed outings, new rhymes and jingles to be introduced and proposed cookery activities.
- A small display of older children's representations in painting,

drawing or construction can be used to demonstrate the skills and concepts involved. For example:

Joe (3 years, 11 months) made this model of his dad's new car. He had to learn to choose the materials he needed, making sure that they were the right shape and size. He learned how to apply glue and stick one surface to another. He controlled scissors to cut the shapes for the wheels. Joe concentrated for twelve minutes on his work and used the following words to describe his model: 'fast', 'zoomy', 'zippy', 'brakes', 'wheels', 'petrol'.

- A display of new apparatus or equipment purchased can be accompanied by a brief explanation of its learning potential.

Make personal contacts

- Regular informal discussions/workshops will work best for a group of about eight parents. The teacher who is 'responsible' for these parents gives a talk, shows equipment or uses a video to demonstrate the value of an activity and the level of development of the children involved. Over a cup of tea parents and teacher can discuss how the learning in this activity can be followed up at home, e.g. visual memory – the child can be asked to remember one or two items the parent must buy when they go shopping; what items does he or she remember best?
- Make individual contact. During the first term ensure you have spoken with each new parent to check they are clear about the routines and activities in the nursery. The amount and level of understanding required to satisfy each parent will differ and will require a flexible response from you. Be sure to gain some feedback from parents. How do they feel their child is benefiting? What information does he or she share with them at home?

SERVICES AND SUPPORT FOR YOUNG FAMILIES

If the nursery teacher recognizes the strong link between the quality of family life and the child's well-being and progress, there must be concern to respect and acknowledge parents in their work. In a review of child care for the European Commission, 1986–8, Britain was seen to regard children as exclusively the responsibility of their parents. This contrasted strongly with other countries such as Denmark and France, where the view is that the care of children is a responsibility shared between State and parent. Peter Moss, in reporting this distinction, stressed there is still no recognition in Britain of children being a social asset: 'We also have difficulty with the idea of parenthood as a socially vital task, which brings major responsibilities and demands, in return for which society should provide proper resources and support'.[24] Since that time there have been some indicators of progress that have withered because of a lack of resources. The report of the Committee of Inquiry on Under Fives made some encouraging statements about the significance of provision for the age-group, but no financial inducements were made available to develop them.[25] More particularly, despite recent interest in providing workplace nurseries in order to encourage mothers back to employment, schools and employers have failed to develop facilities mainly because of the expense involved. Pre-school support services vary from area to area; some excellent facilities are available, but too often the picture is patchy and uncoordinated, with statutory and voluntary services unaware of each other's roles. In the meantime the nursery can be in a key position to work with families. The job of parenting is taxing and stressful in today's climate. Some parents provide for their children's needs admirably and gain great satisfaction from their role. Others want the very best for their children but feel ill equipped to provide it. In these cases, as well as considering parents as educators, there should be some means of support- ing them as people and helping them to enjoy their children. Regular daily contact with parents offers teachers a unique opportunity to keep in touch and, in particular, to monitor how family life is affecting the child.

However, the dilemma for the teacher comes from lack of time and resources to offer adequate support, while recognizing that parents may use the nursery as the first point of contact for help and advice. There is no satisfactory answer to this, but the nurseries that are seen as family supporters are likely to give priority to four factors: (1) having open access to the nursery; (2) recognizing the need for some home contacts; (3) working closely with other agencies involved with young families; and (4) recognizing that parents can help one another.

In nursery centres operating successfully with parents, the main in- gredients appeared to be that parents felt they were welcome.[26] For, although many nurseries consider they do encourage parents to visit freely, this is not always the parents' perception. Some teachers still feel uneasy about the constant presence of parents in the nursery, which can be regarded as a distraction from their work with children. Even if the presence is accepted, attitudes can appear patronizing and of the all-knowing professional bestowing advice. How initial and in-service education can help teachers to view their role in relation to adults as well as children will be discussed later (Chapter 8). Certainly, interpersonal skills of tact, discretion and genuine sympathy with parents are a pre-requisite of the job.

While some parents will just be receptive to facilities offered, others will want to contribute actively and to take some responsibility. Such parents can often provide a range of skills to enhance the nursery.

It is one thing to encourage parents to see the nursery as a warm and welcoming environment, but the problem of making it possible for them to have immediate access to teachers who have no non-contact time is a real one. In some catchment areas parents will appreciate that the teacher is available for them at the end of each day or by appointment; in other areas, apart from making local authorities aware of the urgent need to have extra staffing resources, it is glib to suggest that there is any alternative other than the teacher weighing up the priority of each call for help and suffering the usual pangs of role conflict.

Some parents are rarely seen, because of working commitments or physical or mental illness; others may deliver or collect their child but be unable to reveal anything of themselves in an institutionalized setting, however inviting. The benefits of home visiting to develop the parents' educative role are considered later. Here we suggest that there is a place for the nursery to extend the hand of friendship to those parents who are not seen on nursery premises. Visited at home, on their own 'territory', parents are often more at ease and more open about their own difficulties and in questioning and criticizing the nursery regime. Where home–school liaison teachers have been employed in certain authorities their visits have revealed that, 'as well as informing and advising parents, feedback from home visits helped the school identify the messages it frequently failed to put across effectively to parents'.[27]

Another important role for a home visitor may be to introduce and support parents in visiting the community facilities offered by a nursery. The Haringey Pre-School Centre exists in an area catering for around twenty different ethnic groups. Here home visitors are employed to forge a link with the family and to help them take advantage of the facilities provided. This may involve encouraging a reticent mother to make contact with other mothers at the centre, or befriending a family and helping them cope with the practicalities of life such as form-filling.[28]

In many nurseries there is no additional staffing for home visiting, so teachers must weigh up the need against other priorities. Some teachers see a home-visiting role as crucial to their work, but this is likely to be in an educational context. Nevertheless, a planned visit to welcome a new baby, visit a sick mother or to offer transport to the nursery for a child whose attendance is poor may pay dividends for future working relationships.

A nursery aiming to offer comprehensive support to young families cannot afford to operate in isolation. It needs to be aware of what other support agencies exist and to work closely with these agencies.

The case for a more co-ordinated service for under-5s has already been stressed (see Chapter 1). Gillian Pugh argues for adequate structures that would enable more coherent provision. She also stresses that the polarization between education and care is unhelpful. Young children require both.[29] Nurseries could usefully consider if their own resources would allow them to offer more flexible facilities.

In areas where there is no lead from the top, the practitioners have to take the initiative. Nursery teachers may need information from health visitors, paediatricians, educational psychologists and speech therapists; they also have useful information to pass on. Nurseries also need access to these agencies. Teachers may not see their role as being a marriage guidance counsellor or an expert on obtaining family benefits. They should, however, be able to refer families in need to appropriate sources of advice and information.

Links with statutory agencies may be obvious but the role of voluntary associations is also crucial. Volunteers are in a special position to help families. In describing Home Start, a scheme that introduces volunteer home visitors to families, the role was described as one of 'caring, friendship, mothering and nurturing. Unlike professionals, volunteers are more inclined to be person-orientated rather than problem-orientated. . . . It is a non-threatening role where the mother may identify with the volunteer who herself is not perfect and may share her own fears and triumphs with the family'.[30]

The volunteer can therefore provide a service and offer time in a way that is difficult for a statutory worker with a large case-load. According to Sheila Wolfendale, 'the essence of many of these ventures is the two-way or reciprocal process – that a scheme can only be successful, if it has an inbuilt requisite, the active contribution and participation of the parent.'[31]

It is increasingly realized that parents will retain their dignity and hold on life if they can take an active part in helping themselves. The pre-school playgroup movement is a good example of parents' self-help initially in providing facilities for their young children when nursery places were not available. The vitality of this movement today indicates the need it has met in the community for adults to join together and become involved in their pre-school children's development. The existence of playgroups in no way invalidates the case for nursery education; these two provisions, both voluntary and State funded, could and should complement each other. Ideally parents should have choice of placement for their child – where this does not exist, close collaboration should ensure the best possible use is made of whatever provision is there and that professionals and volunteers learn from one another.

An Australian study on postnatal depression questioned young women about what type of help they had found most effective. The mothers responded that by far the most important was sympathy, reassurance and encouragement received, whilst the least helpful was medication.[32] In extreme cases the time and care offered to young parents and their family may avoid the children being taken into care later. Nurseries need to be aware of the resource many of their parents may provide as volunteer helpers to support particular families. Such groups as Home Start and PPA have institutionalized the support they offer. At a local level nurseries can offer a great deal just by putting people in touch with one another.

Suggested action

Encourage open access in the nursery

- Have bright signs welcoming parents into the nursery.
- Find a space for parents. An attractive room is ideal, but a space in the foyer with easy chairs and magazines at least acknowledges parents have an area for themselves.
- Offer simple services for parents, e.g. a library of knitting patterns, or a scheme for exchanging paperbacks or magazines (this is particularly welcome for parents from different ethnic groups who may exchange their own literature).
- Offer the facilities of a toy library run regularly by volunteers.
- Provide facilities for toddlers and ask a parent to be responsible for seeing equipment is put out and tidied away at the end of a session.
- Organize social occasions, sending personal invitations to every family, e.g. a supper prepared in turn by parents of different cultures; a family barbecue.
- Develop a drop-in centre. According to room available this may have to be a planned weekly occasion using space that is multi-purpose, or a regular provision in a permanent room. Facilities again may vary according to what is practically possible. Parents

may call in with babies and toddlers once weekly for a cup of coffee, or they may use the centre for making snack lunches, ask for it to be open during holiday periods and develop a forum for discussion on issues affecting young families. When possible a member of staff should regularly visit the centre, establishing the link with the nursery. Give new parents invitation cards (illustrated by a child and written in the mother tongue), welcoming them to the centre. The new parent may also be linked with an established parent, who will introduce him or her to the centre and see that he or she makes contact with other parents.

- Develop a support group for parents with particular concerns about their child.

Extend links into the home

- Arrange to receive a list of new births in the locality. Send a nursery representative on a brief home visit with a congratulations card (design your own card using children's artwork and use local-authority printing facilities) and details of any pram club or new parents' support group in the area.
- In an area where parents work and access to the nursery is not easy, a termly home visit by the teacher may be a way of keeping home and nursery in touch.
- Send all parents a news-sheet giving information about any events relevant for young families.

Liaise with statutory and voluntary bodies

- Know what is available. Systematically gather information about the agencies available locally to help young families. Some local authorities publish handbooks offering this information; alternatively the local citizens' advice bureau should be helpful. Using this information, aim to meet a representative of each agency over a period of time to get to know more about the resources each can offer. Ask how the nursery could help for these resources to be better used in the community.
- Maintain the links:

  - Plan termly catchment meetings with representatives of all agencies working with young children and toddlers, together with local headteachers of infant and first schools. Benefits will include people getting to know each other and sharing views on matters of common concern, e.g. early childhood management, diet, support for families under stress.

- Plan regular working lunches with the local health visitor, school nurse, social worker and speech therapist. Make this an opportunity for each in turn to raise some issue of concern or use the time to collect information about certain families and strategies of support being offered.
- Arrange for the health visitor to spend time in the nursery regularly. Where no home visiting takes place from the nursery, the health visitor can provide the link with the home.

- Use the expertise and resources from other agencies:

  - Plan for adult education classes for parents during nursery hours either in the building or located nearby.
  - Persuade the local library to provide you with a permanent resource of books that can be on loan for parents.
  - Persuade the speech therapist to work in the nursery with all the children over a period of time. In this way he or she can keep in touch with children who have a range of language abilities and can have early warning of children with potential difficulties.
  - Use the parents' room and staff-room to develop a monthly family-support service. Have access to an educational psychologist, family social worker and speech therapist on these occasions and make it possible for parents to drop in and take the initiative in asking for advice and help rather than being directed to these agencies.
  - Establish a register of childminders in the locality. Aim to build up a linked care and education provision for those parents who need extended day care. Having established the links, a community volunteer might be responsible for maintaining communication and keeping an updated list of childminding vacancies.

- Offer support to other agencies:

  - Develop exchange visits with local playgroups and, where practical, arrange to exchange pieces of equipment, e.g. jigsaw puzzles and equipment for gross motor play.
  - In some cases playgroups will appreciate a brief loan of a piece of equipment before deciding to buy it for themselves.

- Offer simple in-service sessions for childminders and playgroup personnel.

Help parents to 'use the system'

- Keep updated lists of childminders and playgroups on the parents' noticeboard, with a local road map showing their where-abouts. Keep in touch with playgroup numbers so you can advise a parent of a vacancy if on coming to register they find a long waiting-list for the nursery.
- Invite personnel to offer information to parents, e.g. a marriage guidance counsellor, or a representative from the DHSS to talk about applications for family benefits.
- Give practical help to a group of parents who are prepared to run a holiday play scheme for their children.
- Encourage a baby-sitting service for evenings and short periods of time during school holidays.
- Sow seeds and give encouragement to a variety of parental self-help schemes, e.g. a second-hand clothes shop, arrangements for holiday outings, monthly use of the parents' room as a hair-dressing salon.

DEVELOPING A FULL PARTNERSHIP

So far we have dealt with less questioned aspects of working with parents. Teachers will readily accept the need for a sensitive transition from home to nursery, for parents to be well informed about what their children are doing and that parents have valuable information about their own children. The principle of offering support to parents is also usually acknowledged but tempered in the belief that this must vary with the resources available. Nurseries in mainstream schools are of course directly affected by legal requirements to inform parents and to offer them a more central role in school management through governor in-volvement and attendance at annual governors' meetings. These initiatives may or may not be effective; in some cases, certainly, schools believe they are 'going through motions', which do little to reach parents' real needs for involvement.

These developments reflect a general recognition at all levels that parents have rights and responsibilities. However, if we accept Warnock's view of the parents' central role in their child's education, a particular

approach to working with parents becomes clear. All the contact, information and support given is ultimately in the recognition of this role.
Whether affected by legislation or not, those schools that have a real
reciprocal relationship realize the value of parents as an educational
resource. If teachers and their headteachers have a conviction for col-
laborating with parents, they will be prepared to treat the work as a
serious curriculum commitment that needs resourcing and planning.

These professionals acknowledge the crucial nature of the earliest years
and that this sensitive time for intervention coincides with the young
child's attachment to his or her family. There is now plenty of action
research indicating that children are significantly affected by their parents'
intervention in their learning. Many of these studies in the Eighties
related to children's literacy and language development.[33,34] The more
recent HMI survey on reading standards identified parental involvement
as one of the main criteria to be found in those schools with good
standards of reading.[35] The important part parents play in the general
intellectual development of their children is stressed by Katz,[36] and
Tizard found strong links between the amount of home support received
by children and their attainment in nursery schools and classes.[37] Sylva
believes that any future evaluation of early childhood programmes must
include a study of the parent's role.[38]

Despite this, evidence indicates that some teachers continue to be
sceptical of the preparedness of parents to participate actively in their
child's learning. In Tizard's study of 31 infant teachers in inner London, a
number had a low perception of the interest and involvement parents
would have in their child's education once they started school. Of these
teachers, 29 per cent anticipated that none or very few of their parents
would do anything to help their child. A further 16 per cent felt unable to
suggest whether there would be any involvement. This view of what
would be likely to happen contrasted strongly with the parents' expressed
intentions. With very few exceptions, the 202 parents interviewed said
they would want to continue to help their child at home once he or she
had started school.[39] This interest appears to be shared by parents of
younger children.

Smith's earlier study of pre-school groups reports that more than half
of the parents involved would have liked to have played a larger part in
their child's group and to share his or her experience more closely: 'this is
the strongest possible indication of the waste of interest on the part of
parents – interest in their children's experience and development that
could have been built on for both parent and child'.[40] Hannon's more
recent nursery study revealed not only that parents are interested in

helping to develop literacy skills but also that they are already involved in many reading and writing activities. Although not central to this study, Hannon again found some of the headteachers from the nurseries involved expressing doubts about parents having such interests.[41]

Apart from perceived lack of motivation, some teachers have concerns about parents not having a correct approach to educating their children. In the Tizard study one in four of the reception teachers said they disapproved of parents teaching any reading, writing or number to children under the age of 5; those who said they approved were anxious that nothing was taught that would be incompatible with school teaching.[42] Hannon reports that the nursery teachers in his study believed that parental involvement in developing literacy skills could result in children being placed under too much pressure and being taught by wrong methods.

Both these studies also reveal that, despite these anxieties, teachers only gave very limited advice as to what assistance should be given in the home. In the Tizard study, parents had to take the intitiative to find out about teaching methods for reading and writing. Hannon reported the main advice given to parents in his study was to read and to talk to the children. He suggested that parents did this already but lacked specific guidance as how to develop their practices: 'In the absence of any constructive advice they [the parents] muddle through, with the uneasy feeling that they are "doing it wrong".'[43]

A picture emerges of parents keen to offer their children help but often uncertain what to do, and receiving insufficient information from school. This calls for teachers to acknowledge and welcome the potential commitment, and to help parents develop confidence in what they do. Katz suggests that the function of work with parents should be to help them 'think through their own goals for their own children' and offer parents 'insights and various kinds of information while encouraging them to accept only what makes sense to them and what is consistent with their own preferences'.[44] Where teachers do not have a high expectation of the parental role, there is danger of a self-fulfilling prophecy. Parents who do not have a stake in their children's early education place a heavy responsibility on the nursery school to succeed alone.

One particularly successful venture was the model of shared learning by parents and teachers developed in the Froebel Early Education Project. This research study aimed at producing information on the ways in which knowledge is acquired by young children at home and in school. It noted developmental sequences of behaviour from early motor actions to thought. This information was freely shared with parents who were asked

to take a fully active part in attending sessions and outings with their
children, and in sharing their own understandings of their children's
development with staff. Chris Athey (who directed the project) admits
that initially parents treated the professionals as the experts and they
also lacked sufficient knowledge of the project's intentions to help with
collecting data. However, as they were given information and gained
confidence, parents were able to take an equal part with staff in tracking
their child's patterns of understanding. Athey reports that parents
became increasingly able to recognize and extend conceptual behaviour
having been introduced to them by the professionals. The partnership
throughout the project was genuinely equal. Parents were recognized as
being the best-informed parties regarding their own child, while the
professionals were equipped to look at children as a group and compare
patterns of behaviour. Although parents' levels of understanding and
participation in the project varied, Athey stresses that all became more
and more interested in observing their child's behaviour: 'nothing gets
under a parent's skin more quickly and more permanently than the
illumination of his or her own child's behaviour. The effect of participation
can be profound'.[45]

Suggested action

Help parents to acknowledge their own educational role

- Have an introductory pamphlet available for new parents, stressing the importance of their role.
- Provide a range of simple games and books for parents to use with their children at home. These may be left by a home visitor, who will first have demonstrated how to use them, or they may be part of a library in the nursery. Parents and children can choose the material together and use it with the teacher in the nursery before taking it home.
- Run a series of weekly sessions for new parents using activity sheets suggesting suitable things to do with their children at home.
- Listen carefully to parents' own experiences as these may have valuable messages for you in school. During the sessions parents can discuss the effectiveness of the activities tackled during the previous week as well as raising general issues of child management and learning.
- Indicate the range of learning opportunities available for young

children. For example, talk with parents about the learning involved in daily home routines; use video material to demonstrate the sequencing involved in dressing, making a bed, making a cup of tea, doing the washing-up.

- Offer a range of simple handouts indicating the range of activity and potential learning involved in family outings: on the beach, in the car, shopping, in the garden.
- Devise a simple document that allows both parents and teachers to state their expectations for the child in the nursery/reception class and that clarifies the respective roles each can play in helping to fulfil those expectations.

Develop parents' expertise

- When parents help in the nursery, offer models of managing children and introduce them to new experiences. It may be necessary to make these models explicit, stressing the approach is not a teacher's prerogative but that it will work successfully for parents as well, e.g. avoiding confrontation; sharing a task with a child; aiming to see the child's viewpoint (remembering of course that many parents use these approaches very well intuitively, but may find it helpful to have them identified).
- Run curriculum workshops, e.g. 'story-time with your child'. Include ways of offering stories through pictures, reading texts and telling stories; show some visual aids to use, such as stick, hand and finger puppets, a picture chart hung in the child's bedroom or a 'magic bag' in which a special book or object linked to a story can be found.
- Run workshops on child development: e.g. five one-hour sessions including topics such as 'your child is unique', 'what happens to your child between 1 month and 5 years', 'communicating with your child', 'learning with you at home'.

Make resources available for parents

- Run a weekly bookshop for parents and children. Include useful resource books for parents.
- Build up a lending library of books on child development and learning (parents' fund can be used for this purpose).
- Demonstrate some simple games parents can play with children at home. Run workshops for parents to make some of these games for use at home. (A realistic charge may be made for materials, or costs may be met from school funds.)

- Display information about and addresses for the Advisory Centre for Education, the British Association for Early Childhood Education and other organizations of interest.
- Encourage parents to plan their own reading study groups and allow them to have access to the Open University and National Curriculum Council video-cassettes, which can be used in each other's homes.

Give parents responsibility for their children's learning

- Provide a 'link card' to accompany any books and games going home. Encourage parents to record their comments after using this material with their child. It may be helpful to discuss what comments are useful to record and why, e.g. a comment simply indicating to the child that his or her parent would like you, his or her teacher, to share something positive, such as how much they enjoyed a game together or how well he or she behaved when losing the game. Comments may record what a child wants his or her teacher to know but wants to communicate through his or her parent. Comments may record something of developmental interest the parent has observed. It should also be accepted that only some parents will see written dialogue as relevant and all parents need to have a positive response to their comments.
- Hold a regular 'surgery' at the end of the day or in the early evening, when parents can share with you any particular observed developments or delays in their child's learning and behaviour. Provide parents with a simple record booklet in which they can jot down any observed behaviour of interest.
- Having explained nursery routines fully to new parents, ask each parent to take responsibility for explaining these routines to their own child and checking the child is conversant with them.
- Encourage parents to share in planning the child's daily programme. Keep a planning book for each child in which he is helped to think through and record selected activities and intentions for the session. Suggest that parents discuss and describe these plans for the child at the beginning of each session. These plans will be used later by the teacher when monitoring activities and in shared group review. (See Chapter 7 for shared planning and assessment with parents.)
- Be clear to parents that you do not have all the answers, but need to share the privilege of educating and caring for their child with them.

REFERENCES

1. I. Lazar and R. Darlington (1982) *Lasting Effects of Early Education*: a Report from the Consortium for Longitudinal Studies, Monographs of the Society for Research in Child Development, Serial no. 195, Vol. 47.
2. A. F. Osborn and J. E. Millbank (1987) *The Effects of Early Education*, Clarendon Press, Oxford.
3. HMI (1989) *Aspects of Primary Education. The Education of Children Under Five*, DES, London, p. 7.
4. House of Commons, Education, Science and Arts Committee (1990) *Report of the Committee of Inquiry into Under-Fives*, HMSO, London, para. 6.11.
5. DES (1977) *A New Partnership for Our Schools* (the Taylor Report), HMSO, London.
6. P. Blatchford, S. Battle and J. Mays (1982) *The First Transition; Home to Pre-School*, NFER/Nelson, Slough.
7. G. Pugh (1986) *Coordination of Services for Under Fives*, NFER/Nelson. Slough.
8. Blatchford, Battle and Mays (1982) op. cit. (note 6).
9. B. Tizard, J. Mortimore and B. Burchell (1981) *Involving Parents in Nursery and Infant Schools*, Grant McIntyre, London.
10. *Ibid.*
11. *Ibid.*
12. F. Macleod (1985) *Parents in Partnership; Involving Muslim Parents in their Children's Education*, Community Education Development Centre, Briton Road, Coventry CV2 4LF.
13. Blatchford, Battle and Mays (1982) op. cit. (note 6); Tizard, Mortimore and Burchell (1981) op. cit. (note 9).
14. M. Young and P. McGeeney (1968) *Learning Begins at Home*, Routledge & Kegan Paul, London.
15. G. Wells (1984) *Language Development in the Pre-School Years*, Cambridge University Press.
16. B. Tizard and M. Hughes (1984) *Young Children Learning*, Fontana, London.
17. Tizard, Mortimore and Burchell (1981) op. cit. (note 9).
18. *Ibid.*
19. Blatchford, Battle and Mays (1982) op. cit. (note 6).
20. *Ibid.*
21. J. Atkin, J. Bastiani and J. Goode (1988) *Listening to Parents. An Approach to the Improvement of Home–School Relations*, Croom Helm, Beckenham.
22. Blatchford, Battle and Mays (1982) op. cit. (note 6).
23. K. Sylva and E. Moore (1984) *Record Keeping in Nurseries*, unpublished MS.
24. P. Moss (1988) Services for under fives in context: issues and lessons from Europe (paper given at the NES/NCB Conference, East Midlands Conference Centre, 14–15 July).
25. DES (1990) *Starting with Quality* (The Report of the Committee of Inquiry into the Quality of the Educational Experience Offered to 3 and 4 Year Olds), HMSO, London.
26. E. Ferri, B. Birchell and Y. Gingell (1981) *Combined Nursery Centres*,

National Children's Bureau, London.

27. Macleod (1985) op. cit. (note 12).

28. M. Stacey (1983) Partnership in a multi-cultural pre-school centre, in *Partnership Paper 1*, National Children's Bureau, London.

29. G. Pugh (1990) Developing a policy for early childhood education; challenges and constraints, *Early Childhood Development and Care*, Vol. 58, pp. 3–13.

30. L. Wright (1985) Parents as home visitors, in *Partnership Paper 5*, National Children's Bureau, London.

31. S. Wolfendale (1983) A framework for action; professional and parents as partners, in *Partnership Paper 1*, National Children's Bureau, London.

32. *New Parent* (Australia) (1983) Postnatal depression: a medical or cultural problem?, June.

33. B. Tizard, W. N. Schofield and J. Hewison (1982) Collaboration between teachers and parents in assisting children's reading, *British Journal of Educational Psychology*, Vol. 52, pp. 1–15.

34. B. Tizard and M. Hughes (1984) *Young Children Learning*, Fontana, London.

35. HMI (1990) *The Teaching and Learning of Reading in Primary Schools*, DES, London, p. 2.

36. L. Katz (1976) Contemporary perspectives on the roles of mothers and teachers, *Australian Journal of Early Childhood*, Vol. 7, no. 1, pp. 4–15.

37. B. Tizard, P. Blatchford, J. Burke, C. Farquhar and I. Plewis (1988) *Young Children at School in the Inner City*, Lawrence Erlbaum Associates, Hove and London.

38. K. Sylva (1990) Evaluating early education programmes, *Early Child Development and Care*, Vol. 58, pp. 97–107.

39. Tizard *et al.* (1988) op. cit. (note 37).

40. T. Smith (1980) *Parents and Pre-School*, Grant McIntyre, London.

41. P. Hannon and S. James (1990) Parents' and teachers' perspectives on pre-school literacy development, *British Educational Research Journal*, Vol. 16, no. 3, pp. 259–71.

42. Tizard *et al.* (1988) op. cit. (note 37).

43. Hannon and James (1990) op. cit. (note 41).

44. Katz (1976) op. cit. (note 36).

45. C. Athey (1990) *Extending Thought in Young Children*, Paul Chapman Publishing, London.

3

CURRICULUM PRINCIPLES TO
SUPPORT LEARNING

In pioneering nursery education early in the twentieth century, the McMillan sisters and Maria Montessori were working at a time of tremendous social disadvantage, with children who were ill fed, poorly clothed and badly housed. The accent was on social rescue, and this played a part in nursery pedagogy for some years. Respect, care and a range of play activities were offered to young children, together with a heavy emphasis on good hygiene and daily routines. Susan Isaacs,[1,2] working in the Malting House School, built on these practices but added the very clear message that provision was not sufficient in itself and that the adult's role is crucial in developing the child's learning. Detailed and sensitive observations produced evidence of children thriving on these practices, and today's nursery practice still remains rooted in these early approaches. However there is today a need for an even closer scrutiny of practice to ensure that nursery education is recognized and valued.

In 1974 Barbara Tizard described the nursery curriculum as 'essentially one of free play supplemented by music and stories'. She also regarded it as hardly distinguishable from that offered in the home.[3] This would not be an accurate statement of the nursery curriculum in the Nineties. The implications of the National Curriculum have made nursery teachers consider carefully how their content links into statutory programmes of study. LEAs have developed nursery curriculum guidelines and groups of practitioners have shared in-service deliberating about nursery content and their own role in bringing about cognitive change. The result in most nursery classes and schools is a planned programme of experiences that acknowledges and builds on home experiences but that is professionally tailored to support learning systematically.

The onus is on nursery teachers to retain the good aspects of traditional practice but to set these within a clear framework of thinking for their work. A purposeful rigour with the accent on extending children intellectually is required to justify provision. The public increasingly wants to know what children are learning in a nursery, rather than being satisfied with the provision of a place of social care and safety. Nursery practice must therefore be based on principles that have developed from the increased research and knowledge now available about the nature of learning and the needs of young children.

Today's nursery teachers will develop their principles as the pegs on which to hang their practice. No principle, however fine, is any good unless it can be directly translated into classroom action. Conversely, teachers should be able to look at their curriculum content and the way they organize their teaching and link all this to their educational principles. Theory and practice need to go hand in hand.

It is also necessary to be strictly honest when linking practices and principles. Are some routines adhered to because they promote children's learning or because they are convenient for the adults managing children? Are some messy activities withdrawn half-way through a nursery session because it is in the interests of children to limit curriculum choices at this stage, or because the adults find it easier to clear these up before the lunch hour? Providing an honest reason for all nursery activity can be a painful exercise, but is necessary in clarifying the purposes of provision. This chapter is concerned with identifying some key principles that might be taken as a basis for planning a nursery curriculum.

THE CHILD AS AN INDIVIDUAL

In every child genetic endowment and environment have combined to make him or her unique and special. Because young children are relatively unsocialized and because of their limited experience and egocentric stage of development their individual characteristics will be particularly noticeable. Every nursery teacher knows this and will also accept that, while the pattern of growth and development follows a universal sequence, the rate and progress of this development differ for each child.

It is the child's developmental stage that is significant for his or her learning, rather than chronological age. The wide variation in developmental stage can affect all aspects of a child's growth. It may relate to the child's understanding of concepts, to gross or fine motor control and to social and emotional level of development. What are the implications of this knowledge for the nursery teacher? John Brierley states that

> The important point is that each child is born unique because of 'nature's gifts' and he or she needs a unique environment to maximize them. It follows from this that in the home and at school it is *just* to treat different children differently as long as each is treated as well as possible. Blanket treatment is no good.[4]

If children are individuals, each will possess his or her own particular route to learning. It is the skill of teachers to identify that route, to discover exactly how they can help that child to be motivated to learn.

Certain groups of children have always been particularly vulnerable because their unique characteristics have been overlooked or because they have been singled out for discrimination. Society continues to communicate negative messages to some individuals on the grounds of their class, race or gender. The nursery teacher must try to ensure that each child's self-worth is acknowledged and strengthened to provide a resilience against bias and prejudice.

Studies in the 1960s[5] highlighted the fact that children from working-class backgrounds were not succeeding in school. Subsequent compensatory work with these children and their families indicated that they were as competent as those from other social classes, given they were allowed to demonstrate their understandings relevant to their background experiences. Chris Athey describes how two groups of children from different socio-economic backgrounds showed their understanding of a path of progress with a starting-point, stopping-off points and an end-point. One group pretended to be dustmen, collecting rubbish, with houses as stopping-off points, while the other group collected skiers from various hotels in order to transport them to the ski lift. Athey emphasized that both examples of play reflected common forms of thought.[6]

Children from ethnic-minority groups may also have their abilities under-estimated on account of their behaviour or their difficulties with English as a second language. Children who are facing a new culture as well as being new to a nursery will need time to accommodate themselves. However, reflection and puzzlement may be interpreted as sulky and uncommunicative behaviour. Similarly, bilingual children may be grouped with younger and less able children, and given cognitively easy tasks because their lack of English vocabulary limits the teacher's understanding of their capabilities.

Misunderstandings about the needs of children from different ethnic groups may arise because of lack of acceptance or understanding of their cultural background. This is often the case with black children. Schools often take for granted that all children feel positively about their colour or believe colour of skin is insignificant and not apparent to young children. These misapprehensions are dangerous. Research has shown that young black children reject their colour and show a clear preference for their white peers.[8] As Durrant suggests, 'For young children to reject and be embarrassed by what they are has implications for future self-esteem and mental health'.[9] One Scottish study of multicultural nursery schools suggests that, in the absence of working with individual ethnic-minority children, teachers judged them in terms of their ethnic-group membership. They also made assessments of children's abilities based on their behaviour: thus a quiet, well-behaved Asian child's difficulties with language tended to be overlooked.[10]

Children from different classes, races and cultures need to be helped to develop positive self-images. If a child is not allowed to use his or her home language or have some aspects of his or her home and family life acknowledged in the nursery, the child is essentially being ignored.

While teachers will acknowledge the importance of treating children as individuals, all too often their management and interactions are in response to gender differences. Primary-school studies show that teachers have more interactions with boys. The reasons for this include the fact that boys are more visible in class, by talking more, by volunteering information and in developing more attention-seeking strategies to which teachers respond. Morgan and Dunn point out that children will arrive at school having already learnt a great deal about how society regards men and women. Given a large class of children, the teacher's easiest means of management control will be to follow children's expectations of sex roles. However, if that happens the authors stress that 'during their early years at school they will almost inevitably become resolutely set in a framework which makes explicit the different expectations of the two sexes and continues the vicious circle of deeply engendered biases in adult be-haviour and instincts'.[11]

If all children are to be given the full range of learning opportunities, the nursery must aim to redress any discrimination or inequalities that might result from their class, race, culture or sex.

As well as regarding learning needs, the teacher must be aware of the individual's personal, social and physical requirements. Children differ in their personal make-up; the transition they make to school is partly determined by their approach to change and their ability to adapt to a new situation. Nursery teachers, in acknowledging differing needs, must offer support where it is most needed. They have to recognize that not all children are willing or able to join in a large ring game, for example, and must provide a quiet table activity as an alternative. Not all children in the nursery wish to absorb themselves with messy activities, and such preferences should be respected when voiced by a child as they would be if they came from an adult. A wide choice of activities needs to be available to provide for all tastes. Some children revel in boisterous outside play that challenges physical skills; others are cautious and tentative in their efforts to master body skills. It must be accepted that some children prefer to stay inside rather than face the elements, and within reason and the constraints of practical circumstances this choice should be available.

Physical needs are also individual. If drinks are provided for a mid-morning break, children will vary in their ability to consume a standard amount. Likewise, despite the desirability of developing 'good habits', individual bladder capacity and sphincter control do not make it sensible for children to go to the lavatory at set times.

Every nursery teacher, then, needs regularly to ask him or herself how his or her acceptance of children as individuals is reflected in his or her practice. This is not to say that the entire nursery programme will be geared to responding on an individual basis at all times. One of the processes of maturation is for the child to become socialized, but this process needs to be tackled sensitively and at the appropriate developmental stage.

If children are truly seen as individuals, every one can be regarded as having 'special needs'. Many handicapping conditions involve developmental delays in one or more aspects of growth. This delay must be identified by the teacher with specialist help, but the child will require the same rich nursery provision with the opportunity to operate at the appropriate level of development reached. Thus, the 5-year-old who has a developmental delay of two years in intellectual ability is likely to be playing with concrete materials of clay, water and sand, exploring them through the senses. The 5-year-old whose development is two years ahead may still be using these materials but will be beginning to represent his or her experiences in many abstract ways.

Every child's uniqueness and the ways in which he or she is best able to flourish in a nursery setting need to be answered by the teacher at the earliest possible opportunity.

Essential	Important	Unimportant

Figure 3.1

Suggested action

Determining principles

Each member of staff should list ten curriculum principles relating to nursery practice, each principle to be copied on a small card. All cards are then shuffled and distributed equally among the group. A large sheet of paper should be prepared as indicated in Figure 3.1. Each member of staff is required to read out the principle on one of his or her cards in turn and indicate in which column he or she wishes to place it. He or she is required to justify the decision to the group. All cards should be placed in this way. The aim of the activity is to allow no more than ten statements in either the 'essential' or 'important' columns, and this will be achieved through clarification of terms and negotiation within the group.

Acknowledge children as individuals

- On admission to the nursery, ask parents to share what they consider to be unique and special about their child.

- Select a child at random and write down all you know about him or her as an individual, including ethnic origins. Identify how you attempt to meet his or her particular needs by a programme of activities/adjustment of routines/your behaviour towards him or her.
- Gain an accurate total picture of each child through close observation. For example, a child who has particular ability in one area of development may be expected to have good all-round development; the child from a poor social background with behavioural difficulties may be expected to achieve less than he or she is able.

Acknowledge the child's home background

- Provide for language diversity through story-telling sessions in other languages using familiar folk tales, having story tapes in different languages and dialects.
- Provide for ethnic diversity through providing paint and crayons that allow for the depiction of all skin tones; by checking all activities with an aim to include pictorial material that shows different skin tones and facial features; requesting school-meals services to provide a variety of ethnic dishes children may have had at home.
- Help children's understanding of different behaviours by encouraging individuals to bring in items of clothing and utensils worn and used in their homes; by asking parents from different cultures to explain and to help children in the nursery share different ways of celebrating birthdays and other festivals.

Meet individual needs through the curriculum

- Consider how you meet children's individual needs during story-time, e.g. introducing stories ranging in length and content; ensuring a group of children of manageable size and identifying those who can still receive a story only on an individual basis; focusing on particular stories that match children's own situations.
- Mark each child's cloakroom peg with his or her photograph (this can be a photograph requested from home or one taken on admission to the nursery).
- Set up an obstacle course for children that gives scope for them to crawl through a tunnel, balance along planks, jump and climb. Carefully observe individual children's reactions to this activity.

Which of them refuse to attempt the course? Who is willing
to try with support and encouragement? Who becomes very
competitive?
• Provide a range of materials in painting, sticking and cookery
areas to encourage children to exercise individual choice when
producing something of their own.

LEARNING IS CONTINUOUS

Sound learning should be based on what is already known and should
move cautiously and gently toward the unknown. Learning is best fostered
when there is sufficient challenge to stimulate and interest but not so
much that too dramatic an adjustment is required. This is particularly
important with young children, whose experience is necessarily limited
and who are even less equipped to make jumps in their learning.

In the past there have been remarkable discontinuities in our school
system. Nurseries considered themselves to be something special and
apart. Parents were respected and there were some links but, despite
Margaret McMillan's own philosophy, there was little acknowledgement
of the power of the home environment. Nurseries were cut off from the
rest of the school system, largely because of their own modest, complacent and insular attitudes. Within the infant school, teachers tended to
be autonomous; they had their own children and their own approach to
the curriculum, using their own resources that were firmly kept in their
own cupboards. Children were often subjected to totally different approaches to learning, and it is a tribute to the resilience of some that they
ended up literate and numerate.

In recent years a tremendous amount has happened as a result of the
growing awareness of the need to promote continuity of experience at all
levels of learning. Although for teachers the first transition in which they
are involved is the child's move to the nursery, in fact it may be far from
the first move for the child – he or she can arrive in a nursery from a
variety of placements. Possible transitions experienced before transfer to
a nursery are

1. home to nursery,
2. home to playgroup to nursery,
3. home to childminder to nursery, or
4. home to childminder to playgroup to nursery.

Clearly the regimes and messages offered to children in these different placements will affect the nature of the move to the nursery. The nursery, unlike other phases of education, accepts children who have not shared a previous common experience. In coping with this diversity of background and personality the nursery teacher has a particularly challenging job. The NFER study, *The First Transition* (from home to nursery), found that in the main the children who had come from high-scoring backgrounds (enabling, warm, loving homes) tended to relate better to other children, were found less in solitary and unoccupied activities in free play and showed less lost or negative behaviour in a directed session such as story or register time.[12] These findings reinforce the tremendous difference between those best prepared and those least prepared to enter a nursery class.

There is no doubt that all children have had a fund of experience before they come to school and have learnt a great deal in their own way. It is essential that each child is accepted from where he or she is. It is not enough to allow the learning to continue in the rather random and *ad hoc* way it has to date – it is certainly not satisfactory to ignore what has happened before. The emphasis must be on a planned intervention based on previous learning.

A child has to learn a tremendous amount when he or she moves from home to school. Mary Willes indicates the range of language skills that has to be acquired:

> In taking on his new role of pupil, the newcomer to school has to be put to the test of using the language learned in interaction at home. He has to find, or to extend his resources to include, the language of a learner, one among many, in an institutionalized setting. He has to wait his turn, and recognize it when it comes, to compete, to assert his rights and sometimes to give ground. He has, in short, to discover what the rules of classroom interaction and behaviour are, what sort of priority obtains among them, and how and when and with what consequences they can be broken.[13]

Some children will attune to these requirements smoothly and easily; for others they will constitute a major stumbling-block. Until the young child adapts fully to his or her first transition there is no doubt that his or her learning will be arrested or will take a backward step.

When looking at the entry to nursery, a general pattern emerged from the NFER study. The experience was that quite close attention was paid to the child and family initially. Phased visits to the nursery were planned, with encouragement for parents to be involved. Once the child had appeared to settle, however, the study describes his or her two worlds as 'slipping apart'. Parents were interested in their child's nursery experiences, but they were very wary of doing at home anything deemed unacceptable by the school; because they hesitated to request more information about what happened during the nursery sessions, they remained uninformed. The research team said it interviewed too many parents who had no more information about their child's progress than 'he's happy' or 'getting along satisfactorily'. A fair amount of work was undertaken by nurseries to involve parents, but there were often not enough individual requests to parents for them to do specific tasks. The study also highlighted a lack of liaison between playgroups and nurseries. Little information was received from playgroups when children entered the nursery, and a number of nursery staff were unaware of what experiences had been offered in the previous setting.[14]

More recently, the report of the committee of inquiry recommended that 'Understanding of each others' priorities, purposes and practices can be forged by increased liaison including regular visits and attempts to plan common curriculum experiences as well as record-keeping systems. Increased access to LEA advisory services would be invaluable in enabling this to happen'.[15] This is a worthy aim but no more than that in many areas where different providing groups are still not familiar with each other. However, it is important to consider what initiatives are resource dependent and what might develop as a result of positive attitudes and energy. In recognizing concerns about the possible lack of educational stimulus in some day nurseries, the committee of inquiry suggests that, while it might not be possible to employ full-time teachers in these settings, a useful compromise would be for nursery teachers and day nursery staff to work in each other's settings on a regular basis.

The move to mainstream school can be traumatic if insensitively handled: the move involves adapting to a class that does not have a nursery staffing and may lack the space and material resources of a nursery. The closest possible liaison with feeder schools will aid a smooth transition (see Chapter 5).

There is, in addition, the need to ensure continuity of experience for young children within the nursery. Does the nursery team ensure there is consistency in handling children? Are the expected standards of behaviour, noise and tidying-up common to all? A consistent approach to common situations needs to be agreed. For instance, how do we react to a child who insists on taking every painting and model home with him or her? There should be opportunities for continuous activities from one day to another; can the nursery teacher ensure that a construction of bricks can be left to be completed the next day?

All nursery teachers work on different aspects of liaison and continuity within and between schools. The question remains of how much more can be achieved. Regarding the transitions to and from the nursery, teachers should ask themselves how much they know about what any one child has experienced before he or she becomes a nursery pupil, and how much they know about what he or she is going to experience after the child leaves the nursery.

There is need for more research into how different home and institutional settings support children learning and how links between these settings might enhance continuity. Margaret Clark suggests that children from ethnic-minority groups and those living in rural areas should be considered and that priority should be given to long-term studies: 'In this way the interrelatedness of the children's apparent competence, the contexts in which they are placed and the expectations of the adults can be assessed'.[16]

Suggested action

Find out about the child's home background

There is no single successful strategy for acquiring relevant information about the child's home background, but the following approaches are likely to be useful for different catchment areas.

- An initial home visit offering an invitation card for the child to start at the nursery. Home visits remain controversial and, in practice, some teachers are more highly motivated and more suited to the job than others. However, there is no doubt that some parents are more at ease on their own territory when meeting their child's teacher for the first time – and this can equally apply to the child.
- There should be an opportunity in school or at home for the parents to talk to an interested adult about the unique characteristics of their child. Some parents may respond very well to completing detailed questionnaires, while others will find it easier to chat. Whatever the approach the emphasis should be on communicating positive traits rather than just potential problems.
- A range of occasions for social, fund-raising and curriculum purposes can encourage teachers and parents to meet and can foster trusting relationships (see Chapter 2).

Find out about previous playgroup experience

Previous attendance at a playgroup may indicate experience of a
small home-group offering security but mainly sedentary activity, or
the other extreme of a large group accommodated in a hall with
adults providing few boundaries for learning and socialization – with
a range of other provisions in between. The teacher's knowledge of
this experience can be extremely useful. Good established relationships with playgroups can ease communication.

- Aim to visit playgroups in your catchment area each term to build
  up a picture of their style of management and expectations of
  children.
- Invite playgroups to visit the nursery in session; use opportunities
  to discuss different styles of working with children.
- Link with childminders: aim to involve both parents and childminder in all meetings prior to and at the point of admission.
  As the parents' representative, the childminder should be given
  copies of all newsletters, be encouraged to attend all school
  events and, with the parents' consent, contribute to information
  for the child's portfolio.

Offer the child information

Use an initial home visit to prepare the child for coming to the
nursery. Using a large book of photographs and miniature play
people, tell him the story of Ben's (substitute child's name) first day
at nursery. The story and photographs could include details of the
journey from home, the arrival of other children and parents, the
physical characteristics of the building including cloakrooms and
lavatories, the activities, the routines, and photographs of the adults
who would be available to take care of the child. A special chair
could be identified as a place for mummy (daddy) to sit.

Observe children during their first week in the nursery

- How do they leave their parents at the start of the session?
- How do they settle to activities?
- How do they relate to other children and adults?
- How do they greet their parents at the end of the day?

Check you have sufficient information

Select three children at random who have entered the nursery
during the last term. Make a list of all you know about each child's

previous learning and relevant home experience. Make a note of any additional information you need to enable you to work more effectively with these children. Consider the best strategies for gaining this information, e.g. home visits with the aim of asking parents specific questions about their children; invitations to individual parents to visit the nursery and to talk generally about their child.

Check that parents have sufficient information

Having settled their child in the nursery, invite parents in to discuss effects of the transition. Are parents clear about their child's daily programme – if not, what additional information would they like? A video depicting new entrants during their initial weeks may be an effective way of offering this information.

Plan for individual need

- The child who finds transition to the nursery difficult may require (1) parents to stay with him or her until he or she has settled; (2) flexibility in attendance, gradually building up to a daily attendance; (3) substitute parent attached to the child during initial sessions (this role could be given to a volunteer parent or National Nursery Examination Board (NNEB) student).
- The child who finds it difficult to relate to other children may need (1) the initial security of one adult; (2) gradual introduction to work on a specific task with one other child, with adult present; (3) withdrawal of the adult as he or she gains confidence.
- The non-English-speaking child will be helped by the initial presence of a parent or volunteer helper who is bilingual, and by early involvement in repetitious rhymes and jingles and familiarization with regular routines with associated labels, e.g. 'wash your hands', 'time for lunch'; introduction to one or two socially responsible children who will involve the child in play.

Aim for a smooth transition from nursery to main school

- Both nursery and infant teachers must learn to appreciate each other's work in meeting the developmental needs of the children. This can be facilitated by nursery teachers leading main-staff in-service sessions focusing on nursery practice and by infant teachers joining nursery staff discussions. Occasions should be available for joint discussion of children. Regular exchange visits and exchange of nursery and infant posts will enable a better understanding of each other's age-group.

- Compare the information about your children you wish to pass on to the infant teacher with the information he or she requires. Consider carefully where there is a mismatch and why.
- Where a nursery class is attached to a school, any curriculum policies must be developed with the nursery as the starting-point.
- Continuity of experience should be developed through daily routines. The entry to school in the morning, procedures for playtimes, gathering for story-time and collecting and returning resources – these routines can be eased for the child entering the main school if an attempt has been made to follow the procedures previously established in the nursery. Discuss your daily programme with your infant colleague and compare and contrast your routines, your expectations of children and your priorities during the day.
- Foster continuity of experience by deliberately duplicating pieces of equipment used in the nursery for the child to recognize in the infant classroom. A favourite teddy found in the home corner, or familiar books, can be reassuring to the less confident child when he or she is settling into the new placement.
- Encourage the infant teacher to use additional adults to help children with unfamiliar routines. Parents can be very helpful during the initial move into the infant classroom: during undressing and dressing for PE; helping children to adapt to lunchtime procedures, including meal-time supervision in small groups; involvement with supervisory assistants in organizing small-group games after lunch.
- Use the opportunities offered by an attached nursery unit to allow older children with developmental delay to spend some time back in the nursery and younger able children occasionally to join appropriate sessions in the reception class.

CHILDREN LEARN THROUGH ACTION AND TALK

Young children learn most effectively through their actions and through talk. They will continue to learn without entering a nursery – the power of the home environment has already been mentioned – but the nursery teacher should clarify the particular sort of experience he or she can offer that will nurture learning.

Young children are very ready to please and to learn certain things through imitation. It is possible through regular practice and repetition for a group of 4-year-olds to recite a numerical table or to recognize a number of flashcards. While this 'performance' may impress a lay person it is highly likely that only an image of learning is being seen, with children incapable of making sense of the symbols or of being able to apply their knowledge. In such cases the learners have been required to receive certain information to regurgitate at a later date. No independent learning has taken place.

How do young children learn best? Piaget's main findings remain as valid as ever, even if some aspects of his work are increasingly challenged. Young children gain information through having active encounters with their world, and they process this information into theories and assumptions that form their mental structures. These structures are in turn extended and amended in the light of new information being gathered and fed into what already exists.[17]

John Brierley suggests that 'Through exploration, play and speech the young brain seems to strengthen. A child needs this two-way dynamic relationship with the environment.'[18] Ausabel supports this view, arguing that, although discovery learning and problem-solving are relatively complex forms of learning, they are the most effective means of intellectual functioning for the young child. Received learning through symbols and verbally presented concepts, although simple in cognitive terms, will come only at a later stage of maturity.[19] Thus, a 3-year-old may competently sort out household items in the home corner, classifying and matching. He or she is not yet able, however, to make sense of the code of arithmetic (see page 94).

Having offered the case for young children to learn through concrete experiences, it may be helpful to consider the different roles of exploration, play and talk in development. In exploration the concern is with finding out about reality. Corinne Hutt's study of play and exploration illustrates that exploration precedes play; her sample of nursery-aged children were given a novel box for the first time:

> When a child had thoroughly explored the novel object, he then sometimes used it in symbolic play, for example by pretending it was a bridge or a seat. It was only when the child had apparently learned all there was to know about the object that it was incorporated in play activities, and any further learning was purely incidental.[20]

Thus, through exploration the young child gains information from an experience and modifies or accommodates his or her learning accordingly.

There is a tacit acceptance among educators that play is a useful educational method to promote in a nursery. However, a distinction must be made between closely structured, target-oriented activity and unstructured, child-initiated play. There is a place for both approaches in a nursery programme, but the teacher needs to be clear about their respective benefits.

While highly structured play has a clear purpose, and exploration leaves the child more open to discover what he or she will from materials and apparatus, they are similar in that the aim is for the child to find out something new and modify his or her experience accordingly. In highly structured play, apparatus is used for a specific purpose, giving little space for the child's creative thought. The Montessori approach is a good example of children tackling activities in a way prescribed by the adult. This may be valid as part of a learning programme designed for an individual child, but it is limited as a general diet for children.

Conversely, child-initiated, spontaneous play is open. This approach allows the child to engage freely in pleasurable activity and thus to consolidate skills, actions and meanings previously acquired through exploration. Spontaneous play allows the child to take his or her knowledge of the real world and to try to make sense of it. The child will assimilate this play into his or her framework of experience, but it requires less modification or accommodation, since his or her activity is based on practising or representing what he or she already knows.

The most obvious example of this is in pretend play. Vygotsky has in mind this play, which he considers important for young children because it frees them from the constraints they constantly meet in real life; in a world of all-powerful adults the 4-year-old can escape to become master of his or her world through play.[21] Vygotsky sees play as necessarily involving the creation of an imaginary situation, and Joan Tamburrini suggests that his work creates a link between spontaneous play and the development of imagination at a later stage. The young child creates a situation but needs concrete props to represent different objects and settings. As he matures he is able to relinquish these props and to create meanings and situations through mental activity.[22]

It can be argued, then, that opportunities for exploration and for structured and unstructured play all have a place in the nursery. Sylva, Roy and Painter considered the educational value of play and defined complex play as an activity that is goal oriented, whether the goals are imposed by adult or child. For them the important consideration was that the child felt he or she had accomplished something. They also looked for evidence that the child in his or her play is able to link a series of actions and engage in long-range planning and organization of behaviour. Play was also regarded as complex where an object or act was seen to represent something else – that is, through symbolic or pretend play. These authors also considered the child's concentration span; where there was evidence of absorption and resistance to distraction the task was rated as more intellectually demanding.[23]

Turning to John Brierley's third requirement, a great deal has been written on the significance and structure of language. Suffice it to say that it provides a powerful means for personal development, for reflecting on experiences and for communicating thoughts to others. How this facility is developed has been hotly debated. In 1965 Chomsky put forward a strongly supported notion that the child possesses a 'language acquisition device' which enables him or her to absorb scraps of conversation and discourse, and through this sensitive mechanism the child can make out grammatical rules and thus build up a framework of knowledge.[24] While this was more than acceptable at the time, with the benefit of further investigation the emphasis turned from the view that language was acquired as something accelerated and apart from other aspects of development; interest turned to the whole child and his or her range of experiences. John Macnamara suggested in 1972 that language develops precisely because the child uses all his or her previous knowledge and experience to make sense of a situation.[25]

Margaret Donaldson offers the following example:

> An English woman is in the company of an Arab woman and her two children, a boy of seven and a little girl of thirteen months who is just beginning to walk but is afraid to take more than a few steps without help. The English woman speaks no Arabic, the Arab woman and her son speak no English. The little girl walks to the English woman and back to her mother. Then she turns as if to start off in the direction of the English woman once again. But the latter now smiles, points to the boy and says: 'Walk to your brother this time'. At once the boy, understanding the situation though he understands not a word of the language, holds out his arm. The baby smiles, changes direction and walks to her brother. Like the older child she appears to have understood the situation perfectly.[26]

Donaldson stresses that, as far as the two children were concerned, both were in a position to understand the intentions of the group; the meaning of words was extracted from the behaviour of the people. Thus, language learning is now seen to be very closely tied up with other aspects of development. The child must be placed in a position where he or she can understand what is happening – which will depend on what has happened to the child before and how he or she has accommodated and assimilated these experiences.

Emphasis thus falls on the child as an active learner. The child is required to make links between events and behaviours and then to draw his or her own conclusions. In so doing, the child discovers that language represents these events and behaviours.

The next stage is one of practice and consolidation; developing linguistic skills are used in a range of contexts with other people. In the nursery the child learns according to his or her stage of development to use and practise language for the purposes outlined by Joan Tough.[27] The child will use it to maintain and promote his or her interests and well-being, and then as a vehicle for developing thinking – to examine a range of possible solutions to problems, to predict, hypothesize and plan. As the child learns to use talk for these purposes, language gradually becomes detached from immediate experience. The emphasis has so far been on the particular effects of exploration, play and language on children's learning. The practitioner, it is hoped, convinced of these key ingredients, now needs to reflect on how he or she can plan to include them.

Any richly resourced nursery environment provides a range of opportunities for exploration. The traditional provisions of sand, water, clay, dough, paint and blocks will all initially be explored by the young child, leading to discoveries of their various properties. Dry sand is usually explored first with the hands. The child may poke, press and trickle it and bury his or her hands in a heap of sand. He or she may delight in the cold, heavy feel of the sand and let the fine grains tickle the skin. Clay is not visually attractive and it requires to be touched to discover its capabilities. The cold, clammy nature of clay may repel some children until they meet the challenge of prodding and pushing it to change its shape. Natural potter's clay is most satisfactory for the young child. The intention is to provide not a modelling material but something to work with and explore. Exploration can be staged and guided through provision. Clay should initially be offered to children without water or tools; harder lumps of clay can then be presented with a bowl of water. The child is able to change the substance from something unmalleable to an oozing semi-liquid. The further addition of blunt knives, clean lolly-sticks and pieces of cut-off broom handle will then allow children to explore clay with equipment.

As we have seen with sand and clay, the young child's explorations will be through the senses. He or she needs to see, listen, taste, touch and smell the environment until he or she is ready to accommodate to these experiences.

In structured play, planning will play a large part, because some outcomes are predetermined for the child. In extreme forms of structured play apparatus is required to be used for one purpose only, and any other uses are discouraged. An inset jigsaw is an example of structured apparatus. The teacher who is determined to channel the learning along his or her lines will gently dissuade the child from using the inset pieces to stand up and represent animals and people – the teacher regards the task of completing the jigsaw as the aim. Unstructured apparatus may also be used for structured play. Blocks may be provided with a request for children to build a car. The teacher may return to the group on a number of occasions to check that all the car body parts are being assembled. There is thus restricted space for children's creativity in this task, although there is value in seeing how the group tackles the activity and in observing who emerges as a leader.

Provision of an extreme form of unstructured play requires the adult to be present but passive. Practitioners who subscribe to this approach have no clear ideas how they can promote children's cognitive development through play. They tend to concentrate on the therapeutic value of the activity. Almy suggests that a symptom of their preoccupation with the emotional is apparent lack of involvement in the intellectual life of the child.[28] Tizard states that in nursery schools where teachers adopted this passive role the play was generally of short duration and poorly elaborated.[29]

Where symbolic play is recognized as valuable in promoting children's learning, the teacher needs to take a more active role. This play is increasingly valued for helping consolidation skills and meanings, aiding imaginative development and revealing language structures. The teacher can structure the environment by arranging a setting for an imaginative play area or by limiting the range of blocks available; by actively observing the level of play, the teacher can also obtain diagnostic information.

The teacher may also choose to be involved in children's self-initiated play by playing alongside and offering a reassuring presence, by questioning, suggesting or providing additional props. The 'daddy' who has hurt his leg at work will be better able to play out his role with the addition of a bandage and a walking-stick. The adult needs to be aware of the potential for learning in children's play, but this is a different matter from predetermining the play. The teacher may have set up a structure in his or her provision for home play with graded sizes of saucepans and lids. The teacher must accept, however, that the child is not necessarily going to seize on this graded equipment and develop an understanding of relative size. The play may be purely imaginative, with the purpose of getting the meal cooked and served on the table. If this is so then intrusion would be counter-productive. If, however, the teacher observed the child selecting a wrong size of lid that he or she tries to fit on to the saucepan, it may be appropriate to suggest trying an alternative and to observe the fruits of this in future play.

The teacher should also be influenced by research findings pointing to the most profitable areas of play. Sylva saw the most challenging and complex play in child-initiated music, small-scale construction, art (where the child selects his or her own medium), large-scale construction and structured materials such as jigsaws. Here she observed children working with care, using imagination, planning in a systematic way, learning a skill and working towards a goal. However, she admits a further necessary dimension to worthwhile play, that of 'sustained commitment': 'The ability to manage one's own attention is a prerequisite to effective and satisfying social relations. And of course the ability to concentrate is crucial to later school work'. Pretend play scores highly on this dimension. While it is regarded as an activity of only moderate cognitive challenge, children were found to be absorbed, and this play was seen, together with miniature play and sand and water activity, as a means of encouraging children's talk. Sylva suggests that these activities may be more relaxed and less goal oriented, thus providing an easy setting for conversation.[30]

A somewhat gloomy picture of the nursery as nurturing ground for young children's spoken language is offered to us by recent research. Thomas observed a small group of children for a day and managed to record every utterance from them and from the adults. She found that the teachers were prepared to accept minimal comments from children and that their own exchanges with children rarely helped to develop discourse or thinking skills.[31] In the Oxford Preschool Research Study, Woods reports that 'incidence of really interesting talk is rare',[32] and Sylva supports this in her study: 'Its finding suggests that the pre-school is not an ideal environment for teaching children the many skills of conversation, since coherent conversations are few and far between'.[33] Tizard's studies, too, indicate that children's speech at home is likely to be richer than in a day nursery or nursery school.[34] Tizard refers to the 'puzzling mind' and 'persistent curiosity' of the 4-year-old and suggests that the individual attention and intimate setting of home are more likely to satisfy these needs.[35]

We need to look critically at these findings. In both the Oxford studies mixed samples of playgroups and nurseries were used. Tizard's 1975 work was based on day nurseries, and the 1984 research used a sample of only thirty 4-year-old girls. It is valid to ask in this latter case just how far the findings can be related to other children. The research nevertheless does offer some clear messages to nursery teachers, who can only benefit from comparing their own practice with these findings.

Although the adult's role in promoting conversation has been emphasized, there is much to be said for encouraging children to talk together. Clark, Robson and Browning indicated that peer-group settings often provided opportunities for children to play with words and to initiate conversations in a way that does not happen with an adult present. Peer groups can also be helpful to children with more limited language and to those from non-English-speaking backgrounds. In these cases it has been found that children will help others to pronounce words and understand meanings.[36]

The nursery environment itself can influence talk. Sylva observed some of the richest dialogue in home corners or dens where an enclosed, intimate space had been created. She also noted that there were more instances of children conversing with one another in nursery rather than playgroup settings. Sylva recommends that teachers review their programmes and materials to encourage children to interact in pairs.[37] Pairing of children was seen to have potential for challenging play as well as for dialogue. The teacher's specific role in promoting talk is discussed in Chapter 4. If teachers are to be convinced of the importance of this work and to feel relaxed in giving time to it, they must be supported by their headteacher, parents and policy-makers. Katz refers to 'the institutional imperative which presses teachers to "cover" the curriculum and prepare their pupils for "the next life"'. She suggests that where teachers are under such pressures to develop academic skills, the communication skills that aid intellectual growth will not be nurtured.[38] Bearing in mind that infant teachers have great difficulty in nurturing communication skills with large groups of children, the nursery should act as a 'bridge' between home and school.

The Bristol Language Development Study of 1972–81 focused on children's talk in the home as well as their spoken language development in the transition to school. Although the role of the nursery is not considered, the study has implications for nursery teachers. MacLure and French found that some similar language strategies were employed in the home and at school, such as 'pseudo-questions' where a request for information is made to which the questioner already has the answer. Differences were nevertheless found in that in the home children were likely to question the adult but this was rare in school. Children's spoken language is corrected both in school and at home, but the study found that, while the child might correct the parent at home, it was very uncommon to find the teacher corrected by a child in a reception class in school. The authors conclude that the school setting may, if anything, present the child with a more limited set of conversational options than he or she has become familiar with at home:

> Just as the child at home has more latitude to ask questions and evaluate and correct his adult interlocutor, so also he has more opportunity to introduce new topics and to attempt to change the topic of conversation. . . . Such opportunities are much less frequently available to children in school, firstly because much of the talk is done for pedagogical purposes . . . and secondly because of the complexities involved in handling conversation involving large numbers of participants.[39]

The nursery is surely in the ideal position to ease this transition and to provide plentiful opportunities for the type of talk that already occurs at home, at the same time guiding some conversation into pedagogical channels.

Suggested action

Exploration

- Check that all activity areas have provision for exploring materials in a variety of ways. For example, painting and sticking: cardboard boxes of different sizes, stapler, polystyrene shapes, corks, pipe-cleaners, feathers, wool, paint, glue, sticky tape, fabrics; home corner: variety of kitchen implements, flour sieves, beaters, whiskers, equipment to 'mend' including a large box of spare parts from washing-machines, typewriters, radios and vacuum-cleaners, with tools for mending; outside area: mud patch with digging implements and encouragement to use hands to find as many treasures as you can; 'bicycle maintenance shop' with spare parts, cycle pumps, spanners and cleaning equipment; large construction corner with ropes, wooden boxes and planks, plastic milk crates, barrels and blown-up tractor inner-tube.
- Introduce an interesting artefact, e.g. muscial box, by placing it without comment in the home area and observe the way individual children find out about it. Note how their approach alters according to the stage of development of each child.

Structured play

- Consider how much of your apparatus and materials has a defined use for the child, e.g. some fitting and grading apparatus, jigsaws, miniature dolls with specific dressing-up outfits.
- Assess when these materials are particularly useful, e.g. in helping a child acquire and practise a specific skill.
- Consider how you as a teacher structure children's play:

  - Through your provision and by setting up situations.
  - By requiring that apparatus is used in a particular way, e.g. Lego is for building and not to be used as pretend food in the home corner.
  - Through time, e.g. the allotted time for children to become involved in inside and outside play.
  - Through determining use of space, e.g. a very small home corner may allow only one or two children to play freely.
  - Through your own involvement in the play, e.g. taking a role, initiating actions and suggesting actions for the children, linking one child with another in play.

- Consider how much of this structure inhibits or enriches children's play. This will depend on particular circumstances and particular children.

Spontaneous play

- Observe a child's spontaneous play and note how often he or she initiates action, through suggestions or his or her own activity; how often he or she leads; how often he or she follows; how long he or she sustains the play; his or her use of talk to extend and enrich the play.
- Use this observation as a means of planning curricular opportunities for specific children, e.g. the 'dominant' child to work in a collaborative activity with other strong personalities; the child who 'flits' to be encouraged to sustain involvement in other situations.

Talk

- Move around the various activity areas to determine the most fruitful activities for promoting talk, e.g. large-scale, boisterous play is unlikely to give children time to use language as a tool for thinking, although they may need briefly to communicate with one another.

- Focus on productive areas for play as indicated in research studies, e.g. clay, sand, water, construction and home play. Spend some time in each of these activities listening to the quality of conversation.

- Identify those children who help to foster conversations in groups. Aim to 'use' those children in other situations to assist their peers.

- Set up situations that require children of different linguistic abilities to communicate and collaborate, e.g. two children to mix the dough and colour it with paint, to sort out painting aprons and identify those that need mending, to lay out the drinks at break time.

- Help children to develop social conventions with one another, e.g. waiting to enter a discussion and listening to another point of view.

- Carefully observe children with limited English-language skills. Learn to interpret the basics of their first language, their body language or, if the child is deaf, any utterances. Help these children feel secure in knowing you understand their needs and will help them attach appropriate words to express their needs.

CHILDREN MUST EXPERIENCE SUCCESS

Nursery teachers accept that young children make mistakes and learn valuable lessons in this way. Children must also learn that in many matters there are no right or wrong answers. However, to foster children who are confident to 'have a go' and express their views, and eager to explore new learning, a nursery curriculum must allow experience of success and for these successful experiences to outweigh all others. The learning offered must therefore be manageable and broken into manageable parts. The great skill of teaching at any level is to facilitate learning – to identify what has been previously learnt and the next required step in learning: to find the right match of curriculum content and the appropriate learning route. It is impossible to provide a correct match for all children all the time, but reflection on why an approach did not work with a child, or why a line of inquiry proved especially successful, is the very essence of self-evaluation (see Chapter 7).

The particular skill of nursery teachers lies in their getting to know about the competencies of their age-group of children. In judging what a young children understands, the teacher needs to know about his or her past experiences and observe his or her use of oral language and his or her actions. In this work it is important to consider research findings, some of which develop Piaget's notions about young children's competencies. While Piaget stressed the kind of thinking young children could not manage, current studies indicate that, given the appropriate working conditions, these same children are capable of functioning at a much higher level.

Two major shifts in thinking have been dominant: first the importance of the child's social interactions in developing his or her thinking. Children will make sense of the world not only through their actions but also in discussion with other children and with adults. Specifically, adults can play a very important part as more experienced learners. Second, there is increased recognition of the need for children to start to become aware of their own thought processes. This will include an individual's awareness of how well he or she understands a task, how well equipped he or she is to deal with it and how he or she sets about tackling it in a planned and systematic way. Young children have only rudimentary abilities in these areas (which are collectively termed 'metacognition'). Studies show that they tend to be impulsive, adopting a trial-and-error approach to a task.[40] The adult's role in helping children to develop is discussed in Chapter 6. Here we look at how children can be placed in the best position to reveal what they know.

One major finding of Piaget's was that most children younger than 7 are unable to appreciate another point of view – they are totally egocentric.[41] The test for this was to show the young child a three-dimensional model of a mountain with three distinctly different sides, to place the child on one side of the mountain and put a small doll looking at a different side. The child was then given three photographs showing each perspective of the mountain and was asked to select the view the doll had. On this standard test most children under 7 are unable to select the correct photograph: most selected the view they had. Borke repeated this test, but instead of the photographs the child was asked to demonstrate the doll's view by turning the mountain, which was mounted on a turntable. Using this means many 4-year-olds and some children of 3 were able to select the correct side of the mountain.[42] Thus, given the opportunity to express their understanding appropriately, young children will, it seems, give us a clearer picture of their capabilities. Their thinking will be better expressed if they are dealing with a familiar situation.

Borke continued to modify Piaget's test by using the turntable but substituting animals and people in home settings in place of the mountain. This situation was presumably more like home than the Swiss Alps, and even more children responded favourably to seeing another viewpoint.

A further point regarding young children's thinking relates to their understanding of our intentions. In Piaget's experiment on conservation, children were asked to check two sets of five counters. When the sets were aligned, the children said they were the same; when the second set of counters was pushed apart by the teacher, the children mainly considered that this second row contained more counters.[43] In a modified version of this test McGarrigle used a naughty teddy to push the counters apart and shuffle them around. This time more children gave the correct response than in the previous test.[44]

Margaret Donaldson contends that young children's actions are affected by them trying to make sense of human situations and of people's intentions.[45] She suggests that in the Piagetian test the child tries to make sense of the adult's intention by drawing on his or her experience of them usually doing something for a purpose. Thus, the child's expectation would be that the adult had caused something to happen. With the introduction of a naughty teddy the children were more likely to be open-minded about the result of his actions.

Young children's understanding of the teacher's use of language is also important – the way the adult phrases his or her talk. Margaret Donaldson suggests that a young child may be seen to fail to carry out a task or to respond to an instruction, not because he or she is incapable of that task but because the child cannot comprehend the adult's use of language.

Children are better placed to reveal their competencies if they are given the means to express their understanding, if they are dealing with a situation familiar to them and if they can make sense of the adult's use of language. If the teacher is to move close to the child's thinking he or she should be aware that young children comprehend their surroundings by making their own meanings, which are consistent in their own terms. These meanings are not always clear to adults. The teacher needs to get inside the child's own frame of reference. Vygotsky's statement made more than fifty years ago is still relevant: 'It is not sufficient to understand his words – we must also understand his thoughts. But even that is not enough – we must also know its motivation. No analysis of an utterance is complete until that plane is reached.'[46]

One of the most effective ways of getting close to a child's thinking is through dialogue. David Woods suggests that 'Conversations with young children at best give an insight into their needs, feelings, fears and attitudes. They are a primary basis for reaching an understanding of each child'.[47] But, as Woods points out, not all adults have the natural ability to handle the demands of conversation with a group of young children effectively. It is a skill for the nursery teacher to refine and use as a major tool of work. It is one thing to get a child to talk but quite another to involve and interest the child in a sustained conversation. Most young children, given a gently persistent questioner, will respond, but the response is likely to be limited to answering the question.

Woods describes the 'programmatic' style of conversation, which consists of the adult asking questions and the child replying. Thus the dialogue at a dough table might be as follows:

Teacher: 'What are you making, Rachel?'
Child: 'Eggs.'
Teacher: 'Oh, they do look nice. How many are you making?' (No response).
Teacher: 'How many, Rachel?'
Child: 'Two.'
Teacher: 'Yes, and what colour are they?'
Child: 'Red.'

The teacher is evidently working hard, but to little effect. The child feels under pressure to answer and is feeding back the minimum information. The teacher controls the conversation, and the child plays a secondary, responsive role. Woods's analysis of many transcripts of conversations shows that where the adult or teacher had less of a controlling style of conversation, children asked more questions and made more contributions of their own. From this study he suggests that adults who offer children their own views and ideas receive a great deal more from children.

Thus we may see a rather different approach to conversation at the dough table:

Teacher: 'Oh, those look interesting, Rachel. They are like some red marbles that I played with when I was a little girl.'
Child: 'Was you a little girl?'
Teacher: 'Yes, just like you, with long hair.'
Child: 'When you was a little girl, does you ... does you play?'
Teacher: 'Oh yes, I played with lots of things. But I didn't play with dough.'
Child: 'I made one dough with Jason. Jason made it blue ... Jason made it all blue ... his hands was blue ... my mum ... mum was cross 'cos it was all blue and Jason cried.'
Teacher: 'Oh dear, paint can be very messy. I expect it was a bit difficult for your mum to clear it up.'

The adult's use of language will change according to circumstances. There is a place for questioning a child and for giving direct instructions. The very pace of work often dictates the need for a brief response to a child. However, here we are considering how it is possible to place children in the best possible circumstances to enable them to voice their views and feelings, and this is most likely to be achieved by the teacher adopting a partnership approach in conversation.

A great deal of work has focused on early language development through adult–child interaction, but less attention has been paid to children talking together. Yet nursery settings put a great deal of emphasis on making this possible through the arrangement of furniture and the organization of activities. Although one of the aims of nursery provision is to help the child become socially confident, as Sylva suggests, 'A child's social participation is not only the "classroom" for acquiring interpersonal skills, it is also the scene of his most complex and creative thought'.[48]

Robson's study of nursery children talking together involved recording dialogue by means of attaching radio microphones to target children. The work suggests that younger, more immature children learn a great deal from older peers both by imitating their actions and language and also through being directly taught by older children. Children are often also very good at understanding another child's indistinct speech an adult may find incomprehensible.

Robson suggests that teachers can learn a great deal by studying children's conversations. Ideally this means recording the dialogue and studying transcripts afterwards. However, recognizing the difficulties in managing this, Robson believes that certain points arising from her own study are applicable to other nursery settings. One major factor was the complexity of children's language used in conversation with one another. Robson suggests that teachers tend to use simple, concrete language, being aware of their least capable children in the nursery. Inevitably the children with good linguistic skills are not stretched: these children often appeared to avoid or misunderstand adult conversations, probably, the author suggests, because they were bored with the lack of challenge.

A further point reinforces Woods's work on dialogue. Children's conversations with one another contrasted starkly with adult–child talk. Children's conversations were more on the lines of balanced conversation, but adult–child talk tended to focus on questions and answers.

Robson says that by observing children's talk it is possible to deduce the best settings to promote the richest exchanges.[49] Sylva's study found that in the Oxford nursery classes there was a particularly high incidence of children conversing with one another. Sylva concludes that one reason for this was the popular provision for manipulative activities and pretend play, which provide excellent settings for dialogue.

Perhaps the key ingredient in enabling children to succeed is the role motivation plays in learning. This must surely be a priority for any nursery teacher and a particular challenge in view of the very wide developmental span the teacher may be coping with at any one time. We have mentioned the importance of matching activities and methods to each child's need. Children can respond to very challenging learning if the approach is interesting and enticing. Martin Hughes successfully introduced a group of 4-year-olds to the code of arithmetic. He found they were capable of understanding and using a simple form of arithmetical symbolism and he attributed this success to the work being introduced through an enjoyable game. Hughes reports that by his final session the children were as keen to participate in the game as they were in the beginning, if not keener. He comments that 'Many pre-school children appear to appreciate and enjoy intellectual problems which are pitched at the limits of their understanding'.[50]

To summarize: if young children have successful experiences at the earliest stage of their education this has implications for a spiral of success at later stages in their development. Success breeds confidence and a willingness to be open to learning. To help children to be successful the nursery teacher should make their learning manageable, by breaking it down to meet individual needs, and should place children in the best possible position to reveal their learning and to express their thoughts, views and actions through talk with adults and other children. Aspects of research suggest that teachers can expect more of young children in terms of their learning as long as the teaching is embodied in exciting and relevant modes that are within the child's frame of reference.

Suggested action

Help the child express his or her understanding

- Observe how a child chooses to represent an experience and draw the child's attention back to the experience to crystallize the link, e.g. 'You are flying an aeroplane like the man in the story, Darren. Can you land in the field as he did?'
- Ask a child to show you how a model works if he or she is hesitant in telling how. You can then help the child translate the action into language.

Plan the learning in a familiar context

When checking a child's competencies always aim to use familiar materials and to make the context of work the usual nursery setting, preferably with other children.

Help the child understand the adult's intentions

- Check that your own behaviour and comments are as consistent as possible.
- If you plan to be absent, tell the children in advance and try to explain why you will be away.

Check the child understands the adult's use of language

- Having given an instruction, check from the child's actions that he or she has understood.
- On entry to the nursery, check with parents about the child's understanding of terms for going to the lavatory.
- Listen to parents talking with their children; note the use of special phrases and words.

Enable children to help one another

- Encourage one child to show another what he or she is doing.
- Having shown a small group of children how to use a new piece of apparatus, introduce a younger or less able child and ask the group to show him or her.
- Ask an able child to do specific things for a new or less able child, e.g. 'Chloe, will you do up Peter's coat, please, and show him where to put his shoes. Alex, could you read a story to Jude and show him the pictures?'
- Refer one child to another, e.g. 'Joe is wondering where he can put this dinosaur. Sean, can you help him?'

Nurture motivation

- Keep in touch with children's interests at home.
- Observe where children choose to spend their time and follow this up, e.g. the children who build a lot can be shown some architects' plans and offered the materials to make their own.
- Observe when behaviour indicates boredom or frustration – it is the moment for adult intervention.
- Be ready to help a child through an activity, e.g. completing a jigsaw, supporting an unstable model.

- Make tasks manageable, e.g. a child may enjoy sharpening a few pencils but may want to hand over the task after a time.
- Praise generously but with discretion – children know when they have achieved.

CHILDREN MUST BE HELPED TO BE IN CONTROL

We have seen that, in order to best view the young child's capabilities, it is necessary to check the child's learning in situations that make sense to him or her. Bruner suggests that in order to understand what the child is doing there is a need to observe the child dealing with a familiar task in which he or she is 'holding up his own end' of things.[51]

Piaget's view of the child interpreting the world simply through his or her own investigation is now adapted to accept the need for this to happen in an understandable social context where the child has access to other people who can help the child with his or her learning. In the nursery these other people will be the children and adults with whom the child is in daily contact. The role the adult plays in supporting and extending learning is explored in Chapter 5. However, in order to be an active investigator the child needs to be confident and independent. While we agree with Margaret Donaldson that there is a fundamental human need to develop these qualities[52] by the time they are 3, children will have had many experiences that will have reinforced or dampened their self-belief and extended or reduced their abilities to do things for themselves. Even where children have had good experiences that have encouraged them to be self-standing individuals at home, there is evidence to show that they do not always adopt this approach automatically in school. Studies show that, partly because of the way the pupil role is perceived by young children (often based on what they have learnt from parents, peers and the media), they will often adopt a passive attitude, be reluctant to take risks in their learning and be anxious about their inadequacies being revealed.[53] This is of course more likely to happen when the transition to school is traumatic and young children feel themselves to be passive recipients of a strange school culture. The nursery should help children to know that their views matter, that they are capable of solving a problem and that they know where to go to find the resources to help them. This means helping them to develop a good self-image and the ability to work in a self-sufficient way.

Developing children's self-esteem

The beliefs children have about themselves will not only affect what they can do but also how they react to others. Because this belief is so closely linked with the individual's perceptions of how others view him or her, parents and teachers have a particularly powerful role to play with young children. Tina Bruce suggests that some children have to ask themselves who they are more than others and this can undermine their own sense of worth.[54] It is particularly important that nursery teachers are aware of the need to support children who are members of groups that might encounter discrimination (see pp. 47–48).

Susan Fountain reports the findings of a group of primary teachers who identified behaviours they considered to characterize children with positive self-esteem. These included a realistic assessment of their own work; recognition of the worth of others including giving them positive feedback; the ability to accept contructive criticsm; the ability to work co-operatively in a group, accepting the contributions of each member; and the ability to react reasonably and assertively in conflict situations.[55] Early manifestations of these behaviours are very evident in young nursery-age children who feel secure in themselves. On the other hand behaviour problems may reflect a poor self-esteem, and children who seek attention in negative ways have a particular need for praise and recognition.

There is no recent research supporting the effect of teacher expectations on children's subsequent achievements. However, common sense dictates that, if adults have realistic but high beliefs about what children can do, this will beneficially affect performance in both behaviour and learning, and the reverse will also apply. Praise is, of course, a powerful tool in motivation, particularly with regard to young children who are so eager to please adults. There is, though, a danger of overuse:

> Lavishing praise indiscriminately . . . does not enhance self-esteem, but gives rise to suspicion about the motives of the praiser. True self-esteem comes from inside, from accepting our strengths, and is reinforced by an affirming and positive atmosphere, where we are encouraged to think positively about ourselves and build on our strengths.[56]

Independent learning supports achievement

Young children need to become agents in their own learning. A young child's level of dependence is greatly affected by his or her inherited endowment as well as by the style of parenting. Studies have indicated the effects of restricting toddlers from normal developmental experiences such as climbing stairs and exploring objects, or of other extreme behaviour in pushing 2- and 3-year-olds towards more mature habits; both these attitudes are likely to cause overdependency.[57] The development of independence is aided by a degree of permissiveness and warmth rather than punitive treatment.[58] Erikson writes that the first task of facing a child's personality is to learn to trust.[59] When the child is assured that his or her physical and emotional needs are being met by an adult, the child is then able to turn his or her attention to the wider world.

On entry to nursery school children vary in their adaptation and activity. Each child has his or her own stage of readiness with regard to developing emotional independence from parents, being socially confident in mixing and co-operating with peers, and being physically capable and intellectually self-reliant in making choices, solving problems and initiating actions. Schweinhart, Weikart and Larner regard these achievements as life skills: 'We must recognise that children are capable of taking some responsibility for their own learning and that in giving them that responsibility we not only assist their present cognitive growth but, perhaps more importantly, are laying foundations for their greater conformity and achievement in later years'.[60]

The nursery teacher must expect to spend more time with the child who is emotionally over-dependent. The researchers concerned with the transition study found it somewhat surprising that the total adult time given to all new children was less than 10 per cent.[61] Some new children and less confident 'established' children undoubtedly benefit from a more obvious staff presence in helping them to understand the nursery setting and to take an active part in it. The parent substitute should thus be available to each individual as long as he or she is needed. Social dependence is closely related to emotional stability. An anxious, insecure child will have difficulty in relating to new adults or children. However, a child who is highly dependent on the nursery adult may not find it so easy to relate to other children.

The skills of making and maintaining friendships in the nursery are many and complex. They include the ability to offer friendship, manage conflicts and maintain one's rights while being sensitive to those of others.[62] Although the child will learn many skills from peers, the adult should engineer situations to help children who are in danger of becoming isolates. Any special circumstances need to be considered. As we have seen, a new child may need initially to spend a considerable amount of time 'on the fringe' of activities, watching the play of other children before he or she can take part. Social interaction also depends on the stage of development and the personality of the child. A child of 2 years will normally play by him or herself and be unable to co-operate with others, but solitary play in 4-year-olds is related to dependency; if this is a persistent and dominant form of play it is likely to relate to a poor self-image and to a low level of attention-seeking. However, where a 4-year-old plays alone and actively resists any interference this can reflect purposeful play and a level of sociability.

Carefully monitored group activity enables children to grow from an egocentric state to become group members. In their play children learn to lead, to follow and co-operate, to wait and take turns. Opportunities for this type of growth need to be an integral part of a nursery programme. Where children find this learning particularly difficult, specific planning should provide for individual need. In helping children develop social skills the teacher must be aware that not all people are capable of being, or even wish to be, friendly and outgoing. However, the nursery has responsibility to provide children with a range of life skills. If a child is able to communicate and interact easily with others, he or she may still choose his or her own company, but the child who lacks these social skills does not have this choice.

A degree of physical independence assists all young children in gaining confidence. The 3-year-old who can cope with his or her own personal needs ceases to look to the teacher to support him or her in this aspect of life. For this reason games need to be played that teach the fastening of buttons and buckles; painting aprons need to have strips of Velcro the child can fix for him or herself; the teacher should ensure that small fingers can attach paper to painting easels by means of clothes pegs and that there is an accessible line where the child can place his or her painting to dry after completing it. Routines should also encourage physical self-control: given conveniently located cloakrooms, nursery children can be encouraged to visit the lavatory as and when needed rather than automatically responding to group set times during the day.

Nurseries need to provide a climate in which a young child can develop emotional resilience and become socially and physically confident before the child can develop his or her thinking skills. Helping young children to take responsibility for their actions involves them in making choices and decisions. They need to be helped to take an increasingly active part in their own learning, and the teacher's planning and provision can assist this process in the following ways.

Choosing play materials

There needs to be an opportunity for children to select their resources for learning. Open, low shelves with apparatus in pictorially coded containers with well-fitted lids mean that play materials are accessible. As children become familiar with using different media for creative work they develop discrimination and are able to choose and reject materials as being more or less appropriate for their particular work. A range of paper of different shapes, sizes, textures and colours should be adjacent to the painting area; a choice of adhesives and a selection of materials for collage should also be freely available. This type of provision will help to enhance the learning opportunities in these activities.

Allocation of time

The nursery session should be planned to enable the child to have choice in the use of time. If a mid-morning snack is provided on a self-service basis, the arrangement allows a child to break off an activity when ready, pour his or her own drink and decide what quantity he or she can manage. Many children initially need help in planning their time; a rich provision of activities can be indigestible for an individual who has had no experience of making decisions at home.

Choice of activities

There may be opportunities for children to choose whether to play indoors or outside and whether to take part in a large group story or music session or to opt for a more solitary occupation. Even the youngest children can be helped to make decisions about their environment and daily activities. A new sand tray arrives; suggestions may be made as to where it can best be sited. The cookery activity for tomorrow can be decided by the group browsing over a pictorial recipe book. Which paintings and models to display in the nursery can be a group decision, as can the selection of seeds to be planted in the garden and the choice of material for new curtains in the home area.

Apart from provision, the teacher's own attitudes are all-important. With the high demands of teaching this age-group it is tempting to reward conforming and complacent behaviour in children. However, in returning to main principles, if the accent is to be on developing personal, rational autonomy the teacher must positively encourage independent thinkers, those who question authoritative statements and sometimes choose to tackle things differently.

The US High Scope programme helps children to accept responsibility for their actions. They are encouraged to make choices about their activities, to carry out these plans and then to discuss the outcomes with an adult.[63] This approach appears to have value in placing the child in an active learning position. However, no one system should become a straitjacket; there is a great difference between seeing the High Scope method as a useful way of helping children to become agents in their learning and imposing this framework on all children. As we have seen, emotional and social confidence is necessary before any child is ready to make choices and decisions about learning. Whatever the activity structure, it should not be allowed to inhibit spontaneity and creativity, which are often the keys to development.

Suggested action

Help children to view themselves positively

- Display photographs and self-portraits of each child in the nursery.
- In small-group times, encourage children to state one particular achievement they have had during the session.
- Provide self-adhesive badges and felt-tip pens for each child to make a badge for themselves: discuss each one in turn.
- Make attractive name cards for each child: use these at small-group times to discuss names and individual characteristics of children.

Help children to develop positive awareness of others

- Give new children a 'friend' on their arrival at the nursery.
- Help them to view each other's achievements, e.g. suggest that 'we all look at Uforma's painting and say what we like about it'.

Help children to develop awareness of different emotions

- Use pictorial displays, stories and personal experiences as a way of helping children understand how people can feel and for what reasons.
- Help children explore emotions through facial expressions and body language.

Offer positive message through curriculum and routines

- Give time to individual children, e.g. where possible stagger beginnings and ends of sessions to allow time for a personal greeting and farewell.
- Give children respect, by offering them undivided attention when they are talking, displaying their work with care and re-membering information and views they have previously offered.
- Make the curriculum meaningful and realisic, e.g. give children reasons for routines and rules.
- Involve children in their nursery, e.g. simple printing on lining-paper can be used as new wallpaper for the home corner; a picnic outside can involve children making sandwiches to eat, having previously chosen and shopped for the ingredients.

Help the child to trust

- Aim to be in the same place every day at the start of every session to welcome the children.
- Be aware when one child feels particularly vulnerable, e.g. transition, large-group time or an outing; use eye contact and physical touch to assure the child of your support.
- Find a special puppet for the insecure child. Make sure the puppet is 'put to bed' by the child when he or she leaves the nursery and is waiting for that child the next morning when he or she arrives.
- Try to introduce the child to another adult at an early stage. A mother substitute is all-important at first, but the aim must be for trust to be established within the wider circle.

Help the child become socially adept

- Introduce two isolated children to a task in the hope they will support one another.
- Help children to learn social skills, e.g. ensure that attention-seeking children have initial brief experiences when they must wait for the adult – praise warmly as the attention-seeking becomes less; encourage and help children to take turns.
- Offer children leadership roles, e.g. 'Now, Tony, you tell us where we are going in this aeroplane.'
- Encourage children to support one another, e.g. suggest that a child bathes a friend's sore knee or helps another clear up a breakage.

Develop self-help skills

- Resource the environment to allow children to become self-sufficient, e.g. provide a dustpan and brush for clearing up dry sand; provide a floor cloth or short-handled mop for coping with spillages.
- Have clear expectations for children and support them in achieving these, e.g. encourage children to take responsibility for their own possessions (clipping wellington boots together with a named wooden peg); give children areas of responsibility such as keeping the book area tidy or checking the painting aprons for repairs; one activity should be tidied away before moving on to another.
- Communicate to parents in the hope that these expectations will be supported at home.

REFERENCES

1. S. Isaacs (1930) *Intellectual Growth in Young Children*, Routledge & Kegan Paul, London.

2. S. Isaacs (1933) *Social Development in Young Children: A Study of Beginnings*, Routledge & Kegan Paul, London.

3. B. Tizard (1974) *Early Childhood Education*, NFER, Slough.

4. J. Brierley (1984) *A Human Birthright; Giving the Young Brain a Chance*, British Association for Early Childhood Education, London.

5. J. W. B. Douglas (1964) *The Home and the School*, MacGibbon & Kee, London.

6. C. Athey (1990) *Extending Thought in Young Children*, Paul Chapman Publishing, London.

7. J. Durrant (1988) Racism and the under-Fives, in A. Cohen and L. Cohen (eds.) *Early Education: The Pre-School Years*, Paul Chapman Publishing, London.

8. V. Morgan and S. Dunn (1990) Management strategies and gender differences in nursery and infant classrooms, *Research in Education*, no. 44, pp. 82–91.

9. Durrant (1988) op. cit. (note 7).

10. C. M. Ogilvy, E. H. Boath, W. M. Cheyne, G. Jahoda and H. R. Schaffer (1990) Staff attitudes and perceptions in multi-cultural nursery schools, *Early Childhood Development and Care*, Vol. 64, pp. 1–13.

11. Morgan and Dunn (1990) op. cit. (note 8).

12. P. Blatchford, S. Battle and J. Mays (1982) *The First Transition: Home to Pre-School*, NFER/Nelson, Slough.

13. M. Willes (1981) Children becoming pupils, in C. Alderman (ed.) *Uttering, Muttering*, Grant McIntyre, London.

14. Blatchford, Battle and Mays (1982) op. cit. (note 12).

15. House of Commons, Education, Science and Arts Committee, *Report of the Committee of Inquiry into Under-Fives*, HMSO, London (conclusions and recommendations).

16. M. Clark (1989) Continuity, discontinuity and conflict in the education of under fives, *Education 3–13*, June, pp. 44–8.

17. J. Piaget and B. Inhelder (1969) *The Psychology of the Child*, Basic Books, New York, NY.

18. Brierley (1984) op. cit. (note 4).

19. D. Ausabel *et al.* (1978) *Educational Psychology: A Cognitive View* (2nd edn.), Holt, Rinehart & Winston, New York, NY.

20. C. Hutt (1971) Exploration and play in children, in R. E. Herron and B. Sutton-Smith (eds.) *Child's Play*, Wiley, Chichester.

21. L. S. Vygotsky (1966) Play and its role in the mental development of the child, *Voprosy Psikhologii* (from a record of a lecture delivered in 1933).

22. J. Tamburrini (1974) Play and intellectual development, *Paedaogica Europaea*, Vol. 9, no. 1, pp. 5708.

23. K. Sylva, C. Roy and M. Painter (1980) *Child Watching at Playgroup and Nursery School*, Grant McIntyre, London.

24. N. A. Chomsky (1976) *Reflections on Language*, Temple Smith, London.

25. J. Macnamara (1972) Cognitive basis of language learning in infants, *Psychological Review*, Vol. 7, no. 9, pp. 1–13.

26. M. Donaldson (1981) Learning language, in M. Robert and J. Tamburrini (eds.) *Child Development 0–5*, Holmes McDougall, Edinburgh.

27. J. Tough (1976) *Listening to Children Talking*, Ward Lock, London.

28. M. Almy (1966) Spontaneous play: an avenue for intellectual development, *Bulletin of the Institute of Child Study*, Vol. 28, no. 2, p. 2.

29. B. Tizard (1977) Play: the child's way of learning, in B. Tizard and D. Harvey (eds.) *The Biology of Play*, Heinemann, London.

30. Sylva, Roy and Painter (1980) op. cit. (note 23).

31. V. Thomas (1973) Children's use of language in the nursery, *Educational Research*, Vol. 15, no. 3, pp. 209–16.

32. D. Woods, L. McMahan and Y. Cranstoun (1980) *Working with Under-Fives*, Grant McIntyre, London.

33. Sylva, Roy and Painter (1980) op. cit. (note 23).

34. B. Tizard (1979) Language at home and at school, in C. B. Cazden (ed.) *Language and Early Childhood Education*, US National Association for Young Children, Washington, DC.

35. B. Tizard and M. Hughes (1984) *Young Children Learning*, Fontana, London.

36. B. Robson (1983) Encouraging interaction between staff and children in pre-school units, in M. M. Clark (ed.) *Special Educational Needs and Children under Five* (*Educational Review*, Occasional Publications 9), Faculty of Education, University of Birmingham.

37. Sylva, Roy and Painter (1980) op. cit. (note 23).

38. L. G. Katz (1985) Fostering communicative competence in young children. in M. M. Clark (ed.) *Helping Communication in Early Education* (*Educational Research*, Occasional Publications 11), Faculty of Education, University of Birmingham.

39. M. MacLure and P. French (1981) A comparison of talk at home and at school, in G. Wells (ed.) *Learning through Interaction*, Cambridge University Press.
40. D. Woods (1988) *How Children Think and Learn*, Blackwell, Oxford.
41. J. Piaget and B. Inhelder (1956) *The Child's Conception of Space*, Routledge & Kegan Paul, London.
42. H. Borke (1983) Piaget's mountains revisited: changes in the egocentric landscape, in M. Donaldson (ed.) *Early Childhood Development and Education*, Blackwell, Oxford.
43. J. Piaget (1952) *The Child's Conception of Number*, Routledge & Kegan Paul, London.
44. J. McGarrigle and M. Donaldson (1974) Conservation accidents, *Cognition*, Vol. 3, pp. 341–50.
45. M. Donaldson (1978) *Children's Minds*, Fontana, London.
46. Vygotsky (1966) op. cit. (note 21).
47. Woods, McMahan and Cranstoun (1980) op. cit. (note 32).
48. Sylva, Roy and Painter (1980) op. cit. (note 23).
49. B. Robson (1983) Encouraging interaction between staff and children with communication problems in pre-school, in M. M. Clark (ed.) *Special Educational Needs and Children Under Five* (*Educational Review*, Occasional Paper no. 9) Faculty of Education, University of Birmingham.
50. M. Hughes (1983) What is difficult about learning arithmetic, in M. Donaldson (ed.) *Early Childhood Development and Education*, Blackwell, Oxford.
51. J. Bruner (1983) *Child's Talk: Learning to Use Language*, Oxford University Press.
52. Donaldson (1978) op. cit. (note 45).
53. G. Barrett (1986) *Starting School: An Evaluation of the Experience*, AMMA/UEA, Norwich.
54. T. Bruce (1987) *Early Childhood Education*, Hodder & Stoughton, Sevenoaks.
55. S. Fountain (1990) *Learning Together, Global Education 407*, Stanley Thornes, Cheltenham.
56. P. Galloway, quoted in Fountain (1990) op. cit. (note 55), p. 7.
57. D. B. Stendler (1952) Critical periods in socialisation and overdependency, *Child Development*, Vol. 23, pp. 3–13.
58. J. and E. Newson (1968) *Four Years Old in an Urban Community*, Allen & Unwin, London.
59. E. Erikson (1963) *Childhood and Society*, Penguin Books, Harmondsworth.
60. L. J. Schweinhart, D. P. Weikart and M. B. Larner (1986) Consequences of three preschool curriculum models through age 15, *Early Childhood Quarterly*, Vol. 1, no. 1, pp. 15–45.
61. Blatchford, Battle and Mays (1982) op. cit. (note 12).
62. Z. Rubin (1983) The skills of friendship, in M. Donaldson (ed.) *Early Childhood Development and Education*, Blackwell, Oxford.
63. M. Hohmann, B. Banet and D. Weikart (1979) *Young Children in Action*, High Scope Press, Ypsilanti, Mich.

4

AREAS OF CURRICULUM EXPERIENCE

When considering a framework for the nursery curriculum, priority must be given to ensuring that the general principles are applied. The characteristics and learning needs of young children are paramount and experiences offered and methodology used must reflect this. This chapter is concerned with the types of experiences that will comprise the curriculum. It is offered under seven headings, each of which supports learning possibilities that will combine to contribute to the child's whole development. The headings are for the teacher's use only as a framework for planning and analysis. They will help the teacher to link some experiences into the National Curriculum subjects and so provide continuity of learning. The material in Chapters 3 and 4 is designed to be used in a complementary way. The young child's need to be self-monitoring and responsibly autonomous in learning is acknowledged and must be fostered. Using cues from his or her interests, the teacher will also have planned intentions for the child and ensure there is monitored progress in development. Moreover, young children do not learn in a subject based and fragmented manner. Later sections in the book deal with how, by using these headings, the curriculum is offered as a totality to the child.

LANGUAGE AND LITERACY

The four language modes of talking, listening, reading and writing are important things to develop in any nursery curriculum. Children's oral language has already been discussed. This underpins all developments with written language and will be the focus of work with younger nursery children (see Chapter 3). However, evidence points to children's early language and literacy experiences being closely linked to subsequent achievement in this area. Books and stories are particularly powerful in helping children to become literate. Margaret Clark emphasized the correlation between children's knowledge of, and familiarity with, books, and their later success in reading.[1] Wells stressed the link between children sharing books at home and their subsequent understanding of print when they started school.[2]

Another study found that young children can learn uncommon and difficult words such as 'precarious' and 'embellish' without additional explanation if they were heard in the context of simple stories. The context required that the meaning of the word was self-evident, and learning was more effective if the word was repeated in several different contexts.[3] Apart from new words learnt, Dombey suggests that through stories young children will learn about new syntactic forms, meanings and ways of organizing language.[4] As well as intellectual benefits, a sensitive introduction to books will motivate young children to want to read.[5]

As with oral language, children will bring a range of knowledge about books into the nursery with them. A 3-year-old may demonstrate clear tastes for particular stories and be very familiar with certain literature. To other children stories may be unknown and the starting-point will be to interest them and help them to learn how to handle books.

Children will learn only gradually to take on the role of audience and to listen quietly to a story. Initially, story-telling is interactive. Young children will want, and should be encouraged, to share their experiences and relate these to the story content. In addition, the teacher might want to raise some questions to tempt children into the story and also to assess their understandings. Certain types of questions have been suggested to promote this.[6] These would include helping children to understand the meanings of difficult words; make predictions about events in the story; interpret the thoughts and feelings of characters; and to understand any difficult concepts in the plot. It is important, of course, that any questions do not interrupt the story flow and destroy the children's interest.

As well as receiving group stories, children need the opportunity to share books with one another and on an individual basis with an adult. These times will provide the adult with valuable insights into children's book-handling skills and their abilities to initiate and sustain a story. One small-scale study found that, when given the opportunity to demonstrate these abilities, reception-class children proved to be both interested and competent.[7]

There is a strong case for creating a well-resourced and well-used book environment in any nursery. The first requirement appears at least to be recognized. The Child Health and Education Study reported in 1984 that 95 per cent of playgroups, 99 per cent of nursery classes and 99 per cent of nursery schools provided a book corner for 'most' or 'all' of their sessions. This emphasis on provision is supported by other studies as reported in Meadows and Cashdan.[8] However, an equally clear message appears that little planned use is made of book corners. More usually, children were given free access to use books; they visited the area infrequently and briefly. Where books and stories are central in the nursery curriculum attention must be given both to bring them to children's attention and to make them a focus for learning. Meadows and Cashdan describe a fascinating case study of a teacher who uses a challenging book (in this case, *Watership Down*) as a stimulus for other play activities in the nursery. This literary-theme development reportedly led to increased book use, more sustained and complex role play linked to the main characters, a focus for conversation based on shared story experience and impressive recall and use of elaborated language from children as they retold the story.[9] While obvious care should be taken not to allow a heavily structured programme to prevent children from following their own interests, this approach is worth consideration as a way of tempting children into books.

By the time they enter the nursery some children are able to recognize pictures and photographs as representations of real things. Others need lots of experience and discussion at this level. At a later stage they may be able to relate photographs to their own recent experiences of an outing. Through these opportunities, and given experiences of stories, songs and poems, children move towards the interpretation and early representation of written symbols.[10] The starting-point for writing is the child's discovery that language can be written down. Most children will come to the nursery not realizing that it is print and not the pictures that offer the storyline. Marie Clay tests this understanding by requesting the child to 'Put your finger where I should read'. She then checks to see if he or she points to the print or illustration. Children broadly make the same discoveries when starting to write. Marie Clay's work offers detailed information about this process,[11] which are briefly described below:

- The recurring principle refers to the discovery that writing uses the same shapes repeatedly. These shapes are often perceived as sticks and loops. A young child's earliest attempts at writing may consist of a page of such marks.

- The grouping principle results from the discovery that repetition is not sufficient but that writing involves combining a limited number of marks in different ways.
- Understanding of signs. As they encounter writing in the home and local environment, young children come to understand that print stands for certain things. They are seen to apply this principle when, through play, they put marks on paper to represent messages and instructions.
- The flexibility principle refers to the young child's understanding that letters are made up of limited numbers of shapes that may be used in different combinations and positions. It becomes accepted that only some of these combinations are recognized as letters.
- Directionality principle. The conventions of forming letter shapes in certain directions and starting writing from the top left-hand side of the page are very difficult for many young children. Where there is clear confusion over letter orientation, differences should not be emphasized. As the child's visual perception develops adults can help by pointing out letter and page arrangements during book-sharing sessions.

Early writing will be nurtured by the teacher being aware of the child's stage of development and the teacher's provision of a print-rich environment that both informs children and encourages them to write for a purpose. In this environment many children will leave the nursery functioning in the writing attainment target 3, level 1.

Making provision for literacy activities is very important but there is also a place for teaching specific knowledge and skills. Blatchford's two studies[12] showed that children's reading-related knowledge when entering school at 5 correlated with their reading ability both at 7 and 11 years. The significant abilities were those of letter identification, the ability to write their own name and to copy a phrase. The second study, in considering letter sounding as opposed to letter naming, could find no evidence to support the notion that letter sounding is a more valuable strategy in aiding future reading attainment. While accepting that a few children may be developmentally ready to recognize sound–symbol links and to perceive visually different letter shapes, teaching knowledge and skills to a selective group is very different from making blanket provision for all nursery children.

Suggested action
Focus on books

- Agree on a core of stories you will offer to children as a basic minimum during their career in the nursery. Make provision for special educational needs, gender and different cultural requirements. Evaluate this list regularly with a view to amending and updating.
- Offer a model of reading to young children by bringing your newspaper to work and sharing a picture or news item, or showing them your library book.
- Identify those children who, on arrival, are not conversant with books. Ensure that personal and rewarding book experiences are regularly planned for this group.
- When you have read or told a story, observe how many children in the group refer to that story at a later date, or show any signs of representing the characters or play through other activities. Repeat the story-telling with very small groups of children/at a different time of day/using different content. Check the effects on the children again.

Develop a print-rich environment

- Provide and use captions that offer children useful and interesting information, e.g. the lunch menu, details of birthdays and news of a new baby in a family.
- Give children's own writing status by presenting it well.
- Show children how oral language can be 'pinned on paper' by displaying a written account of a shared story-telling or a significant piece of news offered by a child.

Provide play contexts for literacy

The following contexts will offer children opportunities to encounter print and to practise writing for a purpose:

- Hairdressers – price lists, magazines, labels on equipment.
- Doctors/dentists – telephone directory, message pad, appointment book, prescription pad.
- Newsagent – magazines, comics, newspapers; organization of delivery involving naming papers and compiling lists of addresses for rounds.

- Estate agents – commercial brochures (or those made by children), street plans, telephone directories, appointment book.
- Garden centre – commercial seed packets (and home-made), flower and plant catalogues, Interflora message books, price list, account book.

Introduce letter shapes and sounds

- Opportunities should be taken up during the normal course of the day rather than teaching isolated skills. Use book-sharing times and informal games (I spy) to raise awareness.
- Suggest that children establish their own 'sounds' table by collecting a range of items that have the same initial sound.
- Label mid-morning drinks with the child's name.
- Ask children to select their name and 'clock in' when they arrive.
- Encourage them to label their own paintings and models with as many letters of their name as they can manage.

MATHEMATICAL

We have seen how young children start to accommodate to new experiences through spontaneous play and associative language. At the same time these experiences allow them to detect patterns and relationships: they begin to see similarities and differences, and to notice how things are ordered, fit together and correspond. This early mathematical awareness is yet another way young children have of making sense of their world. The National Curriculum attainment target 1, which is concerned with using and applying mathematics, is very appropriate to consider in the nursery. This attainment target relates to all others and emphasizes the need for practical and investigative work.[13]

A recent HMI study revealed that sixth-form girls viewed mathematics as a useful subject but one that did not give scope for creativity. Some girls also recalled haste and pressure from teachers at an earlier stage in school, which had undermined their confidence and understanding of the subject.[14] The nursery mathematics curriculum should take account of these responses. If boys and girls are helped to 'do' mathematics rather than just learn about it,[15] they are more likely to develop understanding of the subject and be motivated towards it.

As with other aspects of learning, the mathematics is embedded in experiences, and related language is gradually learnt. The nursery teacher needs to check that the child's words express true comprehension:

> A facility with mathematical language does not necessarily mean that understanding is present, nor will children learn merely by being presented with words. On the other hand, first-hand experiences are so important that children who have had opportunities to handle and manipulate real things may have considerable mathematical understanding, although they may not necessarily have the linguistic labels to attach to their knowledge. This emphasizes the importance of teachers observing children's actions very closely as well as listening to their language when assessing the level of mathematical understanding.[16]

The teacher must recognize the main elements that constitute early mathematical development and realize the potential for learning in everyday nursery activities and routines. These elements are as follows.

Spatial awareness

The child's earliest experiences are concerned with space: positions in space and shape. Having had opportunities to move around in different spaces, to handle objects of different shapes and sizes and to fit them into spaces, arranging and rearranging things, the child learns about distance. In so doing the child builds up some understanding of such terms as 'near' and 'far', 'in between' and 'behind'. However, it is necessary to be aware of the young child's thinking at this stage. This thinking is quite consistent but influenced by particular events. Piaget's work indicated that children's beliefs about proximity are at this stage influenced by the presence or absence of barriers. For instance, the art easel may be judged to be near to the window; if the distance remains the same but a table is placed between the two, the child will consider the art easel is now further away from the window. Perception of distance is also influenced by the amount of effort and time going into an activity. To the young child, climbing up a steep hill is further than running down it.

Through increasing knowledge of their own body, young children learn different ways of fitting in and moving in space. Most will not yet understand the invariance of space; they cannot accept that a large ball of clay remains the same even when it is broken into small pieces. They are also only just starting to distinguish two-dimensional from three-dimensional shapes, and Piaget's studies indicate that at this stage young children are not yet ready to appreciate another spatial viewpoint. Recent research has challenged this, however, showing that under certain conditions the child's spatial understanding is considerably more mature (see page 69).

The beginnings of measurement

For young children to learn how to measure accurately they need a range of experiences in making judgements about amounts. The experiences should be with weight, length, distance, time, area and capacity and should lead to the use of such words as 'heavy', 'light', 'long', 'short', 'near', 'far', 'today', 'yesterday', 'wide', 'narrow', 'full' and 'empty'. Such early judgements tend to be crude and inaccurate, but it is important to accept them as the child's own and through further experience and discussion to enable the child to refine his or her views. Early judgements are made through comparisons. This happens through children handling materials and conversing with one another, suggesting who has more or less milk or who has collected bigger stones. Children need to judge how much paper or material they require to cover a surface, and the teacher may join in at this stage to ask if the amount is too much or too little.

Early judgements about time and speed may be helped by stopping and starting at a given signal from the teacher and comparing time intervals during the course of activities. At this stage of thinking a young child is likely to confuse the type of task he or she accomplishes with the length of time in which it is accomplished. Thus, if two children paint pictures in the same amount of time, one big and one smaller, the judgement is often that the big picture took longer. Other judgements can be affected by size: a taller person may be considered older than a shorter person.

The young child will not be 'talked out' of this way of thinking. He or she is unable to view time objectively at this stage. Drawing the child's attention to relevant experiences, however, will help to develop understanding; it is useful, for instance, to draw attention to fixed points in the day and the pattern of the week. When listening to the child's comparisons and questioning about the reasons for his or her decisions, the teacher can monitor progression in understanding.

Early logic

The young child develops a mastery of his or her world as he or she becomes able to predict and understand cause and effect. Logical thinking develops as the child starts to distinguish differences and similarities in things and to arrange them accordingly. He or she also starts to see an order in these differences and begins to place items in sequences.

Initial sorting and classifying are random. When the child begins to apply logic, he or she may sort a pile of buttons into many small groups according to size, colour and shape. Gradually, though, the child is able to reduce the number of groups, and buttons may then be sorted according to one common attribute – all green buttons, whatever shape or size, together.

The ability to sequence depends on children being able to recognize differences and compare them. Through using structured fitting and grading apparatus the young child starts to order because of practicalities. For instance, a set of graded building-blocks can be built into a tower only if the largest forms the base. From experiencing this apparatus children move to ordering unstructured materials and become more and more adept at recognizing fine distinctions.

Through these experiences children learn to use some of the following words and phrases: 'belongs to', 'fits', 'does not fit', 'if', 'this will happen', 'when', 'why', 'what'. The 3–5-year-old thus develops the skills of prediction, classification and sequencing; full understanding is accomplished at a later stage. The aim of the nursery teacher should be to provide the environment and teaching to help the child make better judgements and to use these skills in solving problems.

Early number

In the past any early mathematics in the nursery tended to focus on developing number skills: 'Time is devoted to getting young children to repeat the number names, mime the number sequence, and even draw the number symbols. Unfortunately, such activities have no bearing on a child's acquisition of mathematics or appreciation of the "numberness of number"'.[17] However, if seen as just one of the broad headings for developing early mathematical thinking, there is a place for young children to be introduced to numbers. The essential sub-skills to be learnt are one-to-one correspondence and conservation. At the same time, by the attachment of number names to objects and experiences some early understanding of cardinal and ordinal numbers can develop.

Given many different opportunities to match one item against another, the young child gradually comes to understand that, although the objects are different in type, they can be the same in number. By pairing one chair to each child, one knife to each plate and one lid for each pan the nursery teacher gives the child a concrete experience for checking that they are 'the same'; there are more chairs or fewer plates. Piaget contended that the young child is unable to 'conserve' – that is, to appreciate that a number of objects or an amount remains the same regardless of how it is arranged or divided up. Again, current thinking suggests that children are able to be more open-minded about this in particular circumstances (see page 70), but the nursery must concentrate on helping children to experience conservation in a range of different situations. The most effective experiences are for children to handle materials for themselves, matching and comparing quantities. As their understanding develops, they learn to match items in pictures and to see for themselves that six sausages remain the same whether arranged in a line or a circle. Young children enjoy learning number names in rhymes and activities. However, ability to count does not necessarily mean the child can attach a meaningful number label to a concrete group of items. Counting should be incorporated into the nursery session, with the teacher encouraging the child to count an object only once. As the child starts to place items in sequence, ordinal number labels can be attached. Again, understanding develops soundly only if the child makes his or her own order and attaches his or her own labels. The teacher is wise to accept this order and naming from the child even if it is incorrect. The teacher may, however, gently offer his or her own model of counting or suggest that another child finds out if he or she comes to the same conclusions. While all these early number skills are in an embryonic stage it is important to go along with the child, observing his or her mode of thinking and providing appropriate new experiences at opportune moments to help clarify or challenge the child's conclusions.

Although we agree that drilling young children in number does not enhance their understanding of numeracy, recent studies have challenged Piaget's views on children's arithmetical abilities. Martin Hughes's work has revealed that nursery-age children are capable of representing number symbols, albeit in an idiosyncratic way but recognizable to themselves after a week. He also found that children were capable of understanding the use of the symbols + and − under certain conditions, although they could not generalize that understanding.[18] These findings point to the need for nursery teachers to explore their children's levels of understanding in a more open-minded way. Teachers are beginning to realize that the principles that apply in emergent writing can be applied in early mathematics. If young children are offered an environment that is mathematically rich and can observe the adult using mathematics every day, they are more likely to accept the subject as relevant and purposeful and develop an interest themselves.

The nursery can thus provide a seedbed for mathematical thinking. A range of potentially helpful activity can be explored, but as with other aspects of development the cue must come mainly from the child. These cues need to be observed, then taken up and developed by the teacher.

Suggested action

Provide activities with potential for mathematical development

- Spatial awareness:
  - Paper and construction materials of different shapes and sizes for painting, drawing and model-making.
  - Different-shaped cutters for use with clay and dough.
  - Small-scale play figures (dolls' house, farm and road layouts) to be arranged and rearranged in different ways.

- The beginnings of measurement: provision of apparatus and materials of different sizes to invite comparisons, e.g. two planks of unequal length for large construction; long and short brushes for painting; small and large mats for music and movement.
- The beginnings of logic: encourage pattern-making that invites children to think 'what comes next?', e.g. teacher starts a two-colour bead pattern – child continues it; child makes his or her own mosaic grid pattern and asks a friend to copy it; child makes his or her own collection of stones while on a walk and arranges this pattern, which is then displayed with the stone patterns from the rest of the group.
- The beginnings of number:

  - Sorting of miniature play figures and animals, e.g. dolls' house furniture into appropriate rooms; animals into barns and fields.
  - Conservation of number in making the same number of bricks into different shapes.
  - Matching socks, shoes; lotto games matching pictures, textures and symbols.

Provide stories, songs and rhymes to introduce mathematical thinking

- Spatial awareness: 'The Three Billy Goats Gruff', 'Jack and Jill Went up the Hill'.
- The beginnings of measurement: 'Goldilocks and the Three Bears', 'The Magic Porridge Pot'.
- The beginnings of logic: 'The Enormous Turnip', 'The Little Gingerbread Boy'.

- The beginnings of number: a range of rhymes involving cardinal and ordinal numbers in ascending and descending order, e.g. 'One Man Went to Mow a Meadow', 'Five Currant Buns in a Baker's Shop', 'Oats and Beans and Barley Grow'.

Provide a classroom environment and routines to encourage mathematical thinking

- Spatial awareness:

  – Levels of display and storage and the creation of different learning areas should help children to look at their classroom from different spatial viewpoints.
  – Setting up a 'moving day' into the home corner will encourage children to fit and rearrange furniture into a limited space.
  – Sitting on the carpet for a story means that the children must ensure there is space for everyone.

- The beginnings of measurement:

  – Make a pictorial chart of the pattern of the day; regularly draw children's attention to the sequence of events until they accommodate it.
  – Allow children to mix up their own glue and paint using a simple pictorial recipe; encourage them to see what happens when more or less liquid is added.

- The beginnings of logic:

  – Help children to talk about cause and effect, e.g. if a vase is cracked, what will happen to the water? If a beaker is filled to the brim with water, what is likely to happen when it is picked up? What happens if you go out in the rain without a coat?
  – Help children to sort and classify when they put things away, e.g. by providing clearly labelled storage containers for materials with different attributes; by clearly marking a shelf with outlines of where the containers are to be stored in order of size.

- The beginnings of number: encourage routines that involve one-to-one correspondence, e.g. children to play board or card games that involve them handing out one card to each person; children to hand out paintings to others at the end of the day (one to one or many to one) or to distribute one card to each child at the end of the cookery session.

Key questions to promote mathematical thinking

- Spatial awareness: 'Where does this go?' 'How can this fit?' 'Why doesn't this fit?'
- The beginnings of measurement: 'Are they the same?' 'How can you make them the same?' 'How can you make this one smaller?'
- The beginnings of logic: 'Why do you think that has happened?' 'What will happen now?' 'Can we do that another way?'
- The beginnings of number: 'Where does that belong?' 'Is there enough for everyone?' 'What comes next?'

Allow children to demonstrate what they know

- Provide equipment to make a 'bus': suggest children write down all the numbers they know to make bus tickets.
- Make 'families' of miniature soft play toys and observe how children sort and group them.
- Provide mathematical 'tools', e.g. rulers, tape-measures, clocks, scales and observe how they are used.

SCIENTIFIC

Early science initially depends on young children having plenty of things to explore and investigate and, second, on the teacher being aware of the scientific processes involved in this activity.

Wynne Harlen outlines some characteristics of young children's thinking that are relevant to how they are helped towards scientific inquiry:

- They are unable to think through an activity and are dependent on having to carry it out practically for themselves.
- They find it difficult to see a viewpoint other than their own, unless they physically move to the other position.
- They only attend to one aspect of a situation at a time.
- They cannot relate events to one another, only being able to recall the first and last stages in an inquiry.

Harlen concludes from this that first-hand experience in the child's immediate surroundings are essential in helping children to make discoveries that make sense to them.[19]

Having provided a rich environment the teacher must be aware of the scientific skills that should be fostered. HMI suggest that 'observation, investigation and enquiry, pattern seeking, inference drawing and accurate communication are evident in the best circumstances'.[20] This also covers the main aspects of science attainment target one.

Observation

Children are naturally curious and will make detailed and acute observations from the earliest age. These observations will stem from exploring the world through their senses (see p. 62). The teacher should pursue these observations so that, over a period of time, children's increased experience will help them to be aware of similarities and differences.

Investigation and inquiry

A nursery environment will always have plenty of activities for young children to find out about things. General inquiries will naturally arise as they work with sand, water and construction materials and explore the locality. The teacher can then help them to pursue specific lines of inquiry. HMI describe how a group of 4-year-olds playing with bricks were guided into investigating the properties of different bondings. Children built different walls, tested their strength by pushing them with a broom head and then attempted to explain why some walls were stronger than others.[21] At this stage the notion of fair testing may arise; some children will be ready to consider that variables must be controlled to make the test 'proper'.

Pattern seeking

Through exploration young children will naturally sort and group things. Early mathematics work on sets will provide the foundation for classification. Gradually, given prompts from the teacher, children will learn to make links from their experiences and see relationships. Chris Athey describes how a 4-year-old had discovered the rotational working of his watch and linked this pattern to other things that went round including the glass watch-cover, a merry-go-round and a sand wheel. Athey suggests this child is ready to be introduced to other items that demonstrate rotation.[22] At this stage it is important that the teacher allows the child to seek his or her own patterns and notes repetitions rather than for the teacher to impose them.

Communicating findings

Some young children need little encouragement to describe and to question others about their discoveries – others will be more reluctant or even too absorbed to converse. At this stage it is important that communication is encouraged on an individual basis or in small groups. Children need help in ordering their thoughts, and finding appropriate vocabulary to describe phenomena. Children can also record their findings through drawing, painting and construction.

Suggested action

Use natural materials as a focus for scientific activity

For example, leaves – use a tree near to the nursery to observe changes throughout the year; help children to recall changes by using photographs.

Develop scientific thinking from exploratory play

- Add pebbles, buttons and seeds to sand in the sand tray; offer children sieves with different-size meshes and ask them to sort out different items without using their fingers; ask children to describe what they did.
- Suggest that children try to make bubbles in the water tray using a range of different tools, e.g. small plastic containers, bubble pipes, straws of different diameter, commercially produced bubble-blowers, plastic tubing, egg whisk; discuss the different sizes of bubbles and identify the best ways of producing them; add bubble mixture to the water (60 ml detergent and 20 ml glycerine) and suggest that children experiment with making bubbles that float in the air; discuss which tool made the biggest bubbles, how long the bubbles lasted and what happened to them.

TECHNOLOGICAL

Traditional nursery activity has included many elements of designing and making and the National Curriculum has shown how this activity may be staged to lead to more complex later technological development.

The main strands of technology will be provided for through exploration, planning and discussion, making and doing and reviewing. These
are all valid activities for nursery-age children and also cover four of the
National Curriculum attainment targets. In addition, young children are
becoming more familiar and competent with computers. During their
time in the nursery they should experience different modes of control
technology and have opportunities to use them creatively, linking with
attainment target 5 in technology.

Exploration

Young children will initially need to be introduced gradually to a wide
range of materials and guided by the teacher to discover their properties,
limitations and potential. The child will progress in junk modelling and
woodwork in similar ways from simply experiencing the pleasure of using
glue or hammering to using materials randomly, and only then beginning
to learn about what it is possible to achieve. In early exploration the
process is all important: it is only by getting to know about materials that
the young child will be able to use and combine them meaningfully at a
later stage. New technology can also be usefully explored at this stage.
Children will come into the nursery having already observed and experienced the effects of control technology with their toys, in the home
and local environment. This experience can be extended in the nursery by
children being encouraged to use programmable toys and to have early
access to a computer with suitable, pictorial software.

Planning and discussion

'The most distinctive thing about design and technology is that . . . we use
our knowledge of the past and present to speculate about the future. We
are building a mental bridge out from what we know has been made,
towards what we believe might be made.'[23]

Some young children may be capable of representing their intentions
on paper – for most it will be more meaningful if they are helped to
formulate and talk through a plan. Initially this will be very brief – a bus
made with those boxes. In time, the child can be encouraged to describe
the plan in more detail and think through what materials may be most
suitable to use. Young children are naturally impulsive – left to their own
strategies they will usually adopt a trial-and-error approach to their
making. The design aspect involves the teacher in helping them to
develop a more systematic 'mental bridge'.

Making and doing

The child will use his or her previous experience of handling tools and materials when putting plans into action. Despite this the intentions can prove to be too ambitious in practice. When this happens the adult can decide whether the work is best left to be continued or if the adult should help the child to complete his or her model, making it clear to the group that 'John and I made this together'.

Designing and making may involve children working alone or co-operatively. One research project concerned with design and technology in the nursery reported one instance where a group of three children worked on designing a structure for one and a half hours. This class had recently been organized on a High Scope pattern (see p. 92): 'It was particularly noticeable that the children, irrespective of gender, were very cooperative both in planning and execution of the task, freely exchanging ideas and modifying the construction by mutual agreement'.[24]

Reviewing

Evaluation with young children will naturally evolve while they are making. They are likely to change their plans and seek alternative ways of working as they go along. The teacher will help them to monitor these decisions and to share them with others.

Suggested action

Introduce children to control technology

Use concept keyboards and suitable software programmes to enrich young children's IT experience, e.g. use of LOGO to control a turtle and to develop concepts of direction; use of the self-contained robot, Roamer, which responds to simple directions and can sing and dance.

Use familiar stories as starting-points for technology

- After children have played freely with construction materials, use a story as a means of prompting them to use materials to solve a problem. Use a range of stacking and interlocking bricks (Duplo, Lego), planks, ramps, cardboard and paper.
- Tell the story of 'The Three Little Pigs': suggest that two little pigs' houses are made and tested to see if they are strong enough to withstand the wolf; discuss what testing methods to use.

- Tell the story of 'The Three Billy Goats Gruff': use a floor layout to show the fields and the river; ask children to make the bridge and ensure it is strong enough for the big billy goat and the farmer, who will be coming along later in his tractor; test the strength of the bridge with a model tractor.

Extend junk modelling into early technology

- Have cardboard and textile materials clearly sorted, marked, stored and accessible for children to make their selections.
- Have a selection of adhesives and materials for fixing things together, e.g. rubber bands, masking tape, Blu-Tack and split pins.
- Have some small models of vehicles available in order for children to observe the position of wheels and axles when making their own models.
- Encourage children to outline their mental plan before starting work. Help by asking supplementary questions: 'So where will the people sit in this bus?' 'I see, and where is the engine going to be?'
- Encourage one representation to lead to another, e.g. 'Oh, Sandra, that boat looks really good. Would you like to make a special harbour for it in the construction area?'
- Organize models to be built over a period of time; encouraging children to come back to develop and improve them so long as interest is sustained.
- Encourage children to work together and appraise one another's work: 'Ellen, look at Stephen's bus – how could we stop these wheels being so wobbly?'

AESTHETIC AND CREATIVE

Spontaneous play is one way children symbolically represent experience through first imitating what they have seen and heard and later extending these imitations into role play. As the child develops, he or she is able to extend his or her range of symbolic representations, using the materials the child has explored. Art, music, drama, dance and movement all offer young children a means of developing ideas and personal expression through visual and auditory perceptions, and use of materials, media and techniques. Representation is not a matter of copying an adult. The teacher can nevertheless help the child refine and extend his or her own representations by guiding and suggesting, for example, by

- offering appropriate stimulus;
- teaching the subskills of handling tools, mixing and managing materials;
- encouraging the child to talk through his or her activity;
- encouraging the child to combine materials and link different ways of representing experiences; and
- responding to the child's wish to develop his or her representation.

Link to the arts

A booklet, *Arts and Schools*, describes the range of enriching learning opportunities for children that are not available from the usual school resources. These include contributions from artists, people in the theatre and musicians.[25] HMI suggest that such projects are particularly cost effective as they motivate children and serve as a form of indirect in-service training for teachers.[26] Case studies in the former booklet refer to older children. The learning opportunities for 3–5-year-olds are the same and this age-group should have a similar entitlement to such expertise. The most important factor is that professional contributors should have the skills of relating to and communicating with young children. Teachers themselves can, of course, arrange for children to encounter a range of music and art. Some interesting work took place in a small-scale study developing art appreciation with nursery children. Through offering young children opportunities to view and discuss a range of paintings from different periods and cultures, the researcher concluded that their view of art was extended and offered a broader content for their own work.[27]

Painting and drawing

The child's first attempts at writing in fact begin when the child attempts visual representations. Kenneth Jameson describes communication through and about graphic expression as a beginning of academic learning.[28] The teacher should ensure that a variety of thick and fine crayons, charcoal, chalk, lead pencils and felt-tip pens are freely available, together with paper of different sizes, shapes and colours. The wider the choice of materials available, the more children will be able to select the most suitable media for their explorations and experiments.

The accent should be on individual discovery, although the teacher may need to help and encourage the less adventurous child by demonstrating the different effects that can be produced by different media. The teacher may also want occasionally to structure the activity by limiting paint colours or drawing tools, to encourage children to explore the possibilities of using only a few.

Making sounds

After children have had the opportunity to explore a variety of home-made and commercial percussion instruments they may use them to represent sound effects in stories or to depict some recent shared experience. For example, after children have listened to heavy rain pattering on the roof they may select shakers filled with sand or dried peas to represent the sound; or, if the sound of thunder has frightened some children, the teacher may help them play out their fears by talking through with them how they could best represent the noise, given the sounds they make with their body or with instruments.

Young children's musical abilities develop through playing with sounds, inventing songs and using sounds to represent actions.

Suggested action

Make it possible for the child to represent

- Check the number of ways in which children are able to represent experiences in your nursery during the course of a term.
- Provide sufficient resources in each area of representation, e.g. a range of mark-markers and different textures, shapes and sizes of paper; commercial and home-made tuned and untuned percussion instruments; clothes and props to support role play.

Teach the subskills required for making representations

- After children have explored applying paint to paper they should have the chance of mixing their own colours on a palette.
- Teach a range of simple painting techniques, e.g. printing, wax resist to enable the child to choose his or her means of representation.
- Provide a range of brushes of different thicknesses to allow the addition of fine detail to pictures if required.
- Provide opportunities for children to practise copying rhythms with their body and with instruments.

- Play games that require children to imitate and create different sounds, e.g. 'Simon says, "Growl like a dog" '.
- Assume a role in children's play to introduce them to a new character or to help a child clarify his or her own role. Encourage the child to talk through his or her activity.
- Avoid 'what is it?' questions but instead pick out one feature of the child's painting to comment on, e.g. 'What a lovely colour blue in that part of your picture, Leon. Can you tell me about that?'
- Puppet-making is an ideal way of helping a child to express thoughts through a model. Simple puppets can be made from socks or cross-pieces of folded newspaper. You need to talk with the children through your own puppet used in activities and at story time in order to offer a model.
- Have home-made shakers that have different sound effects; each child can ask the others in a small group to close their eyes and guess what his or her sound represents. This is not easy and will require encouragement and sensitive contributions from you to help the children to listen and then relate the sound to a past experience.

Offer children experience of the arts

- Have a professional performer in both to perform and to work with small groups (mime and puppetry are particularly effective means of communication).
- Request the LEA instrumental service to offer appropriate demonstrations with different instruments.
- Use a small selection of good-quality art prints for small-group discussion and comparison; recount simple stories behind the paintings, e.g. the activities of a boy soldier linked to a print of 'The Fifer' (1866) by Manet. Encourage children to look in detail; ask them to select their favourite piece of a painting; encourage them to discover the different techniques used; have materials available for children to experiment with their own techniques.

PHYSICAL

A child's physical growth and the way the child uses his or her body have a very real effect on the way the child operates in his or her environment.

A child whose body hurts or bothers him or her or whose muscles do not function efficiently is likely to be vulnerable emotionally and is unlikely to be receptive to new learning experiences. The child's developing perceptions depend on physical interaction with the world around the child: if the child is limited physically, his or her perceptions will be as well. For instance, the child with spina bifida who cannot lift objects will have difficulty in acquiring a concept of weight. An environment that denies children the opportunities to practise basic body skills can mean these skills will be limited or never develop in later life. A child's progress in reading and writing can be hampered by the failure to develop certain co-ordination skills during the early years.

The teacher needs to be aware of the stages of physical development, because part of the teacher's job should be to keep an eye on the child's health and growth. However, the teacher must also know how to offer the best curriculum that will promote physical competence. Such pro- vision cannot accelerate the rate of competence before the child is physiologically and psychologically ready, but the quality of movement can be refined once that stage is reached.

The curriculum will include all means of developing small and large motor movements that, in turn, lead to increased body awareness and control. It can be offered through planned movement and physical activities and by allowing children regular access to space and appropriate apparatus.

The interrelatedness of each curriculum area has already been stressed. Because physical action is so central for a young child, the effects of learning and development through movement are particularly broad. The interim report for the National Curriculum Physical Education Working Group emphasizes how physical education contributes to the whole curriculum. The following elements are identified and are pertinent in a nursery curriculum: physical competence; physical development; benefits of exercise; establishing self-esteem; artistic and aesthetic understanding; coping with success and failure; lifelong participation in physical acti- vities; problem-solving skills; interpersonal skills; and links with the community and across cultures.[29]

The nursery teacher should approach physical and movement devel- opment in the same way as other areas of learning for this age-group. It is not appropriate to have an organized lesson for gross motor devel- opment, because responding as a group to precise verbal instructions will be beyond the comprehension of most children. Instead, individual past experience should be carefully observed and nurtured to further progression. Opportunities will present themselves through the environment, with the adult to help refine the skill and to help the child describe what he or she is doing. This approach calls for an informed view and sensitivity to intervene at the appropriate moment. A child's fine motor movements develop through his or her developing social skills of dressing and feeding him or herself as well as using purpose-built apparatus and engaging in creative and messy play. Many activities for gross motor development take place out of doors, although strenuous activity will occur through movement and dance and when using indoor physical equipment.

Suggested action

Plan for physical development in fine motor skills

- Check the skills practised during daily routines, e.g. dressing, undressing, pouring drinks, mixing paints, tidying away small apparatus.
- Plan regular practice of rhymes and jingles that involve fine motor skills.
- Check that apparatus is suitable for skill development, e.g. short painting brushes are easier to manage; fine brushes may be required by children who want to add fine detail to their pictures; inset jigsaw puzzles with knobs are easier for less mature children to handle.
- Check progression, e.g. first attempts at painting involve whole-arm movements on large sheets of paper; further experiences should include experiments with a range of painting and drawing tools, being taught the correct grasp of brush/crayon, working on vertical and horizontal surfaces, tracing and drawing objects.

Plan for physical development in gross motor skills

- Ensure that children have opportunities to practise basic movement patterns, e.g. hopping, jumping, rolling, running; provide games and activities that involve these movements, e.g. 'Simon Says'; work with individual children in play contexts to help develop specific movements.
- Check outdoor provision to see (1) the range of equipment provided to develop different body skills; and (2) opportunities offered by the layout, e.g. corners for turning, marked lines for jumping, zebra crossing for stopping.
- Check indoor provision to see (1) that it is always available,

e.g. opportunities to move furniture around, large play area, music-and-movement session in impromptu and large groups; and (2) that specific opportunities are offered, e.g. obstacle course, climbing frame that can be constructed indoors as well as outdoors.

- Check that children are challenged, e.g. a visit to a park gives them the chance to run to the limit of their ability; large construction apparatus enables life-size models to be built.
- Encourage children to use movement as a means of expression:

  - Provide music with distinct rhythms and encourage bodily responses.
  - Use stories, songs and pictures depicting a range of emotions; help children to represent physically these emotions, e.g. the frightened little pig whose house was to be blown down by the big bad wolf.
  - Provide a playback cassette-player with a range of cassettes that children are encouraged to use for themselves for dancing.
  - Offer props as a stimulus to movement, e.g. following a story about the magic shoes that made their owner into a beautiful dancer, leave the shoes in the home corner.
  - Encourage children to respond to their environment, e.g. after experiencing a strong wind and observing the effect on the trees, provide music and suggest children imitate the action of the branches on the trees.

HUMAN, SOCIAL AND PERSONAL

This heading includes the National Curriculum subjects, geography, history and religious education. However these are only applicable to a young child if they are linked to reinforcing his or her sense of identity. The child needs to become informed about family background, the locality in which the child lives and the parameters of social and moral behaviour that will make him or her acceptable to others and that the child, in turn, can learn to expect.

There is little evidence available about young children's understanding of the past but, given that learning is made meaningful, early concepts about time passing, sequence and change can be introduced. Initially references to time will be loose – 'yesterday, a long time ago' – but (importantly) it establishes a notion of a time other than 'now'. Ideas may be developed through reference to the child's own life history reinforced by stories, the handling of artefacts and personal accounts by adults known to the child.

Young children are naturally interested in their locality and the different work people do in the community. These interests can be developed to link with work in the National Curriculum geography attainment targets 2 and 5. Planned local outings will familiarize children with local landmarks, which can later be referred to in discussion or related to similar landmarks in stories. Visits from local workpeople can provide stimulus for role play where children will demonstrate their understandings of the different work tackled.

The geography attainment target 1 (referring to use of geographical skills) is also appropriate to develop with this age-group. Starting with three-dimensional representation, young children can learn about reference points and how they are linked in the locality. Watkin, referring to two-dimensional work, suggests that through 'picture maps' discussion can be centred around place-related vocabulary, particularly in regard to distance of journeys, direction, location and scale.[30] For nursery children this is best developed through using a road layout and miniature buildings and landscape objects. Some young children may move directly to two-dimensional picture maps, indicating landscape features in their paintings and drawings. The way in which these features are drawn will indicate the relative importance they have for the child. These early graphical representations will become more detailed and precise and may start to include elements of a plan by indicating roads and rivers.

Studies of young children at home suggest that homes and families are potent sources for developing social and moral understandings. Dunn shows that by 2 years a child has some knowledge of social rules and how they can be broken.[31] Tizard and Hughes suggest that by 4 years children's home conversations reflect that 'all human experience was grist to their intellectual mill'.[32] By developing these interests, teachers can help young children become aware of the variety in culture and customs in other families, that people behave differently in their various roles in life and that certain social and moral conventions are necessary when living and working with others. Piaget and other psychologists concerned with young children's moral development also believed that social interaction was necessary for the formation of moral judgements. For instance, young children initially base their judgement on the seriousness of an outcome as opposed to the intentions behind it. As they socialize with one another they learn to modify their views and to consider those of other people.

Suggested action

Use the child's own history

Create an individual history book for each child and develop this with the help of the family. Use photographs, names of relatives and the child's drawings and paintings to demonstrate sequence and change, e.g. discuss the order in which photographs should be placed in the book.

Use visits, artefacts and visitors to develop the notion of changed times

Use stories, pictures and related role play

For example, *The Sleeping Beauty*, *Rumplestiltsskin* to discuss the passing of time; *The Magic Porridge Pot* to illustrate past ways of cooking.

Develop a sense of location and direction

- Encourage children to become familiar with their own classroom layout through retrieving and returning apparatus for themselves.
- Use a home-made road layout and miniature buildings to depict the layout of the school. In a small group discuss each child's route to school and help him or her to demonstrate it using miniature play people.
- Make miniature gardens, encouraging individual children to describe their layouts.

Help children move from picture maps to plans

Draw outlines of equipment as it is stored in the classroom, e.g. outlines of woodwork tools/sand tools on a rack, different-size building blocks. The outlines will serve as as aide to tidying up but will also signal that objects can be represented by a shape.

Assist moral development

- Use real nursery experiences to pose moral problems to children, e.g. 'Sharon and Chloe both want to use the "Roamer". They say they don't want to share it. Now what can we do to help them?'
- Observe children's reactions and comments to note their level of thinking, e.g. Q: 'Joe pushed Peter – why?' A: 'Because Peter

had taken his car.' Q: 'What else might Joe have done that would have meant not hurting Peter?'
- Note moral judgements offered by children during role play and, where desirable, offer an opinion.

REFERENCES

1. M. Clark (1976) *Young Fluent Readers*, Heinemann Educational, London.
2. G. Wells (1987) *The Meaning Makers; Children Learning Language and Using Language to Learn*, Hodder & Stoughton, Sevenoaks.
3. I. Farmer (1978) Acquisition of advanced vocabulary by five-year-old children; an experimental study (PhD thesis), University of Hull.
4. H. Dombey (1988) Partners in the telling, in M. Meek and C. Mills (eds.) *Language and Literacy in the Primary School*, Falmer Press, Lewes, pp. 69–81.
5. M. Meek (1982) *Learning to Read*, The Bodley Head, London.
6. J. M. Mason, C. L. Peterman and B. M. Kerr (1989) Reading to kindergarten children, in D. S. Strickland and L. M. Morrow (eds.) *Emerging Literacy; Young Children Learn to Read and Write*, Newark, Del., pp. 52–62.
7. J. Hemming (1991) Book handling in the nursery school, *Education 3–13*, March, pp. 36–40.
8. S. Meadows and A. Cashdan (1988) *Helping Children Learn*, David Fulton Publishers, London.
9. Meadows and Cashdan (1988) op. cit. (note 8).
10. J. Piaget (1951) *Play, Dreams and Imitation in Childhood*, Norton, New York, NY.
11. M. Clay (1975) *What did I Write?*, Heinemann Educational, Portsmouth, NH.
12. P. Blatchford (1990) Pre-school reading-related skills and later reading achievement; further evidence, *British Educational Research Journal*, Vol. 16, no. 4, pp. 425–8.
13. DES (1991) *Mathematics for Ages 5–16*, HMSO, London.
14. HMI (1989) *Education Observed 14, Girls Learning Mathematics*, DES, London, pp. 16–20.
15. M. Metz (1987) The development of mathematical understanding, in G. M. Blenkin and A. V. Kelly (eds.) *Early Childhood Education, A Developmental Curriculum*, Paul Chapman Publishing, London, pp. 84–91.
16. Dorset County Council (1984) *Mathematics with the Youngest Children*, Dorchester.
17. E. Choat (1978) *Children's Acquisition of Mathematics*, NFER, Slough.
18. M. Hughes (1983) What is difficult about learning arithmetic?, in M. Donaldson (ed.) *Early Childhood Development and Education*, Blackwell, Oxford.
19. W. Harlen (1985) *Teaching and Learning Primary Science*, Paul Chapman Publishing, London, pp. 126–7.
20. HMI (1989) *Aspects of Primary Education: The Education of Children under Five*, HMSO, London, para. 46.

21. HMI (1989) *Aspects of Primary Education: The Teaching and Learning of Science*, HMSO, London, para. 58.

22. C. Athey (1990) *Extending Thought in Young Children*, Paul Chapman Publishing, London.

23. Somerset County Council (1991) *National Curriculum Primary Design and Technology Guidelines*, Taunton.

24. A. Bishop and R. C. Simpson (1990) Playing with design and technology: experiences in the nursery, *Education 3–13*, October, pp. 36–7.

25. DES/Office of Arts and Libraries (1991) *Arts and Schools*, HMSO, London.

26. HMI (1991) *The Teaching and Learning of Music*, HMSO, London, para. 75.

27. M. Payne (1990) Teaching art appreciation in the nursery school: its relevance for three and four year olds, *Early Development and Care*, Vol. 61, pp. 93–106.

28. K. Jameson (1974) *Pre-School and Infant Art*, Studio Vista, London.

29. National Curriculum Physical Education Working Group (1991) *Interim Report*, DES, London, pp. 6–9.

30. D. G. Watkin (1990) Pictures to plans: some early map work in the infant curriculum, *Early Years*, Vol. 11, no. 1, pp. 53–66.

31. J. Dunn (1987) Understanding feelings: the early stages, in J. Bruner and H. Haste (eds.) *Making Sense*, Methuen, London.

32. B. Tizard and M. Hughes (1984) *Young Children Learning*, Fontana, London.

5

SPECIAL CIRCUMSTANCES

4-YEAR-OLDS IN MAINSTREAM SCHOOLS

As 62 per cent of 4-year-old children are accommodated in mainstream school it seems right that particular attention is given to this type of provision. The widespread practice of admitting children to school once a year only in September does result in pupils starting school as young as 4 years, 1 month. Other authorities admit children twice yearly or termly as 'rising-5s'. However, the admission of any children under 5 means they are strictly in the nursery age-group and ideally should qualify for the provision and resourcing that is considered developmentally appropriate. The policy of admitting very young 4-year-olds to school is particularly worrying and strikingly emphasized by Martin Woodhead:

> The new policy means that some children are being introduced to the reception class who have had 20% less developmental life experiences than children admitted under statutory admission arrangements . . . (to emphasise its significance, the equivalent might be if some universities proposed to admit young people from the age of 14, rather than 18).[1]

Recent years have seen increased awareness of the need for caution in making admission procedures. Central government has offered some clear messages. The white paper, *Better Schools*, emphasized the dangers of introducing young children too early to formal work.[2] The select committee report stated that annual admission to mainstream classes should only take place where the curriculum and provision was comparable with nurseries.[3] This was strongly endorsed by the report of the

Education, Science and Arts Committee in 1989: 'No further steps should be taken by LEAs towards introducing three and four year olds into inappropriate primary school settings. Policies in LEAs of annual entry of four year olds into school should be explicitly subject to the availability of appropriate provision and should normally be for part-time places'.[4]

LEAs have also received grants from the DES to provide in-service education and training (INSET) 'through training for teachers, nursery nurses and non-specialist advisers with responsibility for such children and through retraining for other teachers'.[5]

Despite this there remains the reality of many infant classes accommodating large numbers of 4-year-olds, who are admitted to school on a full-time basis, accommodated in a room that is too small and that does not have access to any outside area. These children may be in a teaching group of thirty with the one teacher not trained to teach the age-group and lacking paid ancillary help.

No early-years specialist would willingly support this provision and it certainly does not apply in all cases. However, Woodhead predicts 'that if present trends continue, it will not be many years before virtually all children will enter Primary School before they are five. The age of starting school will have become four, in practice, if not in statute'.[6]

The reasons for the introduction of this admissions policy constitute a curious combination of individual school and LEA response to local conditions, political expediency and belief in educational benefit.

Falling school rolls in the 1970s meant that many infant classrooms became available for use and it was at that time that schools, faced with the prospect of contraction, made practical moves to include younger children. Although numbers have recovered somewhat during the 1980s, this upturn is not evenly spread demographically and some inner-city and rural schools still have to seek ways of boosting their numbers. Even where numbers are relatively stable the pressures of financial management are causing other schools seriously to consider admitting a non-statutory age-group as one means of securing their school membership for the future.

By admitting this younger age-group, schools are also aware they are pursuing a course of action popular with parents. Nursery provision remains thin overall and unevenly spread. The growth of pre-school playgroups has meant this is a real option for many more 3- and 4-year-olds but many parents will select a more educative setting if given the opportunity. As we have seen (Chapter 1) the National Curriculum is likely to increase parental demand for earlier school entry.

The availability of space and demand from parents for early admission encouraged some LEAs to respond positively. Even where there were resource implications of staffing and capitation, the development of a 4-year-olds admission to school was seen as relatively cheap when compared to the costs of providing for nursery education and also as an attractive alternative.

In addition to these pragmatic reasons there has been a strong move to have a single admission to school in September as a means of compensating for recognized disadvantages of summer-born children. Where schools have interpreted statutory requirements for admission and admitted children to school within the term they become 5, this has resulted in a pattern of three intakes during the year. This admissions policy contrasts with other year-group transitions that, by convention, are on an annual basis in September. If this policy is followed, children born in the summer will be admitted to the reception class in that term and will experience only one term there before transferring to the next year group. At the end of their infant-school career, older autumn-born children will have received eight or nine terms of schooling as compared to the summer-born children who would have only had six or seven terms as an infant. For twenty-five years now there has been mounting evidence that summer-born children were heavily represented as under-achievers. One LEA, for instance, changed its admissions policy to a single point of entry simply on the basis of this issue being successfully argued.[7]

Under termly admission, summer-born children suffer a dual disadvantage of being both the youngest in a year group throughout their school careers as well as experiencing less schooling. This can have long-term effects. Mortimore *et al.* explored the effects of children's ages in a study of fifty junior schools in inner London. The study revealed that younger pupils demonstrated more behavioural difficulties and poorer attainment in reading, writing and mathematics.[8] In addition, children starting school in the spring and summer terms are often required to join an already-established group admitted earlier in the year. Hughes, Pinkerton and Plewis looked at the nature and extent of children's difficulties when starting school and how admission arrangements might affect them. Their study revealed that the January intake of children demonstrated more difficulties than those admitted in September. The most noticeable difficulties were those with activities requiring co-operation, persistence and language skills, such as following instructions and 'verbalizing'. This work supported findings from earlier studies and also confirmed that a significant number of children experiencing difficulties continued to do so during the first year in school. Clearly some individuals are going to experience some of these problems whenever they enter school. However, admission into a small, discrete group at least means the teacher has the opportunity of observing and addressing particular needs:

> The notion of a single point entry was seen to at least offer these youngest children more school in terms of quantity and the opportunity for them to be part of one group established at the beginning of the year. The way in which this admission is resourced and managed critically determines whether it offers a quality experience.[9]

Osborn and Millbank's research stressed that, while pre-school experience in nursery schools and playgroups had a clear beneficial effect on children's later cognitive performance, there was no evidence to show there is any educational or behavioural advantage or disadvantage linked to early school admission.[10] This study suggests that a standard reception-class programme may not be as appropriate for 4-year-olds as a nursery-type setting.

There is general agreement that quality for 4-year-olds depends on making sensitive admission arrangements, providing an appropriate curriculum and pattern of organization and involving parents in their child's learning programme. Evidence and recommendations for each of these elements will be examined in turn. While stressing that the fundamental principles supporting nursery curriculum and assessment apply equally to this age group (see Chapters 3 and 6) procedures for admitting 4-year-olds are similar to those adopted in the nursery.

However, there will necessarily be some adjustments to take account of factors such as managing a larger intake of children, helping them adjust to a more complex building, having a less generous staffing ratio and realizing the expectations surrounding the culture of 'starting school' rather than entering the nursery.

Of course, 4-year-olds will not share a starting-point of total inexperience. Playgroups and nurseries will have familiarized some children to aspects of institutional life. However, it should not be assumed that where this has happened a child will necessarily find a move to formal school any easier.

In the knowledge that under-5s may be accommodated in so many different types of provision deemed 'nursery', the adjustment to be made in the main school will vary according to circumstances. However, the following areas relating to a move may cause young children anxiety:

1. *The school building* – in particular a vast stretch of playground, long corridors, large lavatory blocks and the complexity of building layout.

2. *Daily routines* – most vulnerable times for young children are the daily transitions: moving into the hall, being in the playground, changing for PE and lunchtimes. These times are most overwhelming when large groups of children are involved.
3. *The learning experience* – in the nursery the most usual procedure is for children to have unlimited choice of available activities while adults supervise or become involved with small groups. In infant classes the most prevalent mode is for children to be engaged in prescribed activities while the teacher is either actively engaged with the class as a whole or working with a group. The transition into main school usually means a restriction of choice for the child.
4. *The ratio of adults* – a further NFER study observed that many young children reacted to being in large groups with few adults in the following ways:
   (a) Impatience at having to wait for the teacher's attention.
   (b) Covering the ears to shut out noise.
   (c) Bewilderment and dismay in mass situations.
   (d) Failure to respond to instructions given *en masse*.
   (e) Inability to keep still and quiet for sustained periods.
   (f) Unwillingness to pool creative work.[11]

The first few days in school are critical and most schools now organize a staggered intake. The length of time involved admitting children will vary according to the numbers of new entrants but the aim should be to offer a gentle introduction appropriate for each child.

The NFER study on admissions policies revealed that the majority of LEAs having 4-year-olds admitted them in the autumn term on a full-time basis.[12] Many parents would support this as a natural progression from the part-time attendance experienced at playgroup or nursery. However, this view neglects to realize the stress involved in making another transition and being a novice once more. Most young 4-year-olds will find five full days a week initially overwhelming and will benefit from part-time placement at least during the first few weeks.

We have already emphasized the importance of the child experiencing a smooth transition to the nursery and from nursery to reception class. Managing the transition of a nursery-age child to a mainstream school class can be an infinitely more challenging proposition because of probable less accommodating circumstances. Evidence indicates that making a school transition at 4 is potentially stressful. Some children have particular difficulties and Willes identified a group who needed assistance in learning how to become pupils.[13] Gill Barratt in her AMMA study looked at young children's perceptions of school and illuminated their concern with 'not knowing what to do'.[14] Margaret Clark suggests that for children who speak a language other than English, transition to the reception class may be particularly stressful.[15] Brenda Robson makes a plea for special educational needs (SEN) children not to be admitted to mainstream school at 4 years, claiming that it is difficult for their needs to be met given the resources available.[16]

Organization of groups in school will affect early admission. One school of thought supports the youngest children being received and accommodated in school as a discrete group. Another argues that a mixed age-group allows 4-year-olds to be accommodated as a smaller number and to be offered the support of a model from the older children in the class. For small primary schools the organization of age-groups is determined for them, and teachers may have their new intake accommodated in an age-range of 4–7 years. Where schools do have a choice, however, it is worth them considering the joint recommendations given by the British Association for Early Childhood Education and the Pre-Schools Playgroups Association that 'the [4-year-olds] are happier with a group of their peers and younger children than with those older than themselves'.[17] The argument for a separate reception class is voiced by teachers involved in a pilot exercise on early entry to infant schools organized in four London boroughs. One teacher accommodating 4-year-olds in a mixed-age class described it as 'like trying to teach a class of bright, motivated and well taught children and run a creche at the same time'.[18]

Clearly a mixed age-group with its wide developmental span of needs will be more challenging for the teacher than one chronological age-group. With the focus on National Curriculum attainment there is an additional danger that the youngest members of the class may be the ones whose needs are addressed last.

Curriculum provision for 4-year-olds has been the subject of much debate. Concern about the disparity between the experience offered to a child in a nursery or in a reception class led the British Association for Early Childhood Education to start its inquiry into the 4-year-old in the classroom. In response to requests for some definition of an appropriate curriculum, one branch of the association responded as follows:

1. To provide a width of experience which will enable the child to communicate in the broadest sense.
2. To enable the child to cope for himself in the world around him by involving the new school situation with home.

3. To provide situations and experiences for the child to make decisions and solve problems.
4. To provide first hand experiences which will enable children to develop their own imaginative situations. Children learn by using all their senses.
5. To provide a rich and stimulating environment in which the four year old can freely explore and experiment to further his understanding of the world.[19]

This statement echoes all that has been argued for in nursery education and it strengthens the case for a common curriculum entitlement for 4-year-olds. However, because of the constraints of resourcing, these aims must be scrutinized and translated into manageable practice. The reception teacher must feel equipped to deal with a class of 4-year-olds in a realistic and positive way.

A positive attitude underpins any successful practice and it is important that the reception teacher is aware of the calibre of his or her pupils. Developmental research shows that children starting school are powerful learners with considerable linguistic and intellectual competencies. Much of this is acknowledged to have been acquired in the home. In one study where such competencies were revealed, it was contrasted with teachers' perceptions of their reception children. The teachers tended to be negative about children's achievements and to focus on their deficiences in learning. They under-estimated the effects of the home and believed that linguistic success could only come through following the teacher's model of instruction.[20] The researchers admitted these teachers were stressed and experiencing low morale. Many teachers of 4-year-olds understandably feel undermined with inadequate resources to tackle their job. However if those teachers are given the time and the opportunity to observe and understand the intellectual capacities contained in their classes they must begin to see how this is the rich foundation for future work.

The parents' power in promoting their child's learning tends to be starkly contrasted with teacher inadequacies: parents, it is argued, have unique information about their children and share common interests. Raven describes some typical 'teacher' behaviour from an educational home visitor when visiting a child at home. The behaviour is partly described by the adult's feeling of being accountable as a paid employee of the local authority and also being under some time pressure: 'then there was the problem that they did not know the children sufficiently well to appreciate their interests and were consequently unable to harness or build on them. Nor did they know how to "read" their innuendoes and body language'.[21] All these difficulties are only too clearly appreciated by the reception teacher. With a large class of young children it is essential to use all means of moving close to each one of them in order to establish communication and trust at an early stage. Barratt's study warns teachers that when special interests and knowledge children have developed at home are not built on in school, children may be in danger of learning not to be learners in their own right.[22]

The reception teacher (like the nursery teacher) will receive children from many different backgrounds and with many degrees of readiness for more formal schooling. The nursery teacher will have a maximum of two years in a specialized setting to identify and address particular needs. The reception teacher may feel under more pressure, having less time, fewer resources and being subject to greater expectations at the end of one year. Whatever the professional understanding about provision for 4-year-olds, parents whose 4-year-old has spent a year in mainstream school will probably expect a higher degree of achievement than they would if that same aged child had been accommodated in a nursery.

It is important to recognize these pressures but essential for teachers to understand how they will promote sound learning. The 4-year-old who comes to school with clearly developed concepts is ready to progress to more formalized symbolic learning. His or her companion may be at a very different starting-point. Chris Athey suggests that 'in infants there appears to be 'a fairly fixed order of "unfolding" of cognitive structures that, over time, can be impeded or enhanced to a marked degree by conditions of poverty or privilege. Some variation stems from differences in nourishment, from food for the body right through to food for the mind'. Athey firmly believes these concepts are fed by experience: 'Common knowledge of the cognitive capacities of privileged and under-privileged children strongly suggests that early enrichment has a cumulative effect in that subsequent experiences are amplified by enriched minds'.[23]

Once the teacher is acquainted with the conceptual starting-points of children, he or she must be aware of those who have been mentally impoverished and require enrichment. Attempts to accelerate learning by force-feeding children, and classroom approaches that ignore gaps in previous experience and that expect children to jump into abstract recording, will not achieve subsequent sound learning. More importantly they will condemn the child to experience failure. On the other hand, increased experience and opportunities for children to express their understandings symbolically will affect intellectual improvement. The argument for focusing on the children who need compensatory enrichment is a strong one. Tizard stresses the predictive link between children's knowledge of literacy and numeracy skills when starting school and their attainment at the age of 7 years.[24] The teacher must aim to 'nourish' the group of children who lack these skills, in order to give them access to the National Curriculum.

In a reception class the need for good organizational skills is paramount. If young children are going to learn confidently they must be helped to support their own learning. As children become more independent, this in turn helps release the reception teacher to focus his or her teaching. The importance of a clearly defined learning environment which children are trained and trusted to use has already been emphasized (see also Chapter 6). Children also need to be clear about the purpose of their activity if they are going to be actively involved and motivated. Bennett and Kell found that in some teacher-directed activities this was not always apparent: 'Lack of teacher clarity, and/or lack of teacher thought about clarity were certainly features of the classroom as we observed, leaving children unclear and unaware and thereby occasionally very anxious about task demands'.[25]

The argument for play (see Chapter 3) remains just as strong for young children in the reception class. However, in addition to it being developmentally sound, good-quality play provision is simply sensible for the reception teacher. Mari Guha goes further and argues for it being cost effective. Efficiency is enhanced 'because teachers have to spend less time trying to motivate children to learn; because teaching is more effective as teachers achieve a better "fit" between their instruction/explanation and the child's thinking; because the quality of the child's learning is enhanced when it is in tune with self-directed, voluntary involvement'.[26]

Suggested action

Develop links between reception and nursery teachers

Organize curriculum groups where practitioners can meet to share expertise and discuss the different settings that enable or constrain provision for 4-year-olds. Aim to agree some common curriculum for 4-year-olds wherever they are accommodated. Stress this common approach to parents.

Develop a sensitive admissions policy

- Organize a staggered entry of children over a period of time, initially on a part-time basis. Admissions in October allow the teacher to visit every home in September and to build on this knowledge of children's past experience.
- Be flexible about patterns of attendance. Four-year-old children may find school very tiring initially, particularly if it is part time. Particular sympathy should be given to irregular attendance if the child is travelling from a rural area to attend school for a full day.
- If possible, arrange for a separate entrance to school, with the opportunity for parents to accompany their children into the classroom.
- Arrange for new children to arrive at school on their first day well after the usual starting time to allow a 'gentle' introduction to the normal school day.
- Appoint a mentor for each new child: this may be an older child in a mixed age-group class or an upper primary pupil (select both girls and boys for this role). The mentors should be very clear about their role, e.g. collecting the child at playtimes, sitting by them at lunchtimes and responding positively to any of their work. This role may be extended to older mentors linking with new children to share books or to write stories for them.

Plan a half-term induction programme for new children

- Decide what information you want to gather about individual children that will help you plan future learning programmes.
- Decide what activities and what form of organization will most clearly reveal young children's competencies.
- Decide what the young child will need to learn during the induction in order to cope successfully as a pupil.
- Organize a programme for yourself and other members of the team that will enable you to work in some depth with one group in turn.
- Provide information for parents explaining the purpose of the induction and the intended programme. Plan a meeting with parents at half term to exchange information: how do they feel their child has settled into school? What you have learnt about their child and your planned actions.

Provide an organization to support the curriculum

- Plan for 4-year-olds to have a separate playtime from the main school and a shortened lunch break, with opportunities for children to be inside or outside.
- Organize one lunchtime supervisory assistant to have particular responsibility for 4-year-olds in the playground. Encourage this assistant to develop ring games and other informal small-group activities with the children.
- Avoid 4-year-olds being involved with large assemblies, particularly with a full primary-age group. Plan for a separate gathering or one shared with another infant class.

Inform parents and governors

- Provide a separate brochure explaining the reception-class curriculum. Explain the induction to school and curriculum provision that will give children the best access to National Curriculum programmes of study. Emphasize that children will start on the National Curriculum programmes when developmentally ready.
- Ensure that governors understand the principles and practices in 4-year-old classes.

YOUNG CHILDREN WITH SPECIAL EDUCATIONAL NEEDS

The idea that nursery provision supports a child's level of development and provides a base for future development has important implications for young children with special educational needs. Carefully planned inclusion of these children into mainstream nurseries offers them the opportunity of a 'normal environment' at a critical time of their life and usually increases their chance of eventually being successfully integrated into a primary school.

Given appropriate resources, and the applications of curriculum principles and assessment (see Chapters 3 and 6), mainstream nurseries can offer a good experience for a wide range of special-needs children. Those with more severe handicaps are more often accommodated in a special unit. In this section we focus on those children with milder conditions, who are seen in varying numbers in ordinary nursery establishments. Very often the teacher has to deal with such individuals, with no additional staffing or regular access to specialized help. The teacher may be required not only to diagnose the nature of the problem but also to provide a programme of remediation.

In 1982 a DES-funded study considered teachers' perceptions of the numbers of SEN children in mainstream nurseries, playgroups and day nurseries and also the type of handicapping condition.[27] The incidence of special needs was reported to be 17, 7 and 15 per cent respectively of the total numbers of children attending. Types of condition included sensory handicap (including partially sighted and partially hearing children); those with speech and language difficulties; mild physical disability; learning difficulty; behaviour problems; multiple handicap; and giftedness. Adults were reluctant to identify gifted or learning-impaired children at such an early age, but highlighted those with language and speech difficulties and behaviour problems as forming the largest SEN intake.

Clearly then, SEN children are already in nurseries and indeed many nurseries have a policy of admitting a proportion of SEN children on their priority list.

The ratio of SEN children to be included in a nursery cannot be stated in hard-and-fast terms. The type and degree of need is critical. Robson makes a case for nurseries being selective: 'it is unrealistic and uneconomical however to expect every nursery to meet every need. Some children require sophisticated and expensive resources, others may require the skills of highly trained and scarce personnel. It is advocated therefore that some nurseries be provided with extra resources to meet specific need'.[28]

While this may previously have been possible to develop as an LEA policy, the decision to target provision to specific needs is now more likely to be made by the headteacher and governors. If this decision is taken then a careful review of human and material resources undertaken by a specialist agency will establish if provision is adequate. Robson also stresses that a designated nursery may face particular problems linked with catering for children within a wide catchment area. The transport of such children by taxi may reinforce the fact of them being 'different' and, more importantly, it may make regular contact with parents more difficult if they do not accompany their children to school.

The decision to limit SEN admission to certain type of disability may well be a sensible use of resources, and access to specialist help may be more realistic if it applies to specific need. It is certainly easier to develop links with one specialist institution, say a school for the deaf or partially sighted, or one advisory teacher for speech and language disorder, than it is to seek contact with a range of support agencies. However for some nurseries this narrow focus may not be possible, and they may see that their provision is better used to accommodate a moderate range of learning needs from children within the catchment area.

Whatever the decision, it is essential that every nursery has a clear admissions policy with a statement outlining the resources available and approach taken with SEN children. This information should enable parents and agencies to make better-informed decisions about the suitability of a placement for a particular child.

While an admissions policy makes clear the principle of integrating SEN, the actual admission of individual children must be done cautiously. In cases of defined physical handicap it should be relatively straightforward to gain information about the condition and the child's needs. In other cases, a clear diagnosis of need may not have been made and it is difficult to assess exactly how demanding on resources the child will be. It is important for teachers to remember their overall responsibility to the group, and also to be aware that some of their 'normal' intake may prove to have special needs.

The acceptance of SEN children implies certain action. Robson reports that staff in ordinary nurseries are well intentioned, but they often lack the skills and resources specialized teachers have.[29] This supports previous findings from HMI in a survey of provision for SEN in 61 nurseries: 'often teachers [in ordinary nurseries] were without the expertise necessary for either diagnosis or educational treatment, unless as in two or three instances, nursery teachers had become proficient because of their close association with special units attached to their nurseries'.[30]

The nursery will need to have maximum advance information from all involved agencies about the child, and to have a good idea of where to receive specialized advice. Too often nurseries have suffered from admitting children without having received clear and full information about the contextual background or nature of the condition. Over-hasty and ill-prepared admissions, often based on well-meaning intentions, may result in the nursery not being able to cope and the family being faced with the experience of rejection. A successful entry will depend on a multi-professional assessment, including close collaboration with a clear understanding of the roles different agencies play to support the child and family, and a joint definition of confidentiality. The overriding aim should be to offer a new child a programme of support that will enable him or her to experience some success in a normal nursery setting.

Once the child is accepted, the transition into the nursery will need to be carefully planned. In addition to the adjustments all new children have to make (see Chapter 3), some SEN children will have already been referred to various agencies and may have been hospitalized. This is likely to affect their attitude to separating from parents. Other children may have communication problems linked to speech and language disorder. Parents may also react variously: some will have already experienced considerable anxieties and may be overprotective when they see their child in a robust nursery setting. Others may not yet have accepted the reality of their child's disorder. Clearly there will be some SEN children who settle into the nursery immediately and who are supported by sensitive and aware parents. However, the nursery teacher must monitor closely the adjustment of all children referred, and make it clear to parents that they are centrally involved in the process.

The nursery teacher will accept that children with SEN have a particular claim on staff expertise but that this must be balanced against the needs of the whole group. Where an additional member of staff has been appointed as a result of an SEN admission, this should be seen as a means of improving the general staffing ratio and deployment should be flexible. While some individuals initially require a full-time adult caregiver, this dependence may lessen, for instance when the child becomes more socially adept. Other children will require one-to-one attention at specific times for help with physical needs. At other times the extra member of staff may be given general duties, to free the teacher to do specific work with the child and to observe his or her activity.

In principle, SEN children should have access to all of the elements of a good-quality nursery curriculum. However, in order for that access to be possible, in some instances additional planning and structure will be required. Clearly this individual programme will depend on a careful diagnosis of need. This may have been done prior to admission, but once in the nursery the child's reaction to and 'take up' of the curriculum will have been carefully observed and these responses will provide valuable additional information.

Children previously identified as having SEN and those admitted with no apparent difficulties, may exhibit behaviour problems. These problems can severely affect other areas of functioning, and merit a programme of remediation in the same way as any other handicap. In order to assess the child's degree of difficulty, reference to a developmental checklist may be helpful. Useful descriptors can be found in *The Pre-School Behaviour Checklist*[31] and *A Schedule of Growing Skills*'.[32] However, these instruments are best regarded as tools to support teacher judgements. Having had this support from assessment materials, teachers may feel better equipped to decide whether they can devise their own individual programmes, or need to seek specialized help.

Nursery teachers should be aware of the repertoire of teaching strategies they employ daily and that they can use selectively to help modify behaviour. Newman and Pitchford stress the potential benefits of compliance training that, under the guise of the game 'Simon Says', requires the child to follow instructions in two settings, both with and without praise. They stress, however, that this technique should be used selectively, and only with the guidance of an educational psychologist.[33] Other approaches recommended could be introduced more simply. These include the teacher ensuring that a child clearly understands a rule required of him or her by providing the child with negative and positive examples of that rule. The use of stories is also seen as an effective way of specifying desired behaviour and the positive outcomes that will probably follow.[34]

A number of studies[35,36,37] have found that both physically handicapped children, and those with developmental delay, commonly experience problems of socializing with their peers. It is not sufficient to simply expose a child to the range of activity in a nursery. As Lindsay and Desforges point out, 'Ultimately, integration must be measured in terms of the actual interaction between the special children and their peers and teachers'.[38]

While it is important that the child is given time and opportunity to develop social contacts in his or her own way, the teacher must also be prepared to step in and assist and structure activity if there is a danger of growing isolation.

Observations of SEN children must be maintained to ensure that social contacts are well secured. Studies of Down's syndrome children showed that although they appeared to settle in and conform, supported by friendly overtures from other children, these interactions were not reciprocated by the Down's syndrome children. One study suggests that this was due to the Down's syndrome group not being able to return verbal exchanges or eye contact. Specific help was required in order to make social interaction possible.[11]

We have already looked at some ways in which talk can be fostered (see pp. 64–6), but more focus on sharper interaction is required where there are specific speech and language difficulties. Robson reported some benefits for children who were accommodated in special nursery classes. The programme provided the following:

1. Time to listen [to children] and wait for a response.
2. Knowledge of speech patterns of individual children.
3. Knowledge of language ability of individual children aided by close liaison and daily contact with speech therapists.
4. Structured activities: each child followed a structured programme for part

of each day devised by the teacher and speech therapist. The materials used were all readily available in ordinary nurseries but were more carefully selected and monitored in the special unit.

5. 'Unstructured' activities: much of the free play time, fantasy play and role taking was, in fact, structured by the staff and they frequently played an active part with the children.[39]

Robson readily admits that this was achieved with a vastly enhanced staff:child ratio but nursery teachers need to look at these programme elements and consider what is possible in their own schools.

Observations of SEN children in a range of pre-school units have revealed that they spend significantly more time than others in watching activity, rather than being involved. This lack of engagement could be helped by a clear framework for action, such as advocated by High Scope. The requirement in this programme for the child to identify his or her intentions at the start of the session and subsequently review the activity will help focus on what has taken place. Although this is initially a difficult requirement for most children the routine of plan–do–review can provided a much needed structure for organizing a child's time.[40]

The general principles and practices for monitoring and assessment apply equally to SEN children. However, the following elements are particularly important.

Other agencies, including parents as well as nursery staff, will contribute information for the assessment. In some cases this may be used as evidence for when a statement of SEN is made. Under the Education Act 1981, 'The Act's definition of SEN applies to children under 5 who are likely to have a learning difficulty when over this age or whose learning difficulty would be likely to persist if special educational provision were not made for them'.[41]

Any SEN programme needs to be monitored and reviewed both regularly and systematically to ensure that it is proving effective. The smallest steps in progression can be very significant for some children.

The involvement of a named person who is the point of contact for the family and acts as their advocate and keyworker was recommended in Warnock and confirmed in the Children Act 1991. Regular liaison with this person should aid communication with the family and other agencies for the nursery teacher.

The case has already been made for developing a full working partnership with parents of all children in the nursery (see Chapter 2). Past reports, however, while advocating the need for working together, have seen parents as the passive partners benefiting from professional expertise. Warnock suggests that parents should be given relief from the daily care of their child and offered skills to help them cope for themselves.[42] Clearly these parents have particular need for professional support but equally they may play a vital part in supporting nursery staff. The experience of handling a child who has had problems since birth will have elicited certain skills based on intimate knowledge of that individual. Moreover, the fullest information is needed in making an accurate assessment of SEN. The parents' knowledge of behaviour and performance in the home will supplement information gained in the nursery.

Teachers who have worked with parents in this way will realize there are shared benefits for all. To be of full value this equal partnership should be recognized at policy level and reflected in ways such as that suggested by Watt and Flett: 'We live in an age when the written word carries authority and credibility. If parental involvement [is an] important concept in early education it is important that [it] should be given status in written regional statements in the same way as other aspects of the curriculum'.[43]

Suggested action

All parties to have relevant information prior to confirming admission

- The parents: should have the opportunity of meeting the teacher in a relaxed setting in order to talk about their child and ask questions about provision; should visit the nursery on more than one occasion both to see the facilities and programme available and to discuss how their child might accommodate and benefit.
- The nursery teacher: should receive a multi-professional diagnosis from all agencies concerned with the family (this should result in a shared view of the child's condition, its attendant characteristics and the specific needs that have to be met); should observe the child in both home and school setting.

Review resources that you have to support specific needs

- Specific staff expertise and INSET received.
- Past experience of specific SEN that would assist in dealing with similar cases.
- Available materials and equipment to support handicap.
- Suitability of building to accommodate physical, behavioural and learning needs.

Analyse the support available from others from other agencies

- The availability of the parent during nursery sessions.
- The availability of specialist help during nursery sessions.
- The degree of support and advice available to nursery staff.
- Specialized help available to parent and child outside the nursery.
- The availability and degree of contact from a named person who will keep you informed of all developments.

Manage the transition

- The parents' presence at initial sessions should help to transfer the child's allegiance to an appointed member of staff.
- During the early days of admission all nursery staff should be particularly aware of the new child's adjustment. In particular, note should be made of situations in which the child is vulnerable or demonstrates particular confidence and ability. These observations should form the basis of an individual programme of support for the child.

Staffing

- Arrange for one member of staff to be the point of contact for parents and child. This role should include devising and maintaining an individual programme and sharing this with the parents.
- Use a parent or student to work regularly with the child. This adult should be briefed about the child's condition and appropriate management having first worked alongside the teacher with the child.

Establish rules and boundaries at an early stage

- Ensure the child's parent or nominated member of staff works with the child during the first weeks to familiarize him or her with codes of conduct and nursery routines.
- Having monitored bouts of disruptive behaviour (see p. 153), arrange for an adult to help the child through vulnerable periods during the session to avoid confrontation.

Secure a social framework for the child

- Ensure that the new SEN child is only left by an adult to be with a supportive group of children.

- Provide disruptive and socially unskilled children with small-group story sessions using material that illustrates examples of social behaviour. Discuss the examples with the children and refer to them subsequently with reference to the child's own behaviour (see also pp. 110–11).

Help the child organize his or her time

- Be sensitive to the child's initial need to watch and to make sense of his or her new environment.
- Monitor the activities in which the child becomes involved. Encourage the child to declare his or her next intentions when he or she leaves one activity.
- Gradually encourage the child to plan activities for the whole session. Some children will need sustained help in making choices, projecting intentions and stating them.
- Use the child's parent or nominated member of staff to record the child's plan, either in writing or graphics.
- Check the child understands the principle of a plan, is fully acquainted with the range of activities from which to choose and is helped to carry out his or her intentions.

Use parents as active curriculum developers

- Share a development checklist with parents, indicating where their child is within the spectrum and outlining planned activities to promote progression.
- Have a home/school book in which any notable activities at home or in the nursery are recorded and shared. These recordings will provide useful evidence when carrying out a half-termly review with parents.

REFERENCES

1. M. Woodhead (1989) School starts at five . . . or four years old?, *Journal of Education Policy*, Vol. 4, no. 1, p. 2.

2. DES (1985) *Better Schools: A Summary*, Publications Dispatch Centre, HMSO, London.

3. House of Commons, Education, Science and Arts Committee (1986) *Achievement in Primary Schools; Third Report* (Vol. 1), HMSO, London.

4. House of Commons Education, Science and Arts Committee (1989) *Education Provision for the Under-Fives*, HMSO, London.

5. Education, Science and Arts Committee (1989) op. cit. (note 4).

6. Woodhead (1989) op. cit. (note 1).

7. Campaign for Advancement of State Education (1984) *First School Admissions; The Case for September Entry for All*, London.

8. P. Mortimore, L. S. Sammons, D. Lewis and R. Ecob (1984) *School Matters*, Open Books, Wells.

9. M. Hughes, G. Pinkerton and I. Plewis (1979) Children's difficulties on starting infant school, *Journal of Child Psychology and Psychiatry*, Vol. 20, no. 3, pp. 187–9.

10. A. F. Osborn and J. E. Millbank (1989) *The Effects of Early Education*, Clarendon Press, Oxford.

11. S. Cleave, S. Jowett and M. Bate (1982) *And So To School*, NFER/Nelson, Slough.

12. C. Sharp (1987) Local authority admissions policies and practices, in *Four Year Olds in School, Policy and Practice*, NFER/Nelson, Slough.

13. M. Willes (1981) Children becoming pupils, in C. Alderman (ed.) *Uttering, Muttering*, Grant McIntyre, London.

14. G. Barratt (1986) *Starting School; An Evaluation of the Experience*, AMMA, University of East Anglia, Norwich.

15. M. Clark (1988) *Children under Five; Educational Research and Evidence*, Gordon & Breach, London.

16. B. Robson (1989) *Special Needs in Ordinary Schools*, Cassell, London.

17. Pre-School Playgroups Association and British Association for Early Childhood Education (1985) *Four Years Old but Not Yet Five*, London.

18. A. West, S. Banfield and A. Varlaam (1990) Evaluation of an early entry to infant school pilot exercise, *Research Papers in Education*, Vol. 5, no. 5, p. 244.

19. G. McCail (1988) *The Four Year Old in the Classroom*, British Association for Early Childhood Education, London.

20. M. Hughes (1990) The child as a learner, *The British Journal of Educational Psychology; Early Childhood Education* (Monograph Series no. 4), p. 149.

21. J. Raven (1990) Parents, education and schooling, op. cit. (note 20), p. 56.

22. Barratt (1986) op. cit. (note 14).

23. C. Athey (1990) *Extending Thought in Young Children*, Paul Chapman Publishing, London.

24. B. Tizard, P. Blatchford, J. Burke, C. Farquhar and I. Plewis (1988) *Young Children at School in the Inner City*, Lawrence Erlbaum Associates, Hove and London.

25. N. Bennett and J. Kell (1989) *A Good Start*, Blackwell, Oxford.

26. M. Guha (1987) Play in school, in G. M. Blenkin and A. V. Kelly (eds.) *Early Childhood Education*, Paul Chapman Publishing, London.

27. M. Clark, B. Robson and M. Browning (1982) *Pre-School Education and Children with Special Needs*, University of Birmingham.

28. B. Robson (1989) op. cit. (note 16).

29. *Ibid.*

30. DES (1983) *Young Children with Special Educational Needs*, HMSO, London.

31. J. McGuire and N. Richmond (1987) *The Pre-School Behaviour Checklist*, NFER/Nelson, Windsor.
32. M. Bellman and J. Cash (1987) *A Schedule of Growing Skills*, NFER/ Nelson, Windsor.
33. V. Newman and M. Pitchford (1988) Modifying aggressive behaviour in a case study of a four year old in a nursery school, *Educational Psychology in Practice*, no. 3, pp. 29–34.
34. *Ibid*.
35. M. McTear (1985) *Children's Conversations*, Blackwell, Oxford.
36. Clark (1988) op. cit. (note 27).
37. J. C. Sinson and N. E. Wetherick (1981) The behaviour of children with Down's syndrome in normal playgroups, *Journal of Mental Deficiency Research*, no. 25, pp. 113–20.
38. G. Lindsay and P. Desforges (1986) Integrated Nurseries for Children with Special Needs, *British Journal of Special Education*, 13, pp. 33–66.
39. Robson (1989) op. cit. (note 16), pp. 42–9.
40. M. Hohmann, B. V. Banet and D. Weikart (1979) *Young Children in Action*, High Scope Press, Ypsilanti, Mich.
41. DES/DHSS (1983) Circular 1/83, sec. V. 65, HMSO, London.
42. DES (1978) *Special Educational Needs: Report of the Committee of Enquiry into the Education of Handicapped Children and Young People under the Chairmanship of Mrs M H Warnock*, HMSO, London.
43. J. Watt and M. Flett (1985) Continuity in early education: the role of parents (mimeo), Department of Education, Aberdeen University.

6

MAKING IT WORK

Having looked at some principles that support the learning and experiences young children should have, we must now consider how the curriculum should be offered. Two aspects are important here: curriculum planning and planning and organization of resources.

CURRICULUM PLANNING

'Planning should reflect what a teacher sets out to do after identifying children's initial interests. This will include the activities she or he is prepared to offer, and the aspects of the curriculum which these will allow the children to explore.'[1] Teachers must have planned intentions for children as they are professionally responsible for ensuring progress in learning. Planning does not preclude flexibility. Indeed, careful planning will allow some detours to be made with confidence because the teacher is secure in his or her knowledge of the path towards the next learning goal. The teacher can respond to children's interests and adapt the planned route accordingly.

Plans will be for different purposes and will include intentions for the whole curriculum, particular curriculum aspects and group and individual learning programmes. Plans will be based on learning principles and consideration of what children need to know. Most importantly they will be determined after close observations of individual children, noting their interest, skills and competencies. Ultimately, whatever the plan, it must have some effect on children's learning and development.

Careful planning will help ensure broad and balanced content. A balanced curriculum allows for both sedentary and active physical play, for large-group activity as well as quiet areas to enable the solitary child to withdraw from noise and activity. The primacy of first-hand experience has been stressed but there is also a real place for second-hand experiences, such as listening to stories and music. Varied provision needs to be balanced with fixed curricular points. Children will respond to new stimulus, but some need to know that the painting area or the home bay is always there. The adequacy of any structured learning programme must be considered in the light of the aim to provide for the whole child. The High Scope programme, while providing a good framework for children's cognitive development, does not acknowledge the place for emotional growth or the time needed to adapt to a new nursery environment. Montessori methods provide for well-structured and sequenced activities but leave no room for individual spontaneity. Planning should ensure the best use of all approaches when appropriate for particular children.

Plans should be agreed collaboratively wherever the teacher is working in a team. Volunteer parents working in the nursery will start to see the teacher's overall purposes if they are informed of the teacher's plans. Teachers also need to share their curriculum intentions for a term or half term with all parents and can use individual learning programmes as a focus for discussion in parental consultations. Plans may include the following.

Curriculum map

Every nursery should develop a set of documents that set out the structure and sequence of learning in different areas of experience (in a nursery or reception class these should be distinct aspects of main school documentation). These documents should take account of the range of experiences young children bring to school and, at the other extreme, consider the early levels of attainment in key stage 1 of the National Curriculum. In between lies the nursery curriculum, which needs to be set out in terms of subjects included in areas of experience and chart progression in knowledge, skills, concepts and attitudes. These documents (or document) will comprise a guideline for the offered curriculum: it is in effect the nursery's programme of study. Development of such a guideline will help staff to share understandings of the distinctive learning features in each area of experience. It is, however, very important to see this as no more than a guideline because, although it charts the way, the child's learning route may be circuitous and the pace of the journey will not be constant.

Curriculum action plans

With the curriculum map as a framework, plans will then need to focus on how, over a period of time, the child can develop in different ways. It is wise to have a broad view over a term and then to break down planning into weekly and daily components. If these plans are really going to support individual learning they will need to indicate the following:

Content

Content will involve broad decisions about the types of experiences children should have over a week, term or year. Content may be planned and linked through a theme or it may focus on one area of experience.

Content then needs to be considered in terms of the knowledge, concepts, skills and attitudes children might learn. Knowledge, concepts and practical skills will indicate what is to be learned: in the story of 'The Three Bears', children can gain knowledge of the story, develop some concept of number and the skill of matching one to one. Attitudes and procedural skills are those characteristics that help children learn how to learn: learning content about the story of 'The Three Bears' will be reinforced through co-operation and perseverance in role playing through the story and through communication skills in re-presenting it.

The children and the activities

The needs of the whole group, discrete sub-groups and individual children must be regarded. Decisions about content will already have regarded children's interests and abilities. Now decisions will be made about what activities will best promote learning for what children. The term 'activity' encompasses both the more prescriptive teacher-directed activity, which may be offered to a small or large group as in a High Scope programme, or the implicit structure behind the planning of open-ended activity, where the individual child selects what to do.

Learning outcomes

'For the children themselves the effective curriculum is what each child takes away.'[2] Assessment is dealt with later in this chapter and in

Chapter 7. However, plans should identify how children responded to the activities provided. The teacher will use this information as a basis for future planning, bringing the whole process full circle.

Suggested action

Use previous plans to inform future work

Develop an archive of plans including resources used, children's responses and your own evaluation of outcomes. These will be particularly useful for new staff.

Plan for different groupings

- Provide activities to encourage paired work, e.g. making edible people or animals from icing sugar and whisked egg-white with chairs and aprons laid out for two; a table game with two sets of counters.
- Check provision for a child who wishes to retreat, e.g. a large, sturdy, three-sided carton furnished with cushions and a curtain draped over for privacy.
- Check children's interactions and responses in different-size groups.

Plan experiences for target groups

- Identify children who rarely play with water and see they have similar exploratory experiences using dry sand.
- Check that these children's hand/eye co-ordination skills are developed by pouring tea in the home corner or milk at break time.
- Introduce these children to working with water by asking them to wash up the paint pots or wipe down the table after activities.

Plan for depth of experience

- Borrow all available bricks and blocks from neighbouring schools. Set out the environment using only these materials for two or three sessions. Adults will be freed from the managerial demands of overseeing a range of activities and will have more time for observation and interaction.
- A similar focus could be on imitative and role play, including small-scale fantasy play using miniature layouts, people and animals.

Inform everyone of curriculum plans

- Display a copy of your termly plan in the classroom.
- Present plans and reviews of outcomes at governors meetings.
- Send home details of any short-term plans you feel could be reinforced by parents, e.g. 'We are looking at different patterns for a week or so. It would be very helpful if you could share this interest with your child by observing different patterns at home, in the garden or on walks'. (In some catchment areas a suggestion offered in conversation may be more effective than a carefully planned letter.)

PLANNING, ORGANIZATION AND USE OF RESOURCES

John Dewey described organization as 'nothing but getting things into connection with one another so that they work easily, flexibly and fully'.[3] Here we consider organization of the environment, of equipment, of the daily programme and children's learning and the role played by the teacher in effecting learning.

Planning and organizing the nursery environment

The setting in which learning takes place is crucial to the quality of provision. The environment includes both inside and outside areas – furnishings, fitments and equipment. Buildings differ considerably; one teacher may find him or herself in a brand-new purpose-built nursery unit attached to a school, another in a mobile classroom in a remote corner of a school site, and yet another in a nursery school established in the early post-war years. Some teachers have to accommodate young children in a primary classroom offering few concessions to the developmental needs of this age-group. Some of these buildings will present more opportunities than others. The purpose-built classroom may have adjoining toilets, direct access to an outside play area and fixtures at child height, but space may be limited. The mobile classroom is likely to offer the greatest challenge, while the older, separate nursery school is likely to offer greater potential for learning – extra space, small rooms and corners providing ideal areas for small groups of children – although the problem may be that of overseeing all the activity.

Despite the variety of buildings, given space and siting in a self-contained area of any school building, it is possible to develop a nursery ethos. Where decisions are made to bring in children of non-statutory school age, the best possible accommodation must be made available. Teachers have no choice about the buildings they inherit. It is up to them to consider very carefully the opportunities and constraints, to exploit the former and consider how they can compensate for the latter.

The outside space should be considered an integral part of the learning environment for children. Children of nursery age should have their own outside area, even if their accommodation is in a primary school.

Nursery design affects how adults and children work. A small-scale study by Neill suggested that in a large open space adults tended to oversee a range of activities rather than become involved with specific children.[4] That same study supports previous findings by Sylva and by Smith and Connelly that it is harder for children to settle and play profitably in large open spaces and in larger groups.[5] When more space was made available in an experimental playgroup, the children increased running and chasing activity, but there was little or no change in social behaviour.

Whatever the design, the way the building is used reflects the beliefs of the adults who work there. In 1905 an inspector with the Board of Education described a nursery environment:

> Let us now follow the baby of three years through part of one day of school life. He is placed on a hard wooden bench (sometimes it is only a step of a gallery) with a desk in front of him and a window behind him, which is too high up to be instrumental in providing such amusement as watching passers-by. He often cannot reach the floor with his feet, and in many cases he has no back to lean against. He is told to fold his arms and to sit quiet. He is surrounded by a large number of other babies all under similar alarming and incomprehensible conditions.[6]

In 1979 the High Scope classroom was planned somewhat differently: 'The classroom is divided into well-defined work areas and the materials in each area are logically organized and clearly labeled, which enables the child to act independently and with as much control over the classroom environment as possible'.[7] These two examples show that room organization can either hinder or help children's learning.

An aesthetically pleasing environment is part of a nursery heritage. The arrangement of displays, furniture and soft furnishings should, however, reveal a knowledge of child development and provide a stimulus for learning. Because sensory experiences are so crucial at this stage, the environment should provide them, bearing in mind the size of an average

3- or 4-year-old and his or her physical propensities. It is, for instance, a waste of space to provide a chair for every child in the nursery, when children are unlikely all to be seated together except for eating purposes. Provision of a bright carpeted area is essential, however, to allow children to gather together in small groups or as a total group with the adult at certain times of the day.

An emphasis on active learning and choice of activity means a close look at circulation space in the nursery. Different activities need varying amounts of space and different floor surfaces. A building-block area needs to be sited away from circulation space (to avoid accidents). Carpet tiles make an area comfortable for floor work and also reduce noise.

When considering equipment and apparatus for the nursery there is not much research support for clear spending priorities. There is some danger of continuing to provide certain apparatus for children because of an early-years tradition without having hard evidence about how it benefits children's learning and development. In 1978 Bruner queried the traditional nursery rhetoric that praises unstructured materials and emphasizes free physical play.[8] Where studies exist, they tend to support different activities for different purposes. Pulaski investigated the degree of structure of play materials and the level of creativity of children's activity; her work suggests that less structured materials lead to more imaginative play.[9] On the other hand, Sylva, considering intellectually challenging activity for children, argues in favour of activities with a clear goal structure such as small and large construction, art activity and jigsaws.[10]

There is scope for more work in this area. In the meantime the teacher should be clear as to the purpose and potential use of all apparatus used in the nursery. Until the teacher has further information, theories of child development should be the basis of spending priorities. Sensory exploration indicates the need for a range of bought-in and home-made materials and equipment, which will help young children to discriminate through sight, hearing, taste, touch and smell. The physical needs encompassed in large and small motor development demand large and sturdy, indoor and outdoor equipment, and games and apparatus to develop manipulative skills. To represent their experiences in different ways children need access to art and craft materials, music and sound, building-blocks, pictures and a means of symbolic play. Having made these broad decisions, teachers then need to be sufficiently informed to select specific items of equipment that best support each of these learning needs.

With reduced or static capitation meaning less spending power, the onus is on the teacher to spend wisely. This is not easy. There is an increasingly vast amount of material on the market; teachers have limited time and are in danger of making hasty decisions influenced by an attractive photograph and a manufacturer's description in a catalogue. The alternative is to buy tried and trusted products that have been used in the nursery for some years. Teachers themselves often feel less than satisfied with this way of spending, and some clear guidelines regarding planned spending are needed.

Suggested action

The nursery building

The following factors comprise an ideal nursery environment. Check your nursery against this schedule.

- A welcoming entrance for parents and children: this may be a bright display in a humble entry porch or an elaborate foyer; but remember that it creates the first impression of the nursery for visitors and new entrants.
- Some waiting or working space for parents: a room set aside for parents is ideal, but a couple of easy chairs and some parents' books will at least ensure some degree of comfort for a waiting parent or someone working in the nursery away from children.
- A small room that will double as a withdrawal space for working with individual children, counselling parents and a staff sanctuary.
- A small servery to allow full-time children to eat their meals in the nursery even though they may be cooked in the main school kitchen: a nursery school is likely to have its own kitchen; the servery or kitchen can also be used as a cookery area for a small group of children to work with an adult.
- Storage areas should be sufficient for bulky early-years equipment including large wooden apparatus for indoor gross motor activity. A large store with dual access to the nursery and outside area should be provided where there is no separate outside store.
- Cloakroom and lavatory facilities adjoining the classroom enable young children to collect their outdoor wear at will and also to use the lavatory unaided.
- A spacious playroom with an area of not less than eight square metres for each child; south-facing and with access to the outside play area.

The outside area

- Provide for safety. The play area must be fenced off from any vehicle entrance to the school, and any entrances must have safety hooks attached.
- Provide different levels of play; small hillocks allow children a different perspective.
- A grassed area for playing and picnics in dry weather.
- A paved area for wet weather: this should be wide enough for use of wheeled toys.
- Some means of shade.
- Some means of seating: informal log seats fixed into the ground are suitable and cheap.
- Winding tracks using different surfaces, e.g. crazy paving, brick patterns and cobbles.
- A small growing and digging area.
- A wild garden with buddleia bushes, long grass and rotting logs to attract insects.
- A sandpit with paved surroundings and a secure cover.

Use of space

- Visit a range of nursery environments and consider how space is used. Jot down impressions during your visit or take a photograph as an *aide-mémoire*. It is also helpful to visit a setting during a working session and again later without children.
- Consider what is possible. Draw a scale plan of your nursery and a separate list of the experiences you want to offer during a term. Identify the fixed activity areas and see where there is scope for flexibility in other areas.

Check your room arrangement supports your principles

Consider how your room helps

- you to regard children as individuals, e.g. through providing for special needs – a punch-bag in a corner of the room is excellent therapy for some children;
- towards continuity of learning, e.g. there should be some aspect of room arrangement that will be reproduced when the child moves to main school;
- the child learn through his or her actions and through talk, e.g. provision of learning bays to accommodate small groups of children – these may be created with mobile furniture to give the

illusion of privacy for the children but offering the adult the ability to oversee;

- the child develop as an early mathematician, e.g. create enclosed spaces for play and display on different levels to encourage spatial awareness;
- the child learn through a broad curriculum, e.g. low storage lockers with open shelves containing a range of media for children to select in making their representations;
- the child have a balanced curriculum, e.g. arrange for unstructured materials for child-initiated as well as teacher-directed activity;
- the child to become an agent in his or her own learning, e.g. arrange the room for children to have easy access to resources – the painting area should be near the sink to allow for washing hands, and a low washing-line will allow children to hang up their paintings. Provide a cork-tiled wall area at child height for children to display their work;
- the child to learn through success, e.g. some stable activity areas with familiar materials will offer less confident children the opportunity to learn at their own pace; and
- children to be regarded as people, e.g. aim for a comfortable, warm, bright environment that reflects an inviting atmosphere.

Equipment

- Check what you already have. Look systematically at all the apparatus and equipment there is to support different areas of learning, e.g. small construction play – check provision for the most and least able children; throw out incomplete or broken equipment, which will frustrate rather than aid children's learning; enlist parental help to mend equipment where possible.
- Agree priorities for spending in the light of your budget. It is more sensible to opt for resourcing one learning area properly than to spread money thinly across a range of activity.
- Establish clear criteria for purchasing further equipment, e.g. safety, quality, durability, multi-purpose use, easy storage, opportunity to extend learning, supportive to teacher's intention whether prescriptive or open-ended.
- Gather information about what is available. Visit other nurseries to see equipment in use; observe children using it and talk to teachers about specific strengths and limitations; send for sample kits; ask commercial representatives to visit your nursery and

demonstrate what is on the market; press for regular exhibitions
of equipment to be held at local teachers' centres; ask for advice
from local inspectors and advisers.
- Monitor the effects of your decisions. Having made your
purchases, carefully monitor how children use the equipment
for the first term, noting what difference it has made both to
individual children and to the group as a whole.

Consumable stock

- Keep an open stock-cupboard. Staff should be jointly responsible
for keeping it tidy and for leaving a note when stocks of particular materials are low.
- Regularly review the quality and suitability of consumable materials, e.g. is the sand suitable? Should the type of clay be changed?
- Make collections of natural and junk materials, e.g. store collections of pebbles, shells and waste materials throughout the year.
For conservation and learning purposes, the nursery should
where possible grow its own produce to collect seed-heads and
berries.

Planning and organizing the programme

Routines and programme structures are affected not only by how children
are accommodated but also by the ratio of adults, the size of the group
and the length and timing of the session. Children of 3 and 4 years can
have very different experiences: they may be at home with their parents,
with a childminder or attending a playgroup for one or two part-time
sessions a week; they may attend a private or State nursery class or
school, a nursery centre or day nursery, or they may be admitted to an
infant, first or primary school. Programmes may be part time, full time or
for an extended day; they may be accommodated with a full nursery age-
group, as a separate group of 4-year-olds or with older children of school
age. Circumstances vary even more when geographical location is considered. Some nursery provision may be within walking distance, or
children may have to travel with their parents across an urban area, or
take a circuitous route on the school bus from an outlying area to the
village school, which will greatly affect the length of their day. In such
diverse circumstances, it is impossible to give hard-and-fast guidance on
programmes that will be helpful to all. Once again curriculum principles
and theories of child development must determine the pace and pattern

of the day. Whatever the setting the following organizational factors are important.

Flexibility

Young children and their parents need to be able to enter and leave the nursery informally and in small groups. At the beginning of the day, some young children are still finding the transition from home difficult; both parents and child need access to the teacher at this time. At the end of the session the child is tired. It is important that the physical collection of coats and equipment and the emotional transfer back to home concerns takes place as calmly as possible.

There are different models for a nursery programme. While Lally puts forward a case for children operating at their own pace through self-chosen activity, the High Scope programme identifies blocks of time available for both individual choice and teacher-prescribed group activity. Whatever the emphasis it is important that the activities should interest and challenge children and that the organization should not cut across children's own concentration. Clearly this is not always avoidable as any block of time is finite. However, it is less likely to happen if children become aware of the pattern of the session. A degree of certainty about the daily programme will offer a framework of security, although where routine dominates it can result in monotony for both children and adults. Sylva distinguishes between the regularity of tasks and the structure in the task. She concludes that, where specially planned educational tasks are offered within the framework of a flexible routine, this enhances learning; the daily repetition of activities and schedules, by contrast may have little effect.[11]

Balance

A balanced programme may be planned – it may not be received. What the individual child receives depends on his or her stage of development and personal motivation. A large-group activity poses a particular challenge in ensuring that twenty or thirty egocentric individuals benefit in their learning. For example, the teacher may aim to teach a song. In the group there are likely to be children who are ready to receive group instruction; they are capable of both learning the words and enjoying the joint singing. At the other extreme are those with a very limited concentration span who find it difficult to sit still for more than a few minutes; they may not be ready to cope with the language from an adult other than on a one-to-one basis and the activity is irrelevant for them as it cuts across their own interests. These children will learn other things than what is intended. They may learn from one another by chatting together; they may become skilful at avoiding the teacher's attention by positioning themselves on the outer fringe of the group, requesting to go to the lavatory or keeping quiet while effectively shutting themselves off from the activity.

A balanced programme allows for individual choice, individual need and different levels of learning. Balance also allows for children to play by themselves or in pairs and to be introduced to being one of a group. It ensures an environment that challenges the most confident and reassures the hesitant child who is hovering on the threshold of learning. The High Scope programme usefully provides for different groupings. When the child's self-chosen interests are observed they can be used by the teacher as a focus for small-group activity. In this way interests can be shared and extended. This is a very different matter from requiring the child to fit into a predetermined set of routines.

Targeted teaching

The teacher's role in facilitating children's learning has been subject to a range of interpretation. In past years a polarized view developed. On the one hand, there was a passive style, with the teacher providing the rich environment but viewing any direct involvement with children as intrusive rather than helpful to learning; the opposite style was highly directive, with the teacher teaching from limited objectives and requiring a response. In simple terms, the one can be seen to be an abrogation of responsibility for promoting learning while the other diminishes the child's elective and active role as learner. More recently, the High Scope programme offers a routine that acknowledges both the place of children's self-chosen activity and teacher involvement. Many teachers have found this routine useful with defined periods of time planned for individual and group experiences; others regard such a programme as unnecessarily restrictive. The programme may be adapted; most usefully, the teacher is seen as a vital resource in promoting learning and development. This must mean a close look at how teachers manage their time to work with individuals and groups of children. A nursery environment is undoubtedly a complex and busy one. To bring together a group of children who are egocentric with short concentration spans and a great deal of energy is no easy matter, and to enable them to engage in a variety of first-hand experiences requires the teacher to have high organizational skills. The danger of this is that the organization can become an end in itself. In trying to ensure the nursery programme does not disintegrate, teachers can spend their time overseeing the activities, interacting superficially and briefly with children and neglecting their key role of helping children to develop and understand.

When visiting playgroups, Woods found that where adults took a heavy management role they were approached by children about management matters. The adults who played and talked with the children were more often approached about personal interactions. Thus, he suggests, 'the adult is pulled deeper and deeper into managerial action by the children themselves'.[12]

The number of adults available to children will affect the style of organization. The teacher's role in organizing these other adults is discussed in Chapter 8; as a 'leader' of any team the teacher will deploy nursery assistants and parents in ways that will enhance learning opportunities for children. This will include using paid and voluntary ancillaries in a management role in order to free the teacher to work in depth with children. We have already stressed the need for children to learn to be self-sufficient. This is both in their own interests and also to ensure the teacher does not have to try to cope with all their learning needs at the same time. In a well-organized nursery some children can be profitably involved in activity without the presence of an adult.

Suggested action

Ensure children are affected by the teacher's intentions

- How many children use the art area during the day? If it is underused, try

  - changing its position in the nursery;
  - briefing a group of children about some new colour paint you have set out and show them the effects they can create using different-sized brushes;
  - suggesting the children themselves set up a new art area, deciding where it will be and what will be laid out.

- Ask parents what their children talk about at home relating to nursery activities.

Make daily routines that support the child's well-being and learning

- Avoid wasting time, e.g. plan for children to register themselves at the beginning of the session.

- Allow for children to pursue an activity that can be continued over a period of time.

Plan your programme to allow time for work with children and parents

- Prepare your physical environment and materials well before the beginning of the session. In this way you are free to greet children and parents on arrival.
- Plan for a leisured start and end to the day, e.g. a staggered entry and collection of children are helpful – these are best managed if there is self-initiated activity at the start and end of the day.
- Plan a programme that is manageable, e.g. have a range of self-maintaining activities for children, putting priority on well-resourced construction and role play.
- Plan for children to care for their own environment, e.g. teach them where to find materials and show clear expectations about how they should be returned; allow plenty of time for clearing away at the end of a session and spend time showing children how this is done.

Planning for teaching and learning

Having organized the nursery in order to gain time for the teacher, we are now concerned with how this time is best used – in short, how the teacher works to facilitate learning.

Young children's learning is promoted by the teacher's role as observer, planner and scaffolder. We will briefly consider each of these roles. (The teacher is also an assessor and evaluator, and these aspects of the teacher's work are included in Chapter 7.)

Teacher as observer

Observation is a skill introduced to teachers in training. We would expect the nursery teacher to have internalized this skill and carried it into the classroom as the very pivot for practice. Lesley Webb describes what it involves:

> The seeing eye can be trained, as can most senses, and the more we train ourselves to observe the more we see even when we are not actually making a child-study. Noticing what they really do, how, when and in what order, becomes a habit with the good teacher. Like all habits it can be encouraged by

letting the novice practise it frequently. Once established, the ability to look without prejudice, to note detail, to assess a child's pace, needs and strengths, makes for realistic goal-setting and consequent success and satisfaction for the child and teacher alike.[13]

Observation is time-consuming, but experienced teachers will learn how to fit it into their daily routine and also to identify whom they need to observe. Observation is the basis for developing the learning of all children, but more information is required about some individuals than others.

Although teachers must learn to appear casual and unobtrusive when observing and recording, it is important that the process is structured. The Schools Council project on record-keeping in primary schools offers advice to teachers wanting to improve their observation of children:

1. Determine in advance what to observe but be alert for unusual behaviour.
2. Observe and record enough of the situation to make the behaviour meaningful.
3. Make a record of the incident as soon after the observation as possible.
4. Limit each anecdote to a brief description of a single incident.
5. Keep the factual description of the incident and your interpretation of it separate. Use only non-judgemental words in the description.
6. Record both negative and positive behavioural incidents.
7. Collect a number of anecdotes on a pupil before drawing inferences concerning typical behaviour.[14]

Observations of children must also go hand in hand with a knowledge of child development. This knowledge can help teachers to observe aspects of behaviour that might not otherwise have been noticed: it will help make observations more objective, and will offer a theoretical framework to help interpret and explain the behaviour observed.

Teacher as planner

The teacher's planning will capitalize on his or her observations. Having planned the environment and curriculum and taken into account what assistance he or she has, the teacher can plan where to spend his or her time. He or she may recognize that one particular play area is not very popular, and decide that his or her own involvement and interaction may encourage children to use it more. The teacher will also plan with whom he or she will spend time. Katz draws attention to the 'recursive cycle':

the fact that having a given characteristic or behaviour such as high verbal ability stimulates responses from others which lead to strengthening it. Thus the more verbally able a child, the more verbal input he or she receives from

adults and the more verbally able the child becomes.... Thus a planned
programme of positive discrimination is necessary to support learning and
development in less able children.[15]

Morgan and Dunn's work on 'visible and invisible' children in the
classroom supports a similar argument with some link to gender. In this
infant and nursery study the boys' behaviour tended to be more 'visible'
and assertive and thus demanded teacher time. In so doing the boys
gained from the attention and learnt the value of assertiveness.[16]

The teacher also has an important role in planning for children to
interact with one another. Rubin focuses on the varying social skills
children bring into school, and Scarlett looks at the children who lack
many of these skills and become social isolates. The two studies suggest
that the adult can help children to develop friendship skills by engineering
pairs of children to be together and providing structured play in which
relatively isolated children can interact more with other children. However, promoting this aspect of development is a sensitive area; Rubin
warns that adults should be aware of the fine line that exists between help
and interference: 'Rather than "pushing" social skills indiscriminately,
adults should respect the real differences between children that motivate
some to establish friendly relationships with many others, some to concentrate on one or two close friendships and some to spend a good deal of
time by themselves'.[17]

We previously examined how children can help one another through
interaction and talk (see pp. 64–6). Dewhirst suggests that in planning
these opportunities the teacher's own management style is important. She
found that the more instructional the approach, the less likely children
were to talk together: 'children had time to explore and develop these
contexts [for talk] with maximum teacher support and involvement
in terms of making the settings attractive and available, but with the
minimum of interruption and overt directions.'[18]

Teacher as scaffolder

The teacher will have observed what a child can do competently by him
or herself. Vygotsky suggests that this is one level of achievement but
that, given skilled help, a child can progress to achieve more.[19] The
teacher's role is now threefold: the teacher must observe what is happening now, judge what the child is capable of achieving next and provide
appropriate support for this progress. Bruner uses the term 'scaffolding'
to describe this process.[20] Initially the scaffolding may involve offering

considerable help but this is gradually reduced as the child becomes confident with the new learning.

The teacher will scaffold in different ways according to the particular needs of children. He or she is likely to use the following strategies:

Play tutoring   In his study of socially isolate children, Scarlett found they were less likely to become involved in imaginative play.[21] It may be that these children need active help in learning to play symbolically. Smilansky and Freyburg found that children who received such assistance made noticeable gains in their play. Smilansky called this process 'pump priming'. If the child does not react in an imaginative setting, she suggests the teacher plays and reacts as if the child were role-playing.[22] The teacher might say, 'Good morning, Mrs Brown. Has your husband gone to work today? I am going shopping. Do you want me to buy you anything from the shops? Oh, here is Mrs Green, who is coming to have a cup of coffee with you.'

Freyburg played with a small group of children using pipe-cleaner dolls and other improvised materials. She worked with the children to act out prepared stories. When these children were compared with a control group they were found to have improved their powers of imagination and concentration.[23]

The teacher's role as a play tutor may be necessary as a bridge to enable some children to take part in active role play with their peers. As the child grows in confidence and becomes more responsive, the teacher can take a less obtrusive role but should withdraw only when the target child is established in a group.

Conversing   The teacher's role as play tutor is specific to certain children. His or her role in promoting talk, although easier with some individuals than with others, is important for all. The teacher's aim should be to enable all children to share their feelings, thoughts, ideas and attitudes with him or her. To achieve this a particular style of working is required.

Woods explores how adults can help children converse with them freely and openly. His transcript of many adult–child conversations reveals that the adult who offers his or her own personal views, ideas and observations tends to receive many of the child's views – there is a genuine sharing of experience. Conversely, the adult who controls the conversation and who asks questions persistently may receive answers but seldom elaborations or opinions. The conversation thus becomes dominated by the adult:

The apparent maturity and competence of the pre-school child in conversation, then, is not only dependent upon his language ability or home background, but also upon the framework that the adult sets for him in dialogue. The more she is inclined or driven to ask questions and exercise control to keep him going, the less likely she is to be successful. By leaving the child time to think, and periodically taking the pressure off to reveal something of her thoughts, she is most likely to see him at his linguistically most active.[24]

Both Woods and Sylva argue that the managerial nature of the work of a nursery teacher means that during the day talk tends to comprise brief, trivial comments relating to the control of children and to the organization of activities. It is all too easy for the teacher to spend the day seeing that the water is not spilt, sand not thrown, helping children to put on aprons, do up coats and wash their hands, without having had to engage in sustained talk with an individual or group of children. Scaffolding will require time set aside to listen to children and to promote conversations.

Sylva stresses the need for the 'subtle tutorial' to take place between adult and child or small group. She sees this in the context of an activity with a clear goal structure involving the adult encouraging the child towards elaboration of this task. Thus, with large construction apparatus, the teacher may admire the building of a castle but continue to ask about the location of the entrance, how the castle is made secure and how it is defended. According to Sylva, the adult enters the child's construction task with related conversation, which is what another child cannot do.[25]

Tizard and Hughes suggest that many of the valuable opportunities young children have for conversing occur at home during involvement with routine chores.[26] This too has implications for the way teachers use their time; nursery routines can be productive occasions for dialogue.

Questioning   Woods warns of the danger of imposing too many questions on children, yet teachers are aware of the need to ask questions as a way of checking children's understanding. Marion Blank, for instance, suggests that one valuable area of discussion can centre on materials that undergo changes in state. Questions may centre on the process (considering cakes before and after cooking and seeing what has changed), on memory (children remembering what they could do with sand before they added water to it) and on cause and effect (what has to happen to turn an ice cube back into water?).[27]

However, questioning should not be over-rated as a process. Hughes and Grieve suggest we should not assume children will reveal their lack of knowledge or understanding through questioning. Their study presented 5-year-olds with questions intended to be unanswerable (e.g. 'Is milk heavier than water?' 'Is red bigger than yellow?'). They invariably received some answer and, when asked why, the children responded by adding their own meaning to the question (e.g. milk was found to be heavier than water because it came out of a bottle and water came out of a tap).[28] This study supports another, which indicates young children will respond to questions when the meaning to them may be quite obscure.[29]

All conversation tends to include questions. But these should perhaps stem from the adult's interest in eliciting the child's viewpoint, rather than be a testing technique.

Instructing The teacher's role as instructor is not intended in any formal, restrictive sense but simply to highlight that the teacher should provide information and teach certain skills. Woods suggests that 'where adults do not supply such a framework for a child in a difficult task, he may well become demoralized, losing interest in the activity and confidence in his own ability'.[30]

Modelling We have considered the importance of the teacher as the model through which the young child bases his or her view of the world (see Chapter 3). This modelling influences the child's social abilities and strengthens his or her intellectual skills. Bruner, supporting the place of intuitive thinking in learning, comments: 'it seems unlikely that a student would develop or have confidence in his intuitive methods of thinking if he never saw them used effectively by his elders'.[31]

Katz suggests that offering a model will aid a child's communication skills. She also argues that young children need an adult model of articulateness and the opportunity to share in adult thinking: 'Teachers might be encouraged to speak to children as though they are real people, albeit with limited experiences and vocabularies; they are not pets or dolls and should be spoken to seriously'.[32]

Suggested action

Teacher as observer

Aim to build observation into your programme on a regular basis, particularly using times when you have additional adult help from parents or students.

- Observe children's behaviour:

  - Time-sample a child's total behaviour during the course of a week to gain a general picture of how the child spends his or her time, and with whom. Aim to note and record the behaviour for two minutes every half hour.

– Observe over a period of time. Aim to tackle at least one longitudinal study a year, observing a child weekly from September to July, to check rate of progress in development, e.g. powers of concentration, development of fine motor skills and use of language.

- Observe activity. Study activity areas in the nursery to note who uses them, when they are most used and how the equipment is used. This information will help you make decisions about siting and about the form of the provision and how it might be better used.
- Record information using different formats:

  – Keep duplicated copies of a nursery plan, indicating the location of various activities. Use this plan for charting and recording the child's movements during the course of the session (Figure 6.1).
  – Record children's small-group interactions as a simple sociogram. Draw a line every time a child initiates talk, with the arrow pointing to the child he or she addresses. This is a time-consuming and demanding task but is occasionally worth while, especially in providing a picture of isolates and children who dominate conversations (Figure 6.2).

Teacher as planner

Teacher presence at an activity automatically stimulates children's interest. During term you should aim to spend time at each activity to see the range of play, how the provision is used and how it supports learning.

- Plan to work in depth with children; ensure your nursery assistant keeps an overseeing eye on the nursery as a whole while you work with a target group of children.
- Plan time with new children; arrange to be available to new children and make it a priority to spend part of every session with them until they have settled.
- Plan time to work with children who do not respond easily; make sure these children are regularly involved with you as individuals in shopping trips or in domestic routines such as cleaning the hamster's cage.
- Plan to spend time with the most able children; initiate challenging problems involving small-scale constructions – building an

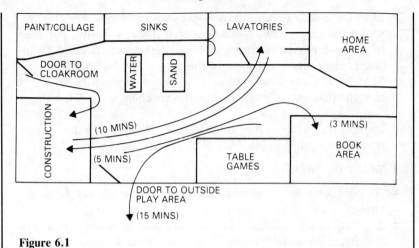

Figure 6.1

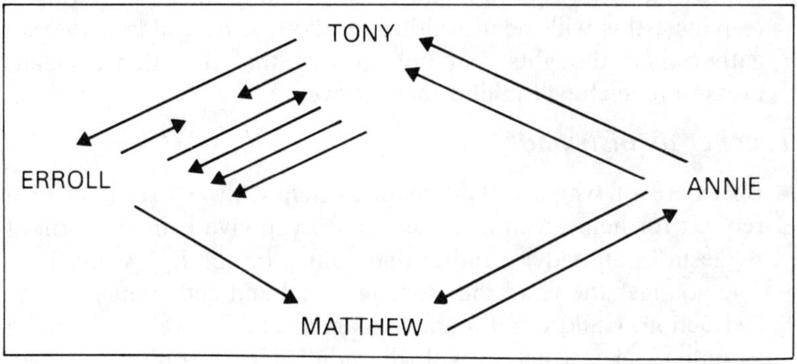

Figure 6.2

obstacle course, creating sound patterns and recording them on cassettes, reading with real books.

- Plan individual programmes for children: if a child is failing in a task, plan a variety of tasks in which he or she is introduced to subskills – e.g. if unable to use scissors, tearing paper; small constructional work and finger-rhymes designed to strengthen small muscles.

Teacher as conversationalist

- Take time to listen to children; make their interests your starting-point.

- Share your own personal experiences with children. They will respond warmly to news about your own children or your purchase of a new dress or new puppy or looking at your holiday photographs (let them bring some of theirs).
- Share your views with children as a way of eliciting theirs, e.g. 'I thought that our ride on the bus this morning was a bit bumpy. Did you, Joe?'
- Include and involve other children, e.g. 'Well, Ros, I don't know what colour paint to use. Ask Neil what he thinks.'

Teacher as questioner

- Avoid questions to which it is obvious you already have the answer.
- Try to question children when you are both involved in a shared activity. This should result in a more natural discourse and a sharing of views rather than interrogation.
- Be sensitive to the time different children need in giving a response; this will mean waiting to allow some children time to gather their thoughts, but not so long that the silence means pressure, which will inhibit their answers.

Teacher as instructor

- Be aware of when a child requires help. Always respond to a request for help, even if the assistance you give is in the form of suggestions and advice rather than taking on the task yourself.
- The younger the child the more personal and active must be the instruction. Children of 3 and 4 years are more likely to respond to individual instruction with the adult demonstrating and then being prepared to assist, e.g. showing the child how to do up his or her coat by standing behind the child and guiding his or her movements.

Teacher as model

- Offer the child a model of questioning, e.g. 'If you want to know how much water you need to mix the paint, why don't you ask James? Say "How much water did you need when you mixed the paint yesterday, James?"'
- Work alongside the child at your own level, offering a model of interest and concentration rather than showing a standard of work to be achieved, e.g. join children when they are drawing from observation or creating patterns.

- Offer a model of thinking for children, e.g. 'I wanted to buy
  some shoes the same colour as my new dress. I wanted exactly
  the same colour, but it was too cold to wear my dress when I
  went to the shop. So I wrapped the dress up in a parcel and took
  it with me. I showed the shop lady and she found me shoes that
  are exactly right. Look – can you see?'

REFERENCES

1. ILEA (1988) *The Early Years: A Curriculum for Young Children*, ILEA
Learning Resources Branch, London.
2. Schools Council (1981) *The Practical Curriculum* (Working Paper 70),
Methuen, London.
3. J. Dewey (1915) *The School and Society*, University of Chicago Press,
Chicago, Ill.
4. S. Neill (1982) Open plan or divided space in pre-school?, *Education 3–13*,
Vol. 10, Autumn, p. 46.
5. K. Sylva, C. Roy and M. Painter (1980) *Child Watching at Playgroup and
Nursery School*, Grant McIntyre, London; P. K. Smith and K. J. Connelly (1981)
The Ecology of Pre-School Behaviour, Cambridge University Press.
6. K. Bathurst (1905) The need for national nurseries, *Nineteenth Century*,
May, pp. 818–27.
7. M. Hohmann, B. Banet and D. Weikart (1979) *Young Children in Action*,
High Scope Press, Ypsilanti, Mich.
8. J. S. Bruner (1978) Child care: science, art and technology (the Gilchrist
Lecture)
9. M. A. Pulaski (1973) Toys and imaginative play', in J. L. Singer (ed.) *The
Child's World of Make Believe*, Academic Press, London.
10. Sylva, Roy and Painter (1980) op. cit. (note 5).
11. *Ibid*.
12. D. Woods, L. McMahan and Y. Cranstoun (1980) *Working with Under
Fives*, Grant McIntyre, London.
13. L. Webb (1975) *Making a Start on a Child Study*, Blackwell, Oxford.
14. P. Shields, G. Weiner and E. Wilson (1981) *Record-Keeping in Primary
Schools*, Schools Council/Macmillan, London.
15. L. G. Katz (1985) Fostering communicative competence in young children,
in M. M. Clark (ed.) *Helping Communication in Early Education* (*Educational
Review* Occasional Publications no. 11), Birmingham.
16. V. Morgan and S. Dunn (1988) Chameleons in the classroom: visible and
invisible children in nursery and infant classrooms, *Educational Review*, Vol. 40,
no. 1, pp. 3–12.
17. Z. Rubin (1983) The skills of friendship, in M. Donaldson (ed.) *Early
Childhood Development and Education*, Blackwell, Oxford.
18. E. Dewhirst (1985) Settings as contexts for dialogue: guidelines for practice
in the management and organization of communication between children, in

Clark (ed.) (1985) op. cit. (note 15).

19. L. S. Vygotsky (1962) School instruction and mental development, in Donaldson (ed.) (1983) op. cit. (note 17).

20. J. S. Bruner (1983) *Child's Talk: Learning to Use Language*, Oxford University Press.

21. W. G. Scarlett (1983) Social isolation from age mates among nursery school children, in Donaldson (ed.) (1983) op. cit. (note 17).

22. S. Smilansky (1968) *The Effects of Sociodramatic Play on Disadvantaged Children*, Wiley, Chichester.

23. J. T. Freyburg (1973) Increasing the imaginative play of urban disadvantaged kindergarten children through systematic training, in Singer (ed.) (1973) op. cit. (note 9).

24. Woods, McMahan and Cranstoun (1980) op. cit. (note 12).

25. Sylva, Roy and Painter (1980) op. cit. (note 5).

26. B. Tizard and M. Hughes (1984) *Young Children Learning*, Fontana, London.

27. M. Blank (1985) Classroom discourse: the neglected topic of the topic, in Clark (ed.) (1985) op. cit. (note 15).

28. M. Hughes and R. Grieve (1983) On asking children bizzare questions, in Donaldson (ed.) (1983) op. cit. (note 17).

29. R. N. Campbell and T. Bowe (1977) Functional asymmetry in early language understanding, in G. Drachman (ed.) *Salzburger Beitrage für Linguistik*, Vol. 3, Gunter Narr, Tubingen.

30. Woods, McMahan and Cranstoun (1980) op. cit. (note 12).

31. Bruner (1978) op. cit. (note 8).

32. Katz (1985) op. cit. (note 15).

7

HOW IS IT PROGRESSING?

The best practitioners have always been concerned about what and how learning is transmitted to children. However, all schools in all phases of education are now aware of the need to look very carefully and to satisfy themselves that they are being effective. This need for greater scrutiny stems from the statutory requirements relating to the Education Reform Act 1988 (ERA) applying to the age-group 5–16. These measures have been concerned with aiming to raise standards in schools, to widen parental choice in using the system and to require schools to be more accountable to the public.

The National Curriculum has offered a framework of content for schools and, although the format for statutory assessment still has to be agreed, there is the intention to check that children are progressing through this curriculum.

Measures encouraging more open enrolment in State schools and encouragement for schools to opt out of the State system and become directly controlled by central government through grant-maintained status are intended to offer parents a wider choice of schools for their child. Under local management, schools are now responsible for their own budgets and can make more decisions about purchasing appropriate resources.

Schools are also required to offer more information to parents. There is now parent representation on governing bodies; all parents receive information about the school curriculum, and an annual report on the school from the governors as well as written reports on their child's progress in attainment through the National Curriculum.

The effects of these policies are mixed. Most schools are responding to curriculum guidance and there are indications that primary-age children are receiving broader and better-planned progressive experiences. Large, entrepreneurial schools in affluent areas where parents are generous contributors are thriving on financial independence. Some are judiciously purchasing additional resources for their schools, which benefit the children and reinforce parental support. Other smaller schools have less money with which to make purchases and, where parents are on very limited incomes, the school has no additional source of income. As more and more schools receive delegated budgets the gap between these types of provision widens.

Information parents now receive by right has always been available to them from schools that have operated in a spirit of partnership. Some information schools are now required to give is not necessarily seen as relevant to parents. This is evidenced by the general poor attendance of parents at annual governors meetings. It is contrasted by the usual very good parental response to consultation meetings about their child's progress. Such information is now rightly an entitlement and is essential if we are expecting parents to take an active part in supporting their child's learning and development.

Teachers of children younger than 5 are not bound by these legal prescripts. However, nursery education is still funded by public money and there is the implicit assumption that this funding will entitle young children to good-quality care and education, which will enable them to have access to later learning programmes. Non-statutory provision is always vulnerable in times of economic restraint, and even if nursery provision is not abandoned it may be 'modified'. Undesirable thrifty measures may be introduced that, in effect, offer 3- and 4-year-olds a travesty of the education they need.

Properly resourced nurseries, with space, good-quality equipment and the right number of well-trained adults, cost money. Where this exists the onus is on the teacher to prove the effectiveness of such provision. Where less is offered, there is still a need for a careful scrutiny of results for teachers to be clear about what they can achieve and where they are forced to compromise because of a lack of funds.

Although the future role of LEAs remains uncertain, they are still centrally concerned with the monitoring of quality in schools. Nurseries are open to inspections by HMI and local-authority officers. Teachers are professionally accountable to those who pay their salaries and morally and professionally accountable to their clients – the parents and children. Teachers need to be told how they are performing, but more than this is required if they are to respond effectively to changing demands or to improve their performance. While external appraisal and prescriptive documents can help to make teachers aware of their strengths and weaknesses, there is no guarantee this knowledge will be accepted and acted upon. In some circumstances it can have adverse effect, causing anxiety and feelings of inadequacy if 'recipes' for improvement are not forthcoming. Conversely, if teachers can be helped to take responsibility for examining their practices and the nursery service offered, they will be strengthened professionally. The confident teacher and school will use information offered from external evaluators to match against their internal judgements. The DES, in looking at the partnership between LEA and school, suggest that both parties will gain if any LEA review fits in with a school development programme, if experienced LEA officers share their monitoring and evaluation skills with the school and if the basis of LEA judgements is made public and is open to debate.[1]

In this chapter we will look at steps nursery teachers can take to develop self-evaluation. They need to decide which aspects of their work merit closer attention or review, and this will involve gathering specific information through a monitoring process. Monitoring of individual learning and development must be the teacher's main concern. Information resulting from assessing, reporting and sharing details of children's progress can usefully contribute to an evaluation of most aspects of nursery provision.

These processes can be brought together in a cycle to form a school development plan, which, as Hargreaves suggests, will help the organization of what is already happening and what needs to be done in a more purposeful and coherent way.[2]

REVIEW AND MONITORING

HMI describe 'review' as 'a retrospective activity [which] implies the collection and examination of evidence and information'.[3] Reviews may be tackled as a team or by individual teachers. The review process can vary from informal staff discussion about some aspect of school life to a highly structured questionnaire offered to the staff to complete to decide which aspects of work merit closer attention. The initial stages in the GRIDS programme are an example of the latter approach and are very suitable for a staff new to monitoring and review.[4] HMI comment: 'For schools that were used to evaluation, the information-gathering stage was less formal and detailed'.[5]

'Monitoring' is the term given to information gathering. In *The Practical Curriculum* monitoring is likened to 'taking an invalid's temperature or checking tyre pressure and oil levels, a thing to be done carefully, from time to time, as a prelude to assessment and review'.[6] Monitoring is something that is built into most teachers' practice, because it involves keeping in touch with the effects of teaching and learning. The process may extend outside the classroom to include parental and community links, continuity and liaison, staff development and all other aspects that impinge on the life of the school. Any systematic approach to monitoring needs to regard each of these strands in turn and to consider the best means of gathering the information required. It may need to take into account information from children, colleagues, parents and governors, as well as one's own behaviour and responses.

Monitoring thus requires skills that can be learnt but that should not be under-emphasized. Some of the monitoring skills required by teachers engaged in self-evaluation are described in the Open University material, *Curriculum in Action*:

> Ability to carry out observations including: an ability to recognize the selective nature of observations, the implications of selecting a sample of pupils, the implications of using a particular recording technique, the implications of selecting a focus for observation. An ability to categorize data from observations. An ability to recognize inferences made while observing, recording and categorizing information.[7]

Time and planning are needed to identify the area to be monitored. Where observations are made, they need to be structured; an *aide-mémoire* can be helpful. Many of the suggestions for action in this book have focused on issues for teachers to monitor. However, the complexity of classroom life means that self-monitoring can be a difficult and demanding task for the individual teacher. Information gathered from cassette and video recordings can be helpful, as can having an independent observer to gather information for the teacher. This latter approach was explored in a small-scale research project, 'Teachers in partnership'.[8] There the aims were explicit: to look at the ways in which teachers could learn from one another. The project monitored pairs of teachers, who alternated roles of 'observer' and 'teacher' and in turn gathered information for each other on issues they designated as causing concern.

The classroom observer needs to be seen by the teacher as a resource rather than a threat. The emphasis must be on the teacher being presented with objective evidence, which he or she will then use in making his or her own judgements. The team approach established in a nursery should provide a good foundation for this way of working. Nursery staff are used to working in the presence of other adults, and a nursery teacher and nursery assistant could develop 'partnership observation' as a regular aspect of their work, particularly during times when students are in the nursery.

In common with all schools, nurseries benefit from gaining information about themselves from lay people. HMI suggest that

> Greater recognition could also be given to the function of groups external to the school in the process of evaluation. Parents, governors, employers and the wider community have expectations of schools and of individual pupils. These need to be clearly articulated, and schools might do more to seek and consider these views.[9]

Suggested action

Review

- Using a GRIDS approach, devise your own headings to consider with colleagues (one model is suggested in Appendix IV).
- Give each member of staff in turn the responsibility of deciding on an aspect for whole-staff review in the nursery.

Monitoring

- Monitor content: consider the range of stories offered to children in one term; consider the range of imaginative play situations presented.
- Monitor routines:

  - Observe how children enter the nursery at the beginning of a session and what activities they seek.
  - Observe different behaviour of children when they are greeted at the door and when the adults receive them at different activity areas.
  - Monitor the effect of changing a nursery routine; observe how children behave in a traditional whole-group set break-time and then in a self-service snack break-time.

- Monitor use of time:

  - Observe the number of choices children are offered during a nursery session.

- Use a student or teaching colleague to monitor how a nursery headteacher uses his or her time during the course of a day.

• Monitor the environment:

- Observe the effect of display in the nursery; how much do children notice when display is newly presented? After one day? After one week? When the adult has involved them in the presentation?
- Observe the effects of alteration in the building, e.g. different siting of coat pegs.

• Monitor the effect of increasing the nursery team. If additional parent helpers are added to the team, observe the effect on children's behaviour and activity.
• Monitor links with and provision for the community. Use information from governors to monitor the following:

- Provision for parents collecting their children at the end of the session; adequacy of waiting space and space for pushchairs.
- The parents' room; the amount and type of use during a session.
- Communication links; how the messages put out by the nursery are received by parents; questioning parents about how help offered in literature and information in newsletters is regarded.
- Keep a check on parents' responses; check which parents attend parents meetings to see if the meetings are fulfilling majority needs, and note if alternative methods need to be adopted; check how many parents from ethnic-minority groups attend meetings.
- Monitor the effects of helping parents to become more informed about their child's education; keep a record of questions asked by parents before and after workshops.
- Devise a regular system for gaining written information from those parents who are willing to give it; provide a box in the foyer and devise a simple questionnaire for parents to complete, offering their views on arrangements for the transition into the nursery, on the provision of information and on involvement.
- Keep a visitors' list of all those attending a nursery open day.

ASSESSMENT

According to HMI, 'assessment' 'implies the use of measurement and/or grading based on known criteria'.[10] Although nursery teachers may traditionally 'shy away' from measuring children's performance, they more readily accept that systematic checks need to be built into a nursery programme to ensure the children are thriving. Katz reminds us that difficulties and setbacks occur during normal development, but these should not be regarded as permanent: 'Rather, these difficulties help us notice those periods when the child's own life or situation, for a wide variety of possible reasons, is out of adjustment with his or her emerging needs.'[11]

Bearing in mind that all behaviour is testable in a certain sense, the Dorset nursery document offers some useful general guidelines:

1. Appropriate assessment procedures need to be adapted for different areas of development, bearing in mind that part of a child's growth is intangible and difficult to measure.
2. Assessment of young children will vary according to the situation in which the child is working and the people with whom he or she is involved. Thus the context needs to be mentioned as part of the assessment.
3. Any assessment of young children should as far as possible be encompassed within the usual activities of the nursery.[12]

Assessment should be considered an integral part of the teacher's work. It provides the means of deciding what children should receive in their future learning programmes, and also gives some indication of their future progress.

It is particularly important to gain a clear picture of the child at point of entry to the nursery. This will help to ensure that the child is offered well-matched learning opportunities that meet his or her interests, that talents are acknowledged and weaknesses rectified. It also ensures a base line from which teachers can track progress and thus gain a clearer picture of what the nursery curriculum is achieving. Hurst suggests that teachers are very dependent on parents for this initial assessment.[13]

Information parents have gathered and noted down about their own child's early development and progress can be invaluable. Sheila Wolfendale has developed a useful checklist for parents to use, which schools could use as a basis for discussion prior to the child starting school.[14]

Some innovative work is involving parents in ongoing assessment.

Merttens and Vass describe some work from the IMPACT project where parents of infant children are asked to make judgements about their child's understanding of mathematical language, ability to sequence and balance items. These judgements are used to match against the teacher's own assessments.[15] Lally also stresses the value of all members of the nursery team contributing to an assessment and sharing their interpretations.[16] This activity has important implications for moderation; it can be extended to allow groups of nursery practitioners to view children's paintings, models and constructions and share perceptions of developmental levels achieved.

All children should be subject to assessment. In a study of assessment methods and purpose in Dumbartonshire nursery schools, a number of individual child observations revealed that many children were spending up to a quarter of their time in aimless activity.[17] This discovery was a surprise, since the immediate impression was of a nursery setting in which all children were busily occupied. Because of this impression, had the observations been directed at one child only, the finding could have been seen as one indicator of special needs.

Once more we return to the value of an experienced teacher's observations and interpretation of those observations. Because of the complex and interrelated nature of early learning and development, these methods are potent assessment tools. These observations need to be planned, however, and an *aide-mémoire* can help to remind teachers of the various aspects of behaviour they should be aware of. Katz suggests using common-sense headings to highlight aspects of development that should be monitored in all children. Some of these assessment categories, such as 'sleep' and 'eating patterns', will depend on detailed information from parents; in other areas a fuller picture of the child will be realized by parents and teachers pooling information. These include consideration of the child's ability to become interested and involved in different activities, level of play and responses to authority.

Katz also says that any useful assessment must depend on observations planned over a period of time.[18] She suggests that a 4-year-old child will need a four-week period of observation to pick up the behaviour pattern and judge where there may be cause for concern. She warns that these judgements should be made in the knowledge of common deviant behaviour. There is, for instance, little need for concern if a child's appetite is poor due to his or her often being totally absorbed in pursuits the child considers to be more interesting than eating. Warning of potential difficulty comes only where for no clear reason a child scores badly and consistently under a number of headings.

Although well-planned and sensitive observations show what a child is doing, it requires a different approach to reveal capabilities. A structured situation needs to be set up in which the child can respond to a given situation. The setting for this should be as familiar as possible, and the child must find the activity enjoyable. (Some studies of activities that have aimed to 'test' children in this way are mentioned on pp. 69–70.)

There is a limited amount of commercial material available for assessment in nursery education. Where it exists it should be used with discrimination. Maureen Shields, in introducing the NFER assessment material, stresses that 'it is a recognized danger that assessments, instead of producing useful information about children's development and performance, may come to determine what is taught. A central purpose has been to serve the needs of teachers, not to impose external standards on them'.[19] Whatever the approach or material used, the teacher is aiming to identify the learning outcomes resulting from the activity. This information will help in further planning.

Collecting evidence of children's understanding and learning is thus an essential part of nursery work. However, it must be viewed realistically. The rapid pace of development of a young child and his or her responsiveness to his or her environment makes it difficult to form a definitive view about the child's capabilities. David and Lewis suggest that it will be the result of 'best guesses.'[20]

Suggested action

Observation for assessment

- Note the child's personal preferences for activities and companions.
- Determine the times and activities most appropriate to observe specific skills and behaviour, e.g. note what activities encourage children to converse or to use fine motor skills.
- Having observed where the skill or behaviour is best assessed, aim to observe the child across a range of these activities and over a period of time.
- Use a framework for observation of every child to identify those who are generally under-functioning and those who need specific help in certain areas (see Appendix III).
- Analyse information from these observations as soon as possible after the event.

Setting up situations for assessment

- Determine where abilities need to be checked individually and where a task can be set for a small group, e.g. individual children's pictures may be checked for hand/eye co-ordination and the response to requests to add specific attributes – this can take place with a number of children painting at one time; physical skills can easily be checked with groups of children playing together.
- Scrutinize all activities as possible contexts for assessment, e.g. home corner to observe and set up situations to check quality of talk, emergent writing, mathematical sequencing, matching and ordering.
- Use the materials children are already playing with for assessment, e.g. use miniature play people for discussion and a means of assessing a child's knowledge of his or her own family. Never attempt to interrupt absorbed play or you will defeat your purpose.
- Check understanding is sound by transferring the task to other situations, e.g. if a child can sort buttons according to two attributes, can the child use this skill with other sorting materials?
- Be sure the child understands the task expected of him or her; you will need to know individual children well to adjust the wording and approach accordingly, e.g. when checking children's recall of a story, a child may be prompted by others in the group.
- Plan a progressive task; start with a task that is easy for all the children in the group, making it progressively more difficult according to the abilities of the child in question.

Develop checkpoints in learning that will highlight the child's readiness for the National Curriculum programmes of study

For example, plan a series of activities that will check understanding of conservation – with clay, water, sand.

Ensure your assessments result in some action

For example, having checked the level of understanding of conservation, plan other experiences that will ensure the concept is secure.

RECORDS

Although a record is not in itself an assessment process it brings together assessment information to be used for summative, formative, diagnostic and evaluative purposes. Specific benefits of written records will be to

- offer an all-round picture of children's development;
- track the children's progress over a period of time;
- inform curriculum planning; and
- have evidence that can be shared with other interested parties.

The form of records in all phases of education must be the result of team agreement. The School Council project found that 'Satisfaction with and systematic, even enthusiastic use of record-keeping systems seems to be guaranteed only in those schools which had produced a record system as a collaborative exercise involving all staff'.[21] Such an exercise should take into consideration the fact that the same records are not needed for all children. A broad check on development, using an instrument such as the observation assessment schedule in Appendix II, together with progressively graded checkpoints, needs to be used with every child; any deviation from the norm then identified should be followed and noted in detail. Bearing in mind that children's development and progress are uneven and erratic, individual records are likely to vary tremendously between children and over a period of time for many children.

By consulting children's records, the nursery teacher gains important information about his or her practice. Patrick Whittaker suggests that 'a school's record system is essentially a device to monitor the curriculum, although frequently it is regarded as a means of ensuring children's progress'.[22] Teachers need to keep their own records regarding the content, skills, concepts and attitudes they plan to offer their children. This is the forecast of their intentions and it is meaningful only when matched with a review or record of what was actually received. However experienced the teacher, he or she still needs to work within this framework. Records help the teacher to determine the materials or resources needed and to indicate on occasion the method or approach with any particular child. The records should be drawn up jointly with the nursery assistant and other members of the nursery team, and the plans should indicate achievable developmental targets for children.

These documents will also help teachers refresh their memories as to how the team achieved certain objectives and conversely why an approach failed. The teacher's planning records are important but should be simple and easily kept. The key test for any nursery's recording system is to judge if it offers the required information about matching curriculum to needs.

Sharing assessments

Assessment and recording procedures should not only inform the teacher about children's learning and the effectiveness of the teacher's own practices but also offer important information that must be shared with other interested parties, particularly parents and receiving teachers. The Rumbold committee emphasizes that 'parents will need to be assured that the information that they receive about their child's progress is reliable'.[23] It suggests this is most likely to happen if parents have been able to contribute to records and have had clear information about the curriculum map and intended sequence of learning planned for their children.

The receiving teacher will need specific information in order to create a smooth transition and continuous curriculum for her new children. This will include information about the child's personal and emotional development, his attitudes and approaches to learning in a group and his level of achievement including readiness to benefit from a National Curriculum programme.

Where teachers and parents have not been used to having extended dialogue about a child's progress and development, both parties will need time and help to develop. Teachers must be encouraged to offer evidence rather than opinion of achievement and to seek confirmation that this evidence is supported by achievements at home. Parents should understand that the occasion is to be used both to gain and offer information, and that their personal and intuitive observations of their children can contribute powerfully to an overall picture of development.

Receiving teachers must be convinced that the information offered about the child's nursery experience will assist them professionally when planning for the next stage of learning. Without this conviction, the information will not be used. This has implications for close liaison between the phases to agree and implement a policy of transfer information which acknowledges the child's received nursery curriculum, sets clear indicators for next steps in learning and is communicated manageably through documentation and discussion (see also Chapter 3).

Suggested action

Decide as a team the format for recording children's progress

- Consider as a staff what information you need in addition to that required in the local-authority record.
- Discuss the most effective ways of gathering that information (see 'Assessment', earlier) and the most appropriate way of recording – e.g. a checklist or dialogue on individual children's development. Involve infant staff in any discussion on transfer records, e.g. invite reception teachers from schools you feed to come to the nursery for an informal session; encourage them to be frank about any faults they see in the current system and to state what information they require. The aim should be to reach a compromise; satisfactory policies on transfer records develop only when there is shared understanding of the aims and practices of both nursery and infant phases.

Consider different types of record

No single form of record is appropriate for all types of information. The following formats are all useful for some children some of the time.

- A parental profile of the child when he or she enters the nursery. This is a useful starting-point, and the teacher can annotate information during the early weeks at school.
- Individual child studies focusing on particular aspects of behaviour and progress over a period of time.
- Completed checklists, which may have been used as a curricular *aide-mémoire* for the teacher.
- Transfer records, briefly indicating the individual experiences and achievements of each child.
- Selected examples of children's work, dated and kept over a period of time; these give evidence of progression and are useful for enabling continuity of provision for learning at the next stage of schooling. In certain cases it may be helpful to attach teacher comments to this work indicating how the child set about the task and the child's general work attitude.

Use records as transfer documents

- Make sure the material is readable; check the information is clearly set out, with key points highlighted.
- Check the records really do communicate required information and ask for a regular review with infant staff.
- Clearly explain to infant staff the criteria used for obtaining the information; they should see any observation schedules used, and procedures and ratings for checking progress should be explained.
- Ensure information goes to the infant school at an opportune time, e.g. preferably at the end of term preceding the transfer.
- Indicate on records where it would be useful to supplement the written information by meeting and talking with the teacher.

Share records with parents

In many nurseries information is shared informally and regularly with parents. Despite this, consider the benefits of arranging a formal occasion at which it should be possible for all parents to receive information.

- Have a termly occasion entitled 'How Is Your Child Getting On?' Hold this over a period of two days and evenings, using written information on noticeboards, individual letters and a personal approach. Aim for every parent to have an agreed time slot (not less than half an hour). Where parents cannot bring partners, encourage them to bring a friend or translator.

  On this occasion have available the child's personal details; a record of any observations made, with an example of schedules used; results of checks made on progress; and clearly dated samples of children's work including paintings and two- and three-dimensional models.

  The occasion should be used to update any personal details, to inform parents about the nursery view of the child's development and progress and how this view has been gained, and to enable the parent to share concerns and offer views. The interview should end on a positive note, giving a clear indication of future action intended with the child in the nursery and agreed support to be offered at home. Keep notes of this interview.
- In certain areas a written report giving some of this information would be welcomed. However, this should not take the place of

an interview; the record can be handed over at consultation, having formed the basis of discussion or having been taken on a home visit.

EVALUATION

Having gathered information about specific aspects of practice, the teacher can use this to make judgements about current effectiveness. More than that, if this information is to help towards professional growth it needs to inform decisions being made about subsequent action. The evaluation is thus formative rather than just an end in itself.

The Open University evaluation pack suggests six useful questions any teacher can ask him or herself and gain insights into his or her work:

1. What did the pupils actually do?
2. What were they learning?
3. How worth while was it?
4. What did I do?
5. What did I learn?
6. What do I intend to do now?[24]

For our purposes the answers to some of the questions should be available through the monitoring, review and assessment procedures described. The answers to questions (3), (5) and (6) should be tackled at this stage.

As mentioned earlier, good teachers have always been self-critical. They can be helped in this by encouragement to reflect on their practice in a systematic way, to share these reflections with colleagues and to work as a team toward a cyclical policy of information gathering, assessment and recording of outcomes, which determines what happens next. Bernard Spodek summarizes this approach: 'Ultimately the evaluation of early childhood educational evaluation must rest on the degree to which we can help to improve the education of all children by what we come to know about the education of some children'.[25] In a nursery where action is determined in this way, all staff should be refining their skills (the more closely you look at something, the more information you are likely to gain), growing in confidence and becoming better able to withstand uninformed criticism and the whims of society. With this professional strength, any external evaluation from the local authority or HMI should be welcomed. The information offered by these bodies will be a useful comparison with the nursery's own judgements. At present this service is only available to nurseries within the educational service. The Rumbold committee recommended that social services and voluntary provision should have a similar entitlement, but recognize this has resource implications.[26]

Teachers of young children, then, need to be seen not only doing good things (this has always tacitly been accepted) but rigorously reviewing their work and acting on this in a way that characterizes the highest-quality practice in any phase of education. HMI suggest that before schools undertake evaluation they need to have achieved a state of readiness.[27] We shall discuss how that state is reached in Chapter 8.

Suggested action

Be realistic

You will achieve effective evaluation only by focusing on one aspect of work at a time.

- If you are fairly new to evaluation, start with a small-scale study, e.g. what happens to (identify target group of children) when they are playing outside? How does (individual child) use his or her time during the later part of the nursery session? Using this information, measure the effectiveness of your planned programme and judge how it could be improved.
- When you are confident in tackling these studies, work with your nursery assistant and other members of the team on joint ventures.

Act on evaluations

- If the implications for action are wide ranging, they should be broken down into manageable targets, which in turn should be reviewed, e.g. evaluation confirms that children are spending little time in the art area and the quality of their work is poor – implications for action: to improve quality of materials used, to change the position of the art area, to make it possible for children to be more self-sufficient in that area, to have more teacher input. Try not to embark on a further evaluation until some improvement has been seen in the current area of study.

Communicate your approach to parents and governors

- Where appropriate, hold an informal meeting with parents along the lines of 'How our Practice is Improved for your Children'.

Many parents will be interested and impressed to realize how closely you regard the daily aspect of work.

- Regularly report the processes and outcomes of evaluation to your governors and involve them in the whole cycle, e.g. share examples of plans and learning outcomes at governors meetings: encourage governors to take responsibility for evaluating some aspect of the nursery and reporting back with recommendations to the governing body.

Make full use of external evaluation

This can come about as a result of a brief visit from a nursery colleague in a neighbouring school or a lengthy school inspection. In all cases you should welcome comment or constructive criticism but expect evidence to support any statements made. Weigh these statements against knowledge of your own practice; aim to look more closely at the aspects of practice highlighted.

Take every opportunity to look at your practice with fresh eyes.

Agree and present your development plan

- Involve all staff in determining priorities for action for the forthcoming year. Include some realistic timed targets to aim for at the end of each term. Try to specify what should be done and by whom.
- Aim to tackle one major and one minor change, e.g. development of mathematics/organization of small-group times.
- Consider resource implications and staff-development needs when making plans.
- Sketch out development plans for the next three years to give a longer-term frame of reference.
- Present your overall development plan to the governors and display copies in the staffroom and parents foyer, so that everyone can share information about your intentions for managing change.

REFERENCES

1. DES (1991) *School Development Plans Project 2: Development Planning: A Practical Guide*, HMSO, London, p. 17.
2. DES (1989) *School Development Plans Project 1: Planning for School Development*, HMSO, London, p. 4.
3. DES (1985) *Quality in Schools; Evaluation and Appraisal*, HMSO, London.

4. Schools Council (1984) *Guidelines for Internal Review and Development in Schools*, Longman, London.

5. DES (1985) op. cit. (note 3).

6. Schools Council (1981) *The Practical Curriculum* (Working Paper 70), Methuen, London.

7. Open University INSET (1981) *Curriculum in Action*, Open University Press, Milton Keynes.

8. J. Ruddock (1982) Teachers in partnership, *Journal of the National Association of Inspectors and Educational Advisers*, Spring.

9. DES (1985) op. cit. (note 3).

10. *Ibid.*

11. L. G. Katz (1984) *More Talks with Teachers*, ERIC Clearinghouse on Elementary and Early Childhood, Urbana, Ill.

12. Dorset County Council (1982) *The Youngest Children in School*, Dorchester.

13. V. Hurst (1991) *Planning for Early Learning: The Education of the Under Fives*, Paul Chapman Publishing, London.

14. S. Wolfendale (1987) *All About Me*, National Children's Bureau, London.

15. R. Merttens and J. Vass (1990) Assessing the nation: blueprints without tools, *Primary Teaching Studies*, Vol. 5, no. 3, pp. 223–39.

16. M. Lally (1991) *The Nursery Teacher in Action*, Paul Chapman Publishing, London.

17. M. M. Clark and W. N. Cheyne (1979) *Studies in Pre-School Education*, Hodder & Stoughton, London.

18. Katz (1984) op. cit. (note 11).

19. M. Bate and M. Smith (1978) *Manual for Assessment in Nursery Education*, NFER, Slough.

20. T. David and A. Lewis (1991) Assessment in the reception class, in L. Harding and J. R. Beech (eds.) *Educational Assessment of the Primary School Child*, NFER/Nelson, Slough.

21. Schools Council (1981) op. cit. (note 6).

22. P. Whittaker (1983) *The Primary Head*, Heinemann, London.

23. DES (1990) *Starting with Quality* (the Report of the Committee of Inquiry into the Quality of the Educational Experience Offered to 3- and 4-Year-Olds), HMSO, London, para. 129.

24. Open University INSET (1981) op. cit. (note 7).

25. B. Spodek (1982) Early childhood education: an overview, *Studies in Educational Evaluation*, Vol. 1.8, no. 3, p. 24.

26. DES (1990) op. cit. (note 23).

27. DES (1985) op. cit. (note 3).

8

THE PROFESSIONAL
DEVELOPMENT OF STAFF

Work can be one way of achieving what Herzberg describes as 'that unique human characteristic, the ability to achieve and through achievement to experience psychological growth. The stimuli for the growth needs are tasks that induce growth'.[1] Teaching young children is demanding and yet offers many opportunities for psychological growth. Nursery teachers who seize chances to develop in their work are the ones who have job satisfaction and offer the best of themselves to the children and parents.

In this book we have already dealt with many aspects of professional development. Wherever teachers are thinking about the curriculum or forms of organization they are considering whether they can improve on current practice. This type of development has always been present among teachers but previously happened in an individual and *ad hoc* manner. The accent today is on looking at teacher development in a more thorough and systematic way. One reason for this emphasis is linked with the recognition of the rapidly changing nature of society. There is a need to help teachers respond to this change by providing a dynamic and helpful framework of professional support.

This is required across all phases of education. For nursery teachers there are added reasons for looking to professional support. The focus on nursery curriculum and pedagogy during the past twenty years has led to a much higher profile for the teacher, who is now seen as a central resource for the child's learning rather than as just a benevolent provider. Increasing information about child development and learning, together with stress on the need to engage parents in this process, makes the job potentially more demanding in every way. Moreover, all children under 5 share similar needs, and yet, as we have seen, there are different forms of education and care for them. Accommodation of these young children is a good political platform, and some local education authorities have allowed 4-year-olds into school with little consideration for their needs or the training requirements of the adults who are to care for and educate them. An HMI survey in 1987 revealed that six out of every ten newly qualified teachers interviewed felt they were not adequately equipped for teaching such young children.[2] In 1988 there was evidence of unequal in-service support for teachers of younger children.[3] Since then the heavy focus on National Curriculum training has meant that only a minority of education authorities have extended their courses for teachers of 4-year-olds. If these children are to remain in the system it is essential teachers receive some professional help to tackle the job.

All workers with young children require support and, while acknowledging the different levels of expertise involved, there needs to be some coherence and standardization in the training offered to those working in State, private and voluntary settings. The requirements of the Children Act 1991 for training of all those concerned with day care of young children and the introduction of a system of National Vocational Qualifications (NVQs) to introduce nationally agreed standards across professions including child care are significant moves in achieving a more unified approach.[4]

RECENT TRENDS IN TEACHER EDUCATION

Central government's increasing interest and influence in education has included the whole remit of training and development of staff. Certain trends have emerged in initial and continuing teacher education, namely, a departure from the conventional route to becoming a teacher, the move to rationalize and control training and the increased role for the school in teacher training.

Although the conventional forms of primary-teacher training through the four-year BEd and one-year PGCE (Postgraduate Certificate in Education) still predominate, there are some departures from these routes. Shortened BEd courses are now offered for overseas qualified graduates and early-years conversion courses exist to enable secondary and primary teachers to retrain for the younger age-group. Some of these latter courses are as short as one term. More recently, two new schemes have been introduced and are being piloted. The first offers a route to qualified status for graduates through a two-year school-based PGCE developed in collaboration with a teacher-training institution and the school. These candidates are known as 'articled teachers'. The 'licensed teacher' scheme enables people from a variety of backgrounds and experience (including those who have taught overseas) to be employed in a school and undertake a course of training that is monitored by the LEA. As yet the numbers of teachers entering primary schools through these alternative routes is small and will presumably depend on the willingness of schools and LEAs to invest time and money in their training.

The establishment of the Council for the Accreditation of Teacher Education (CATE) to advise the secretaries of state on approval of initial teacher-training courses has meant a rigorous look at the starting-point of the work. Programmes of initial teacher training are not accredited if they do not meet CATE guidelines.[5] Recognizing that local-authority funds for in-service development were not always used in the most effective way, central government now allocates money for this purpose. In so far as this has meant that every school and college has had to consider its present and future in-service needs and submit these to be reflected in a local-authority bid, the move is a good one. Increasingly in-service monies are devolved to individual schools allowing them the opportunity to identify and meet their own needs.

The most positive aspects of CATE are concerned with the relationships to be developed between schools and initial training institutions. Apart from the recommendation that teachers be involved in the selection of students, the DES states that no new initial teacher-training course will be approved unless it is supported by a local committee on which there is teacher representation. The emphasis is one of a close working partnership between institutions, LEAs and schools, with teachers helping to plan and assess students' practical performance and sharing in their training within the institution.[6]

IMPLICATIONS FOR NURSERY TEACHERS

In part, because the schemes are new, the nursery phase is not yet affected by the most recent of the routes to qualified teaching status. Nevertheless, the prospect of such diverse entry routes naturally raises suspicions about diversity of standards in the teaching of young children. Despite the attempts of CATE to regularize the content of initial training, nursery students continue to have different experiences with varying emphases on the theory underpinning work and the practical application. The length of the course also affects the training. In addition to the normal range of professional skills to be learnt, nursery teachers need expertise in managing paid and voluntary ancillary staff, in liaising with other agencies and working with parents. With the current focus on the National Curriculum, the pressures on time increase. Already there is insufficient opportunity to develop a programme of child development and pedagogy appropriate for the nursery age-range and the problem of overload in a one-year PGCE course is particularly acute.

Where training institutions are complying with CATE recommendations there are many instances of nursery teachers taking a central role in determining and supporting the quality of provision for student teachers and their quality of performance. Practices include the arrangements made for the students' practical training in the nursery, nursery teachers being involved as associate tutors in training institutions and their contributions as external examiners or as one of a team of internal assessors appointed to judge student performance. Such a spirit of partnership between training institution and school should help abolish the divide – real or imagined – between ivory towers and chalk faces. Tutors and teachers are becoming better informed about each others' jobs and student teachers have a better opportunity of gaining from shared expertise than ever before.

The quality of a school placement for a student teacher remains crucial. Any nursery that is requested to train students should be aware of both the responsibility for offering a model of practice and the need for the student to have the opportunity to practise his or her skills – with sensitive guidance. This approach means time and planning for the teacher, particularly when working with students during their early period of training. Above all, when taking on these commitments, the needs of the children in the nursery and their parents should not suffer in any way.

To be useful partners with training institutions, teachers will need to become familiar with the aim, content and approach of initial training courses. They will require time to link with tutors and to have the opportunity for feedback from their sessions. This has resource implications that are now emphasized as schools start to manage their own budgets and colleges become self-funding. If these links are to be maintained in the current financial climate, arrangements must ensure that the workload and expertise of teachers and tutors is shared equally to the benefit of young children and students.

In-service funding arrangements now place responsibility on the schools to determine their own priorities and to do so within a framework of planned development. The nursery teacher's needs must be seen within this framework; there must be space for individual opportunity, but the cost of any one teacher's professional gains will be maximized if they fit into a coherent plan for the nursery.

It is heartening that provision for under-5s is now acknowledged and funded by the DES as a priority area. Overall funding is not generous (£4.9 million in total available for 1991–2), but the principles are established and monies are available to all LEAs on the basis of their satisfactory bid that meets certain criteria. The funds are targeted to plan and co-ordinate provision for young children across both the State and voluntary sectors and to improve the quality of their teaching.[7] The ways in which LEAs put these requirements into practice vary considerably according to the legacy of the past work they have on which to build, and the current resources available. However, where funds are held centrally curriculum support and advisory teachers develop and co-ordinate work including the establishment of links with playgroups, health and social-services personnel. In theory, nursery teachers now share an entitlement to professional development throughout their careers. In reality funds are scarce, access to providing institutions is uneven and careful planning is required to enable individuals to receive appropriate help at different stages in their careers. There must also be balance between school-based and external training. A dynamic nursery is the best possible seed-bed for professional growth but wider perspectives can only be gained from viewing other practices, and a depth of understanding acquired through linking practice to educational theory.

NURSERY-NURSE TRAINING

The main qualifying routes for nursery nurses are through the diploma of the National Nursery Examination Board (NNEB), the diploma of the Business and Technical Course in caring services (nursery nursing) (BTEC) and the Diploma in Post-Qualifying Studies (DPQS). Of these qualifications, the NNEB remains the longest and best recognized. Although it has recently changed its qualification from certificate to diploma status, the NNEB continues officially to have no minimum entry requirements and offers students no career structure or opportunity to transfer to more advanced courses in higher or further education. The newer BTEC diploma, however, requires candidates to have four GCSE passes at grade C or the equivalent. It is accepted as a valid alternative to two A-levels and as an appropriate entry qualification for the teacher training BEd. The DPQS is only open to qualified care workers over 21 years. It offers a possible further course of study for NNEB workers but with no automatic assurance of financial support and few openings to a more senior post.

The BTEC diploma now operates in around eighty colleges and has been welcomed as a course that offers students a route into nursery teaching. There remains concern that less flexible entry requirements and the accent on the course as preparation for higher education will debar less academic students from training as nursery assistants and from regarding the work as useful and satisfying in its own right.

The NNEB report in 1981 stressed that, rather than lacking in academic rigour, the certificated course (as then) offered students an essentially practical training as evidence of competence to practise a valuable and particular sort of craft: 'The essential nature of a craft is that the test of its mastery lies in the practical application of the knowledge, skills and attitudes which have been fostered during a period of apprenticeship and training.'[6] The value of this craft is recognized by all who work with good-quality nursery assistants; the need for their ongoing professional development is now at least recognized by allowing them access to funded in-service training. There remains the urgent need for public recognition, reflected through salary increases.

Suggested action

Assistance with student selection

Your contribution should be valued in offering the perspective of the practitioner. Prior to the selection procedures, have in-school discussion on the following:

- What are the main skills required for working with this age-group of children?
- What qualities help teachers to be successful with 'difficult' children?
- Discuss the range of skills needed for managing groups of young children.
- What are the most difficult aspects of working with parents? What personal qualities are required for this work?
- What are the qualities of (1) a good team member and (2) a team leader?

These gathered responses may form the criteria for selection. You will then need to discuss how student potential can be identified to meet these criteria.

The teacher as college tutor

Your strength will be your present practical experience with children and your ability to translate theory into practice.

- When taking a session with students, aim to bring the nursery as close to them as possible by slides; a three-dimensional plan of your room with movable furniture; a video of your practice; an arrangement for students to have one session based in your nursery immediately after school.
- Offer examples of your planning and how it develops into practice by giving a plan of one day and following this with slides and examples of children's work, showing some of the day's outcomes.
- Offer different models of monitoring and recording children's progress.
- Offer experiential learning by taking on the role of nursery teacher, with the students as the children, and running through some large-group activity (e.g. story-telling) and a range of small-group work. In time the students can take turns in the role of teacher; the session may be videoed; the student may take some of the teaching points and be videoed using them with groups of children.

The nursery as a practical training ground

Opportunities for practical training should include the following:

- Introductory days in the nursery to consider selected aspects, e.g. the environment for role play; type, storage and use of large construction toys; the role of the teacher with children who have English as a second language. These limited observations can be written up and discussed with the teacher.
- Blocks of time for a small group of students to work with their tutor on some aspect of nursery practice. The informality and team approach characterizing nursery work make it reasonably easy to accommodate students in this way. The work must be clearly planned with the aim of all parties benefiting from the experience. The focus of study may differ from working on one

aspect of development with children to a more complex area
involving some classroom research and helpful data being fed
back to teachers.

THE NURSERY TEAM

Whatever the situation the teacher finds him or herself in, it is most likely
that the nursery teacher will be working with other adults at some point
during the day. Teachers may be in open-plan buildings where they work
in a team with other teachers; if they work in a bona-fide nursery they
will have a full-time nursery assistant. Even where this full-time assistance
is not available, and the teacher is coping with 4-year-olds in a primary
school, he or she may have some part-time ancillary help and the assistance of students, and the teacher can choose to invite parents into the
classroom to work as volunteer helpers.

All nursery teachers accept the very real difficulties of working alone
with a number of young children; teamwork adds another dimension to
the job. As leader of such a team the nursery teacher is responsible for
the deployment of voluntary and paid staff. The teacher must ensure they
are well briefed and prepared, able to tackle their respective jobs, and
that they receive all the necessary feedback to get satisfaction from
that work. Unless the teacher takes this responsibility for the team, the
nursery is unlikely to reap the full benefit from the shared expertise and
energies of these adults. Certain management and interpersonal skills are
necessary for the team leader, whatever the size of the team.

The nursery teacher's role is essentially no different from that of any
other teacher in that he or she is an educator. However, because the
pupils have very limited experience and undeveloped learning skills, the
teacher must have particular expertise in child development and the
knowledge to plan learning routes for individuals. In a large nursery
the teacher may have other teaching colleagues. If a team is to function, however, there should be one leader. This may be marked with a
post of responsibility, or the leader may be the most experienced teacher.
Alternatively, team leadership may be shared, with each teacher taking
responsibility for a period of time (less than a term each may mean
fragmentation in planning).

The team leader's task is to consult with colleagues, respect their views
and use their expertise, taking responsibility for the overall framework in

which the children learn. The head of a nursery school is also responsible for policy-making, while a nursery teacher in an attached unit represents the nursery when policy is determined for the whole school.

The nursery assistant has a qualification in the education and care of young children, and this expertise complements that of the teacher. The training for a nursery assistant is shorter, more practically oriented and less academic than teacher training; the assistant is, nevertheless, qualified to work alongside the teacher and to offer support. This partnership cannot be successful if there is strict role delineation. The nursery assistant has no more been trained to care only for the physical needs of children than the teacher has been to assist only cognitive development. However, the teacher in charge is ultimately responsible for the group of children and, while consulting with colleagues, must be ultimately responsible for deciding how the nursery will operate in the best interests of each child. Nursery assistants should be allowed full responsibility for planning part of the programme, but this should always be attuned to the overall structure decided by the teacher. Thus, although the nursery assistant is recognized as the teacher's assistant, the true spirit of the partnership comes through with the assistant working as a full team member.

Parents and members of the community can play a valuable part as volunteer helpers in a nursery. We have considered the usefulness of working with parents in order to offer them a model of handling children and promoting learning. We should also accept that in any community there is a great deal of energy, talent and expertise to be harnessed. Given all that we know about developmental and learning possibilities for young children, the basic staffing ratio is not generous, the recommendation being one teacher and nursery assistant to twenty-five children. The resourceful nursery teacher will therefore look to identify the people who are prepared to offer their time and skills and will plan to use them as additional staff. The nature of this involvement can vary from an occasional contribution to play an instrument, or to help children with woodwork, to a regular commitment to work with a group of children or tackle ancillary jobs in the nursery. Whatever the job, the voluntary helper needs to be prepared beforehand about the children, their needs and the nursery routines.

Where there is a regular commitment, the helper should be clear about the purpose of the work, how it fits into curriculum planning and how the helper is succeeding. While working in the nursery, the voluntary helper is a member of a team and should be accorded courtesies as such.

Suggested action

Developing a team

- Meet together to share views on teamwork. What are individual expectations of what can be achieved? What are the expectations of a team leader?
- List your own strengths and weaknesses and ask other team members to do the same.
- Aim to work with another team member who will complement your qualities and skills.
- Develop your own clear picture of the strengths and weaknesses in the team by listening to individuals and observing them at work with children and adults.
- Agree working principles as a result of shared experiences; offer the team shared reading; visit another nursery as a group and talk with them about their principles and practices.

Communicating effectively

- Written communication can be displayed and kept updated on attractive noticeboards or in a daily folder. Team members should be asked to scan these papers regularly.
- Important information should be given to the whole team at the same time.
- Each team member should be clear concerning to whom, for whom and for what he or she is responsible.
- Hold meetings to exchange information and discuss curriculum development. Agree times and dates well in advance and always end the meeting promptly. Never hold a meeting when information can be conveyed just as well in other ways.
- Team planning should occur at the beginning or end of each day to forecast, prepare resources and review the programme and its consequences for children. Arrange some team meetings to include all members of staff; the caretaker, dinner ladies and voluntary helpers each have a contribution to make.

Sharing discussion

- Discuss the children:

  - Select individuals and share information about their development.

- Select a child known to have a particular strength in one area and share views as to how this can be developed.
- Agree on expectations for children regarding issues such as tidying up, resolving arguments, levels of noise, personal autonomy and swearing.
- Share information based on structured observations of children who will require written statements of their needs.

• Discuss the children's products. Consider a range of paintings or models, sharing views on the information they offer about skills and concepts gained.
• Discuss organization. Share views on the pattern of the day; encourage each team member to analyse the strengths and weaknesses of routines.

Working with voluntary helpers

• Recruiting expertise:

- Ask new parents if they would be willing to help in the nursery; keep a card index file of their interests and talents and the most convenient times for them to help. Keep this updated by asking parents to inform you of any changes in their circumstances or any new area of interest.
- Ask parents if they have links with any others in the community who would have particular strengths to offer the nursery.
- Interest potential voluntary helpers by suggesting they spend a trial day with an established helper in the nursery; have a small exhibition of photographed activities involving voluntary helpers with brief explanations indicating the range of work possible; have a simple leaflet for new parents, setting out the above information; include a contribution from a voluntary helper describing their work in one of the nursery newsletters.

• Preparation of voluntary helpers:

- Where the contribution is to be for a single occasion only, ask the visitor to call into the nursery one day previously for coffee to see the nursery in action. The helper will then be a familiar face to the children and will be better informed to judge the timing and approach of the session.
- Regular helpers need a planned induction by attending a briefing meeting; this occasion should be relaxed, with refresh-

ments, but the aim is for the teacher to make clear to the helper how adults work with children and promote learning. Provide the helper with written information; a series of booklets can include topics on 'Cooking with Young Children', 'Working in the Book Area', 'Conversation with Young Children' and 'Mixing Paints and Glues'; these booklets, which can be referred to at leisure in the home, indicate the value placed on the task of the helper.

– Hold a series of workshops showing the range of activity in the nursery, how materials are prepared and the potential of some of the apparatus for learning and development.

• Include voluntary helpers in the team:

– Encourage them to use the staffroom and on the first occasion make sure that a member of staff escorts them to coffee.
– Include them in at least some full team meetings and make sure their views are sought.
– Provide specific as well as general opportunities for voluntary helpers to discuss their anxieties or report on success in their work.
– Show appreciation by having a 'thank you' party for them at the end of year, by offering them a small gift in appreciation of their work, by including them as guests in the end-of-term staff party or supper.

THE NEW TEACHER

However satisfactory the period of initial training, the student takes a big jump in entering his or her first teaching post. Experiencing the world of work full time requires adjustment in itself, and any new job involves establishing oneself with a new group of people, adapting to new routines and having one's competence tested. Hannam suggests that 'because the new teacher feels herself to be an outsider she will tend to see what goes on in the school in sharp outline. Any faults or failings in the system may be uncompromisingly noted and censured'.[8] Most new teachers share some similar experiences of lack of confidence, initial bewilderment and fatigue during the early days. New nursery teachers are no exception, but find themselves in a particularly challenging and responsible position.

These teachers are faced with a new intake of children who are coming to school for the first time. The children need a gentle and sound transition to school, and their parents need to be assured of this and included in the process. These young children have to be assessed at an early stage without the aid of any previous professional records, and the teacher has to keep in touch with their learning and development at a time when the pace of change is rapid. Some of the children's family needs will require the new teacher to liaise and work with other support agencies from an early stage; it can be daunting for an inexperienced teacher to have to attend a case conference and produce relevant evidence in front of other professionals. The nursery teacher also has to assume an immediate leadership role in working with a nursery assistant – a role that can cause anxiety if the assistant is older and more experienced.

There continues to be a shortage of nursery teachers. With so few experienced nursery teachers available, probationary practitioners are in great demand and schools understandably wanting appropriately trained people are sometimes forced to place a new teacher in difficult circumstances. New nursery teachers can be particularly vulnerable if working in a class attached to a primary school whose governors, headteacher and staff are unaware of the needs of the youngest children in terms of content and approach. There is further concern for the new teacher required to take a large class of young 4-year-olds and, despite training and professional convictions, expected to treat them as year-one infants and follow a National Curriculum programme.

A nursery environment can nevertheless also offer particular support by virtue of its informality and teamwork. Young children are highly motivated clients; parents are also generally more interested in their nursery children's all-round development than in later years, and there is the tremendous excitement of working with an age-group at a time of such rapid and fascinating development.

The period of induction is critical. An HMI survey revealed that often induction fell short of what the new teacher expected. Recommendations included the provision of full information from institutions to receiving schools about the teacher's strengths and weaknesses during training in order to facilitate a good match of school-based support; the need for all schools with new teachers to have an induction plan that includes monitoring and evaluation of progress based on classroom observation and structured discussions with a nominated mentor; and for schools to have the benefit of written guidelines on induction from their LEAs.[9] The survey's emphasis on the LEA's role will not apply in future years as schools take on the training role, and the probationary period of teaching is no longer a legal requirement.

It is likely that some cost-conscious governors may be particularly anxious to appoint new teachers to posts as a means of saving on staffing costs. Nursery and reception classes attached to primary schools may be particularly affected where uninformed governors prefer to keep more expensive and experienced practitioners for older children. In these cases the onus is on the headteacher to stress the significance and complexity of working with the youngest age-group. Even the most talented of new teachers needs help, including moral support and teaching expertise, while respecting the teacher's need to adopt his or her own teaching style. Schools can benefit greatly from the addition of a new teacher. They should remember, however, that supporting a new colleague requires time and patience and that, from the viewpoint of established staff, a highly motivated young teacher with current expertise can cause disequilibrium.

Suggested action

Provide information before the new teacher takes up post

- The first visit after appointment should be informal, with an opportunity to get to know the building and the staff and get the 'feel' of the school. In turn the staff should be able to see how the new teacher will fit in as a colleague.
- A teacher 'mentor' should be appointed who will be the probationer's first point of contact. This person's task is to see the new teacher has all the information and resources necessary for the job.
- Provide a range of documents to give to the teacher on the first visit. Encourage the teacher to take these away and read them at leisure, noting points for future clarification or discussion. The following documents will be useful: a job description; a staff handbook giving details of school policies and daily routines; a parents' handbook; a list of school dates for the year; a plan of the school and classroom with a list of equipment; a list of children due to start school, with dates of birth and any records or information gained of past experiences; and professional details regarding the nursery assistant with whom the teacher will be working – including work experience, particular areas of expertise and professional interest, and how the assistant has previously worked as a member of the team.

Provide the new teacher with a manageable job

If teachers are to give of their best, they must have maximum opportunity to succeed during their first year.

- With a class of 4-year-olds in a primary school, the new teacher should have the largest classroom, a reasonable size group (maximum twenty-eight children) and priority call on the ancillary helper if there is no nursery assistant.
- In a nursery, the new teacher should (if possible) be placed with a sympathetic nursery assistant, even if this means staff reorganization.
- The new teacher should enter a classroom that has been well maintained, with adequate apparatus that is in good condition. The teacher should not be expected to make apparatus immediately to supplement resources.
- Offer guidelines to new teachers in coping with the job, e.g. they should not expect to change their displays weekly and maintain the quality; they cannot expect to get to know all the children in the first week – planned in-depth observation and assessment over a period of time are necessary; they should not feel guilty if they do not have the same feelings for all the children but they must try to offer them all their maximum skill and care.

Ensure regular dialogue

The new teacher has been used to sharing professional thinking and practice with others. This is something that should be encouraged and provided for throughout the teacher's career.

- The mentor should meet with the teacher weekly and offer active support. Within the relationship specific questions should be asked and accepted as proper, e.g. 'What children did you observe this week?' 'What information have you gained?' 'How do you propose to change your approach (the curriculum) in the light of this knowledge?' 'How can I help you with this?'
- The new teacher's records should offer the mentor and headteacher insights into his or her understanding of the job, priorities and planning. New teachers often use a lot of time and energy in keeping copious records and will benefit from having a framework for this from the school. It is not sufficient for these records to be handed in and returned with brief written comments. They

should be the basis of professional discussion about the teacher's approach to his or her work.

Provide a variety of support

- Help the new teacher look at children in depth; share other teachers' observations and comments about children with him or her; suggest the most appropriate times when the new teacher should observe children, e.g. when alone, in a group or talking with an adult.
- Prepare the new teacher for particular aspects of the job; take him or her to observe a case conference on a child before the teacher is required to contribute; ask the new teacher to manage the domestic detail for a parents' workshop so that he or she can observe the approach used.
- Give the new teacher the opportunity to see a range of practice; if working alone in a nursery, allow him or her to visit to see other models of practice. These visits should be planned and followed through (see pp. 204–5).
- Help to rectify weaknesses, e.g. relationships – no sound nursery teacher should find this a great problem, but inexperience and anxiety may cause an abrupt or defensive manner. Encourage the new teacher to observe models of counselling and dialogue with parents, which can then be discussed afterwards, helping the teacher to see reasons for the approach.

Respect the new teacher as a valuable colleague

If teachers are professionally sound and have received a good initial training, they should immediately be able to contribute to a nursery. Self-esteem will be raised if this is openly acknowledged.

- After one term of settling in, give the new teacher an area of responsibility, however small, e.g. checking the parents' notice-board, keeping it in good order and ensuring that relevant and up-to-date information is available; or checking the storage and condition of all sand-play equipment in the nursery. Ask the teacher to report anything noteworthy relating to his or her responsibility and make any recommendations at staff meetings.
- Take advantage of new teachers' 'fresh views'; ask them to write a brief report on how they see the nursery during their first few weeks of work. It should be stressed that the work is for the teacher's own use and can be compared with a similar report that he or she writes at the end of the year. This work should

help teachers appreciate their own development and increased understanding during their first year. In a good trusting staff atmosphere, however, they can be asked to share their material.

EXPANDING HORIZONS

New teachers are very much concerned with the 'hows' of the work. They need to feel that they are coping with the children and contributing as a members of staff before they can look further ahead to their development. But when this further stage is reached, nursery teachers need to consider their professional needs carefully, preferably in consultation with the headteacher and in collaboration with the rest of the staff.

The allocation of in-service funds in LEAs according to the size of school has meant that smaller schools have limited monies to support initiatives. Imaginative ways of sharing in-service costs with other schools are being devised as part of support networks being established among school 'clusters' or 'families'. Nursery and infant schools with nurseries and 4-year-old classes have a particular need to share professional development because of the specialized nature of their work. There are also benefits gained from sharing expertise within a larger forum apart from any economic savings made.

Not all in-service developments need be costly to be effective, however, and there have been many past examples of expensive initiatives achieving little long-term benefit for teachers and children. We now look at the range of in-service needs nursery teachers may have.

Identification of professional needs

It is extremely difficult for practitioners who have been working in a particular way for years and who are professionally isolated to be clear about their effectiveness. Before self-evaluation can take place, these teachers need to match their practice against alternative models and to look carefully at their abilities. (Many practitioners are tempted to develop those professional areas where they are already strong rather than to address their weaknesses.) Some teachers can manage this alone; most need the help of colleagues to see where they stand professionally.

Where a group of teachers share common problems it will be easier to discuss needs in the light of shared experience. Within the group there may be individuals with particular strengths who can help others. It can be easier to decide as a group that a visit to study different practice would be helpful rather than coming to that decision alone.

However perceptive, no teacher can be aware of how he or she is performing in all areas of his or her work. Teacher appraisal offers the opportunity to gain further insights. Appraisal has unfortunately had a bad press; it has been equated with accountability and seen in conjunction with conditions of pay. Now that it is mandatory for teachers it is hoped the positive aspects of the process will be highlighted and it be used as a real aid in developing professional needs, recognizing good practices and improving effectiveness. Employees are generally eager to receive honest feedback about their work. The findings of one major study stress that, where an established appraisal system was working in schools, teachers were willing to discuss the procedure, and there was a welcoming open school atmosphere and an enhanced professionalism shared by staff.[10]

Although the emphasis in appraisal regulations is on an appraisal based on classroom observation, nursery teachers should also expect to gain some information about their work with parents and leadership skills with staff – both of which are central aspects of the work.

The mandatory requirements for appraisal apply only to teaching staff and, where the process is new for schools, it may initially be greeted with some trepidation. However, as Lally emphasizes, most nursery teachers are by nature self-critical[11] and, as with other aspects of evaluation already discussed, the emphasis should be on self-appraisal with the appraiser serving as a support. The value of this support will vary in accordance with the quality of the appraiser.

The entitlement of the nursery headteacher to an appraisal by an informed practitioner is aided by the recommendation that the appraiser appointed should, wherever possible, have experience of early-childhood education.[12] There is unfortunately no such safeguard for a nursery teacher who will be appraised by his or her primary headteacher who, though supportive, may have little specialized knowledge of the requirements of nursery work.

Essentially the process should be straightforward, becoming accommodated into the school system and offering practitioners direct professional help. Where this occurs appraisal may naturally be extended to ancillary staff who would wish to benefit from the practical outcomes.

Areas of professional development to consider

Some indication of the range of information available relating to young children learning has been presented in this book. To avoid feeling overwhelmed by the implications, nursery teachers should look critically at each of the different aspects of their work and see what they require to be first-class practitioners. Each area needs to be regarded in turn. Consider how, through your own efforts and with in-service support from the school and the local education authority, you can achieve professional growth. We suggest some of the main areas for consideration.

Child development

A sound knowledge of child development underpins any professional work with children. Roberts and Tamburrini stress that such study should link theoretical issues with practical observation of children: 'The more one knows the theory of child development the less likely one is to fail to notice significant items in children's behaviour'.[13] Any student of child development needs to recognize that these theories are constantly evolving and expanding. The nursery teacher who tackled the subject ten years ago is in need of a major update.

Curriculum principles, planning and organizational skills

Knowing the sequence of development and learning, teachers now need a thorough grasp of how to match the learning opportunities. They need a clear rationale for working based on the processes of learning for young children; a professional repertoire of content and activity and a range of methods to offer the curriculum most effectively. Meticulous planning and organizational skills will ensure they are using all available resources to best effect.

Assessment, recording and reporting

Monitoring of individual children has always been a feature of good nursery practice. This must continue to support systematic assessments, which are closely linked to planning future work for children and recorded in a useful format for both parents and all professionals involved with the child.

Classroom-based research

Teachers who want to know how they are succeeding must be sure their practice is effectively meeting their planned intentions. If they tackle this rigorously using appropriate methods of investigation, they are acting as researchers. Early research studies were mainly by professional researchers who were trying to judge the success of nursery education in global terms. Today, in the knowledge that many different forms of nursery education exist, the focus is on examining strands of practice in turn to see the effects on children, and helping teachers to develop the techniques to do this: 'The aim in teacher research is for the teacher to attain the eyes of the artist, for it is art that teaches the sensitivity of being attentive to significances that normally remain uncelebrated'.[14]

Nursery practitioners have a particularly strong need to develop these techniques for the following reasons. In work that is so packed with activity there is need to stand back and take stock of what is actually happening. The nursery phase is rich in areas of potential inquiry; there is good evidence now of teachers contributing to research, although a worrying lack of funding to support all that needs to be done. Because so much of the young child's learning is private, we need to look at his or her responses in depth to see how teaching and learning are achieved.

Desforges suggests that if teachers are really to promote the development of children as reflective learners, they need to have time to react to individuals and follow their lines of inquiry.[15] This is acknowledged as practically impossible in a class of infants with a ratio of one teacher to thirty children. It is more likely to be achieved in a nursery setting with judicious deployment of paid and voluntary ancillary staff. Research with young children can be very productive, because the children are so unselfconscious, and the presence of an observer is not likely to inhibit their behaviour or responses.

Openness to change

It may be that such classroom study leads to planning and implementing change. Teachers need to feel confident with this process themselves as well as competent in helping colleagues to change their practice.

Personal relationships

A strong thread running through all aspects of nursery work is the teacher's relationships with children, parents, governors and colleagues. Qualities of warmth, humour and empathy, coupled with a real interest in people and an ability to listen, are, we hope, identified in those successful applicants training for teaching. Such qualities are not easy to teach, and their essential nature becomes apparent only when they are seen to be absent in an otherwise competent teacher.

Awareness of educational issues

In today's educational climate no teacher can afford to be insular. A knowledge of what other agencies provide for young children, as well as the aims and approaches of local infant schools, is important. More than that, an extended professional teacher in any phase will be interested in broad educational issues. The last requirement may seem daunting, bearing in mind the heavy work-load of a nursery teacher, but breadth of vision is helpful in putting one's own work in perspective. The informed, clear-thinking and articulate practitioner is the one on whom we pin our faith for young children in the future.

Ways of promoting professional development

How professional needs are met depends very much on the individual teacher's motivation and ambition as well as on the school's and LEA's ability to find resources to meet perceived and identified needs. In-service development used to be seen in terms of the course teachers attended on a voluntary basis after school hours. Today this approach is merely a single strand in a web of initiatives teachers may find relevant to their personal and professional growth.

In-school developments

School-based and focused in-service developments allows staff to identify their own concerns and tailor activity to meet these concerns. The particular difficulties of providing supply cover for nursery staff and the perceived desirability of nursery teams sharing in-service developments are good reasons for this being a current major thrust of in-service work. The five teacher development days allocated for such work are now regarded as an integral part of school life and seen as necessary to allow for whole-school issues to be debated. These occasions have encouraged a staffroom climate where there is discussion of educational and pedagogical matters and the opportunity to learn from others in a relaxed and familiar setting. However, nursery and most infant schools are small units and are aware of the limits of expertise in terms of staff numbers. Collaborative school-focused work offers the opportunities for pairs and small groups of schools to share thinking and practice. This will, of course, be most productive where schools share a similar philosophy and are at a similar stage of development.

Leadership and communication

Any nursery is likely to have a mixed staff of varying personalities with different motives for working and different attitudes, hopes, fears and views of the job. Their competence will also vary. Despite the various moves associated with the Education Reform Act 1988 (ERA) and designed to raise standards, schools continue to vary in effectiveness: some are dynamic institutions offering opportunities for children and staff, while others have atrophied. The ILEA *Junior School Report* identified several key factors in the more effective establishments.[16] Some of these factors that are equally relevant to nurseries include a high-quality headteacher, a supportive deputy headteacher and a good staff climate.

Five years ago, Sir Keith Joseph, in giving evidence to the Commons Select Committee with reference to primary schools, mentioned good headteachers as being the nearest thing to a 'magic wand' for a school. This belief in the effect of leadership from the top is reflected in a number of studies and reports, including the recent report by the School Management Task Force.[17] The headteacher has always provided a model of commitment and standards for the staff; the direction of policy and practice reflects his or her philosophy and how this is communicated in the school. Primary headteachers in particular have an increasingly onerous job and one that takes them away from classroom activity. However, although teachers are less likely to receive regular teaching support from their head, they must be made to feel that their practice is known and supported by a senior member of staff.

Whether in a small nursery or large primary school, nursery teachers need to achieve job satisfaction, as do their other colleagues. Clearly the rewards of contact with young children will contribute to this but satisfaction also largely depends on management structures within.

Nothing is more likely to cause tension in a school than teachers feeling they do not have access to information. Even in a small school there are teachers who are uninformed about developments and unclear about what is expected of them. Nursery assistants who do not receive information cannot possibly perceive themselves as full team members.

Communication takes place with or without proper networks. However, if a school relies on a grapevine system it must expect distorted messages, misunderstandings, lack of response and frustration among the staff. The smallest nursery unit should establish sound information networks through updated noticeboards, regular well-planned staff meetings and clear job descriptions. The staff should share responsibility for the curriculum, including keeping themselves updated and others informed on all information relevant to their curriculum area that has implications for the nursery phase.

The small, intimate nature of a nursery unit is conducive to staff unity. In an organizational climate where staff are encouraged to be personally responsible and interdependent, having a stake in all decision-making, all adults will grow. They will gather strength from one another and, through group identity and increased confidence, will be more inclined to take risks and to innovate.

The resource of extra teacher time is always prized in an establishment with young children. A nursery attached to a primary school may use a supply teacher to release nursery and primary staff to view each others' work.

In the nursery the teacher might need extra time to work with a new member of staff or with the nursery assistant on some specific activity. Alternatively the chance for staff to work together or to observe each others' practices without the responsibility of their class can overcome feelings of professional isolation that may well exist in nursery units.

External courses

No school or group of schools is capable of meeting all the professional needs of its staff. It may be desirable and economically practical to draw together groups of teachers and nursery assistants to offer specific short courses in particular aspects of their work. The short course can be particularly effective in offering training in specific skills, such as different ways of observing children. The relevance of any external course for daily practice is essential as is its role as a tool for change. The recent Leeds evaluation of primary practice project shows only too clearly that even generous funding for course provision, which prescribes certain ways of working, is not effective in itself in changing practice.[18] Teachers should have identified a need for the course themselves and be clear well in advance of content and structure. They should also have some time and ideally have access to advisory teacher support to help them reflect on course input and trial some aspects of work in their class practice.

Longer part-time courses offer staff the chance of a broader and deeper view of their work. There should be more opportunities to link theory with practice and, in some cases, to gain some extrinsic reward in accreditation. Again, relevance is all important: if a written study is involved it should be linked to an aspect of nursery practice; required professional reading should be current, pertinent and manageable.

Full-time secondments are now increasingly rare, the justification being

that funding is spread more equitably across institutions to give all practitioners in-service opportunities. However, the professional development
of our future teaching force, which is promoted mainly through short and
part-time courses, may limit the depth of expertise acquired and restrict
opportunities for reflection.

Considering other practices

Teachers are constantly eager to see how other colleagues manage their
work. The nursery teacher perhaps has a particular need for this support.
In many authorities nursery provision is scarce, and the practitioners feel
isolated; in others where large numbers of children are inadequately
provided for, teachers need every possible support to prevent them from
becoming demoralized by not being able to tackle the job properly.

A visit to another nursery can help the teacher stand back and view
how a different group of children are accommodated and catered for. As
well as looking at other practice in the education system, awareness
of other provisions can broaden vision. Playgroups, day nurseries and
nursery centres have particular work constraints, priorities and related
practices. Nursery teachers may put their own problems into perspective
by visiting a provision that is not purpose-built, in seeing evidence of less
generous capitation allowance in the amount of equipment provided and
in watching colleagues dealing with overwhelming family need. The
ingenuity and flexibility often born from working in difficult circumstances can also help teachers to see more possibilities in their own
setting. A broader knowledge of available provision for young children
should also help teachers to evaluate their own contribution to young
children's development and learning.

The most satisfactory arrangement is for a supply teacher to be available for visiting purposes. This is expensive, however, and puts the onus
on the teacher to ensure the maximum benefit is derived from the visit.
Without careful planning teachers can certainly return from a day's visit
enriched, but remembering few specifics.

A profitable visit can give a teacher 'a lift', but it may not be sufficient
to refresh someone who has been in the same post for a long time.
Despite the current shortage of nursery teachers, in some areas of the
country opportunities to move jobs are rare, and there are often family
reasons for not moving from the area. Nursery assistants have no means
of promotion in education and can remain in one nursery for the whole of
their career. There can be an expressed need to have a different experience, and in this case a temporary exchange of post with a colleague can

be helpful. In the past local authorities have initiated and approved such schemes. It will now be for governing bodies to agree arrangements where they can recognize that two classes and two practitioners can benefit professionally as a result of careful planning without this costing anything.

Curriculum-support teachers

In any area there are always outstanding practitioners who demonstrate particular skills and qualities in their work. Recently these people have been used extensively as curriculum-support and advisory teachers. This move has been well received by schools where there have been tangible benefits of practical classroom support. The work has also been professionally enriching for the teachers who have been challenged to work in a range of different schools and to help effect change. Most advisory teacher posts have been funded to support National Curriculum initiatives and rather fewer allocated to nursery and 4-year-old classes. As the benefits of this form of support are clear, infant and nursery schools could consider making joint bids to LEAs or combining their own funds to allow the teachers of their youngest children to receive this professional help.

However, the future for all advisory teachers is uncertain. Their continued existence will depend both on the ability of LEAs to fund them and the willingness of governors to release them from their teaching post. Some governors are reluctant to risk losing a good practitioner, albeit temporarily, in order to offer them this form of professional and career enhancement.

The 'secret garden' of professional development

Teachers grow and develop in complex fashion. By institutionalizing and funding in-service work, central government and local educational authorities are touching only one aspect. Katz suggests that 'teachers may need occasional renewals of courage to enable them to sustain their efforts'.[19] Bearing in mind that teachers, like children, are individuals, some need these renewals more than others and find them in different ways. Headteachers who care for their staff personally and professionally are probably in the strongest position to influence an individual teacher's outlook; but it may be that a pint in the pub with a trusted colleague, a visit to someone else's classroom or the effect of some thought-provoking comments from a new member of staff will be the catalyst for change.

Whatever it is, the change must be desired if it is to take root and flourish. If the teacher is supported to succeed, he or she is likely to want to continue learning.

However committed he or she is, a nursery teacher has his or her own life, with its personal joys, hopes, fears and problems. These should not be allowed to dominate professional work but they will affect it. Teachers should appreciate the need for a fulfilling personal existence to help them to give of their best to children.

Suggested action

Identification of professional needs through appraisal

- Preparing for appraisal:

  - Prior discussion about the process is important to ensure that all staff know what is entailed and what benefits can accrue; it may be helpful initially to work with those who volunteer to be appraised.
  - Be clear about the area of work to be appraised (e.g. work with parents, curriculum leadership, classroom teaching).
  - Collect evidence to be used at an appraisal interview; ask the appraisee to consider his or her own work with the help of an *aide-mémoire*; the appraisee's work may be observed by the appraiser; consider tangible evidence of the effects of past work.

- The appraisal interview:

  - Give good notice of the date and time of the interview.
  - Allow time for the interview (roughly one to one-and-a-half hours); make sure the venue is comfortable and that you are uninterrupted.
  - Open the interview by encouraging the teacher to give his or her views of work during the past term/year; highlight successes but focus on evidence of weaknesses and steer the discussion toward helping change weaknesses to strengths.
  - The emphasis should be on performance of work rather than personality; but the appraiser should end the interview knowing more about the individual being appraised.

- Action after interview:

  - Practical results of the interview should be clear and realistic; they may include a school visit, change of responsibility, in-

creased apparatus, agreement to alter the daily organization.
- The effect of these outcomes should be monitored, and improvements in work publicly recognized.
- Any suggestions from those being appraised of how the process could be improved should be considered and where possible acted upon.

Checking your own professional needs

Ask yourself the following questions. Your honest responses may help indicate your priorities for professional support:

- When did I last read a book/attend a course on child development?
- How familiar am I with the post-Piagetian studies mentioned in this book?
- When did I last experiment with a new curriculum activity?
- How able am I to relate my practices to defined principles if a visitor arrives tomorrow?
- How often do my children get bored and 'out of hand'?
- How do others (including my nursery assistant) rate me as a teacher?
- How difficult do I find working with adults as opposed to working with children?

Developing classroom-based research

- Develop the skills; request input from your institute of higher education; ask for contributions on 'Ways of Gathering Evidence'.
- Share your work – through reports at staff meetings and governors meetings; through linking with other nurseries and asking the teachers' centre to circulate a termly leaflet on 'Classroom Inquiries in Nurseries'.

Developing as a unit

- Offer leadership to the team; delegate as much as possible to free yourself to be the curriculum leader.
- Communicate clearly:

  - Make sure communication is two-way by giving people the opportunity and time to respond and inviting and respecting their views.
  - Demonstrate your professional concern for all staff by helping them to have a definite and feasible job in which they can

succeed and that has been jointly agreed and documented in a job description.

- Use the most practical and effective means of keeping people informed, e.g. a daily/weekly folder giving details of changes in organization, visitors arriving and after-school meetings.

- Encourage involvement; each member of staff must feel they have a stake in the nursery:

  - Regular curriculum meetings should be after school and based on a well-prepared agenda.
  - Where numbers permit in a nursery school, share responsibility for the curriculum among staff including keeping updated on National Curriculum initiatives in Key Stage One.
  - Persuade each member of staff to share one aspect of their practice with others, e.g. how they work with an individual child, how they manage a music group.
  - Encourage discussions and joint decisions on all major policy; an experienced nursery assistant may have very helpful views on new admission procedures, and a new teacher will add a fresh viewpoint to existing practices.
  - Share reading. Build up a resource of professional books you may share with other nurseries; encourage staff to bring in and share relevant articles and reports, which can be discussed at staff meetings.

- Use outside expertise:

  - Invite local people with relevant expertise to contribute to staff meetings, e.g. family-centre matron, social worker supporting young families, headteacher from neighbouring nursery school.
  - Have occasional joint staff meetings with other nurseries and invite the local adviser or education lecturer to lead a discussion.

Seeing how others work

- Plan a regular and balanced programme of visits for all staff in turn that will support jointly agreed needs.

  - Build up a picture of different local provisions for young children: playgroup, day nursery, family centre, childminder, infant school.
  - Visit your local feeder school as part of a liaison programme.

- Visit other nurseries that are dealing with similar situations to your own.
- Visit other nurseries and schools that have a reputation for different practices.

- Prepare for the visit:

  - Identify the venue to visit that will best meet needs. Prior information on strengths and interests of local nurseries will help you to make the most suitable choice, together with advice from the local inspectorate.
  - Timing and length of visit: determine whether the visit is most useful during the working day or after contact hours, e.g. classroom layout may be best considered first without the children present, then seeing it in use later.
  - Identify the staff to visit. Where possible staff should visit an establishment to follow up their own particular concerns and interests; visiting in pairs is more profitable, and change may be encouraged by suggesting that an enthusiastic member of staff accompanies a more reticent colleague.
  - Gather maximum information. Ask other staff what information they would like you to get for them from the visit; carefully note this and follow up.

- Follow up the visit:

  - Arrange to share the experiences of the visit with other staff in one or more of the following ways: report back informally at a full staff meeting; relay the information requested by members of staff prior to the visit; compile a school archive of records of visits made and points noted to use for future reference.
  - Thank the host school; a thank-you card may be sent to the children of the host school; the host staff will appreciate some account of how the visit was followed up by the visitors, including a courtesy copy of any report.
  - Consider possible long-term benefits; one visit may occasionally lead to further links including joint curriculum planning or an extended time in the host school, e.g. a temporary exchange of teaching or nursery-assistant posts.

External courses

- Seek advice from previous students on the course to check if it is likely to meet your needs.

- A residential course may be most difficult to attend if you have domestic commitments; but it will prove most profitable in terms of developing contacts with others and allowing you to be single-minded and removed from other responsibilities.
- Avoid the danger of feeling overwhelmed by course input and frustrated at not being able to put everything into practice; aim to change one aspect of your work at a time, making sure you feel confident with this before going further.

Curriculum-support teachers

- Offer a group of reception teachers some support with their 4-year-olds.
- Arrange to share support among three infant schools; use shared in-service funds to gain assistance from a nursery teacher.
- Ensure governors are supportive; explain the shared benefits for all including the professional development for the nursery teacher and increased liaison between schools.
- Identify a good-quality supply teacher who is familiar with nursery practice and who would release the nursery teacher for three afternoons a week for an agreed period.
- Plan thoroughly in advance to ensure that all parties are clear about the focus of support needed and the ways in which the nursery teacher will work.
- If funds permit, allow supply cover to provide some planning time for the nursery teacher.
- Outcomes should include an informal evaluation of the support and a brief report to the governors.

REFERENCES

1. F. Herzberg (1972) One more time – how do you motivate employees?, in L. Davis and J. Taylor (eds.) *Design of Jobs*, Penguin Books, Harmondsworth.
2. DES (1987) *The New Teacher in School*, HMSO, London.
3. C. Sharp (1988) Starting school at four: research findings and implications (paper given at NFER Conference, Starting School at Four: Planning for the Future, Solihull Conference Centre).
4. National Council for Vocational Qualifications (1989) *Criteria and Procedures*, London.
5. DES (1984) *Initial Teacher Training: Approval of Courses* (Circular 31/84), London.
6. DES (1984) op. cit. (annex) (note 5).

7. National Nursery Nursing Examination Board (1981) *A Future for Nursery Nursing*, London.

8. DES (1990) *Grants for Education Support and Training 1991–2*, London, pp. 51–2.

9. C. Hannam, P. Smyth and M. Stephenson (1976) *The First Year of Teaching*, Penguin Books, Harmondsworth.

10. Suffolk Education Department (1985) *Those Having Torches... Teacher Appraisal: A Study*, Suffolk County Council, Ipswich.

11. M. Lally (1991) *The Nursery Teacher in Action*, Paul Chapman Publishing, London.

12. DES (1991) *School Teacher Appraisal* (Circular 12/91), London.

13. M. Roberts and J. Tamburrini (1981) *Child Development 0–5*, Holmes McDougall, Edinburgh.

14. J. Ruddock (1985) The improvement of the art of teaching through research, *Cambridge Journal of Education*, Vol. 15, no. 3, p. 122.

15. C. Desforges (1990) Teachers' perspectives on classroom interaction, in C. Desforges (ed.) *Early Childhood Education*, (*British Journal of Educational Psychology*, Monograph Series no. 4), Scottish Academic Press, Edinburgh.

16. ILEA (1986) *The Junior School Report*, Research and Statistics Branch, London.

17. DES (1990) *Developing School Management: The Way forward*, HMSO, London.

18. R. Alexander (1991) *Policy and Practice in Primary Education*, Routledge, London.

19. L. G. Katz (1984) *More Talks with Teachers*, ERIC Clearinghouse on Elementary and Early Childhood, Urbana, Ill.

APPENDIX I

ASSESSMENT ON ENTRY TO THE NURSERY OR RECEPTION CLASS

WHY?

The early assessment of children is essential to help you move close to the child and to match learning experiences to his or her stage of development. Where the assessment is sensitive and accurate the child is more likely to settle comfortably and easily into the nursery or reception class, secure in the knowledge that his or her needs are known. The child will also progress in learning as he or she is faced with appropriate challenges.

SOURCES OF INFORMATION

It is important to gain a broad and full picture of the child. In order to do this a range of people who have particular relationships with the child and see him or her in different contexts should contribute to the assessment. These will include the following.

The parents

All parents have significant knowledge of their child, based on three or four years living with him or her and experiencing the child's development. The fact that their views are partial should not detract from the detailed information they can offer.

Others close to the child

All family and friends who have spent time with the child during these early years will have valuable information about personal characteristics and abilities. It is obviously not possible to talk with the people individually but parents should be encouraged to share with you the views others have of their child. You may also gain valuable insights into the child's interactions with different family members or childminders if they bring or collect him or her from the nursery.

Professional and voluntary pre-school workers

Any health visitors, doctors, social-services personnel and playgroup workers who have had prolonged contact with the child will have made formal or informal assessments according to the nature of their involvement. All staff in the nursery or school will gain insights and information on the basis of their daily contacts.

WHAT INFORMATION?

You need access to any information that will help you professionally in caring for and educating the child. This will include

- significant details about the child's life history, including health and family position;
- the family's cultural and religious involvement and views on education;
- what the child can do by him or herself, in a group with other children and with some help from you;
- attitudes to activities including what particularly motivates the child;
- how the child relates to other children and adults; and
- his or her cognitive learning style, e.g. impulsive, reflective, persistent.

WAYS OF GAINING THIS INFORMATION

Informal discussions with parents

Whether through home visiting or individual consultation at school, parents need time and encouragement to talk freely and positively about their child. The focus should be on what the parents regard as special about their child and their views of his or her achievements. They should be made aware they are the prime source of this information and that their judgements will provide the base-line for helping their child progress in the nursery.

Links with other agencies

Regular and reciprocal visits with playgroups are time consuming but valuable in order to see the child in an environment away from home. Playgroup leaders are often understandably cautious about their role in assessment. However, their descriptions of daily playgroup activity and information about the child's normal pattern of behaviour and play preferences will be a valuable supplement to the teacher's own observations (see also Chapter 2).

Pen portraits of the child

As you observe the child from the time of his or her first visit and subsequently in self-chosen activity, you will build up a picture of what the child likes doing and what he or she can do unaided. You do not have to withdraw from interactions with children in order to note their activity and behaviour. Sometimes as a participant observer you will gain greater insights through noting the child's responses to your comments and questions, e.g. noting individual behaviour in the book area and subsequently sharing a book with the child.

Semi-structured tasks

These will enable you to check the child's aptitudes in a given situation. Any task should be simply an extension of a self-chosen activity, e.g. after observing the child's free play with blocks you may suggest that he or she builds two towers the same and then makes one taller. This will give you information about the child's manual dexterity and understanding of mathematical language; using the child's interest with a miniature play layout, you may wish to check spatial awareness by suggesting he or she places the farmyard animals in a field or parks miniature cars in a car park so they all have lots of space.

Communication networks within the school

Other teachers, nursery assistants and lunchtime supervisory assistants should be encouraged to share their observations about the child. This may be through informal daily discussion; through encouragement to note down anything of significance and place this in an observations box; or through focused meetings when the progress and development of one particular child is discussed. Whatever the method, the emphasis must be on offering insights based on objective information rather than prejudiced comment.

USING THE INFORMATION

By consulting a range of people and observing the child in detail yourself, an overall picture will emerge. This information forms the basis of an individual profile of development, which should be continued in some form throughout the child's primary career.

This profile will be used to inform both parents and professionals of the child's progress. In the nursery it is also a valuable means of communicating with the child. The profile may be further personalized by adding the child's photograph, family photographs, holiday postcards and selected birthday cards. Development and sharing of this personal record is particularly valuable for those children who need to have their sense of identity affirmed.

APPENDIX II

SAMPLE OBSERVATION SCHEDULE FOR ASSESSMENT

It is suggested that this schedule is used to observe the child during the latter part of his or her first term in school, over a period of three weeks to gain a general picture of development.

Child's name: ....

Date observation started: .... Completed: ....

Please circle the number of the statement under each heading which most accurately describes the behaviour of performance observed.

Relationship with peers:

1. Takes a leadership role in a group which includes older children and may invite more reluctant peers to participate.
2. Joins in most group activity with ease.
3. Joins in with group activity when invited to do so but this rarely happens.
4. Shows interest in activity with others but always observes rather than participates.
5. Clearly prefers his or her own company: avoids contacts with other children.

Reactions to authority:

1. Occasionally resistant to adult requests, but cheerfully complies with persuasion and responds to reasons given for request.

t to adult authority if absorbed with his or her own
.
,trongly against adult authority but will temper his or her
ɔ in the light of the responses from peers.
4. Stroɪɪ.ᵧ y resists any implication of adult authority at all times: constantly pushes against boundaries of behaviour.
5. Submissive attitude – never questions adult authority – appears anxious when adult requests are made.

Self-sufficiency:

1. Attempts new tasks with confidence and enjoys new experiences: makes decisions without reference to adult.
2. Usually self-sufficient but sometimes needs adult's support with a new activity.
3. Self-sufficient while there are no problems: in the light of difficulty immediately turns to an adult for help.
4. Needs an adult nearby and requires regular reasssurance to follow a course of action.
5. Clinging and almost totally dependent on one adult.

Involvement in varied activity:

1. Regularly involved with a full range of activities and combines materials from different activity areas for his or her own purposes.
2. Has clear preference for particular activity but will move if new experience or apparatus is on offer.
3. Has clear preference for particular activity but can be persuaded to move.
4. Always starts the day in one activity area and is very reluctant to move.
5. Always stays in one activity area and resists encouragement to move.

Interest and concentration:

1. Regularly takes an active and sustained interest in a task and is oblivious to distractions around.
2. Willing to complete a task with an eye for detail when interested.
3. Will complete a task with encouragement and occasional help from adult.
4. Always wants to try new activities but quickly loses interest and 'flits'.

5. Has little interest in becoming involved in any actiⁱ
   on the sidelines.

Use of language:

1. Converses with ease: initiates talk with adults and peers: is
   capable of explaining his or her own meaning if it is not clear:
   projects and hypothesizes.
2. Takes an equal part in a conversation. With encouragement can
   explain a process and expand points.
3. Responds to conversations: occasionally reports on present and
   past experiences without prompting.
4. Uses talk mainly to direct his or her own actions and those of
   others in play: may bring up a point of interest but is unwilling to
   do this or listen to others.
5. Main use to refer to his or her own physical needs and maintain
   his or her interest: responds with single words or brief phrases if
   approached in conversation.

Personal buoyancy:

1. Constant sunny, resilient disposition – rarely thwarted.
2. Occasionally upset if thwarted by adult or child – otherwise
   cheerful.
3. Often tearful and upset if thwarted but rapidly recovers.
4. Regularly moody and withdrawn for no apparent reason.
5. Prone to outbursts of uncontrollable temper tantrum for no
   apparent reason.

(This sample is a useful starting-point – the schedule will be more valuable for you if the statements are discussed and amended in the light of
your needs.)

APPENDIX III

CARRYING OUT ASSESSMENTS

You need to assess in order to check how the child is responding to certain curricular experiences and to enable you to adjust his learning programme where necessary. Your assessment should indicate whether there is need for

- revisiting and consolidation of previous learning (gaps in understanding observed);
- application of current learning (understanding is only observed in certain contexts);
- further challenge (secure and generalised understandings observed).

The outlined plan suggests one way in which a teacher may assess and record some aspects of learning of twenty children fortnightly.

1. A rota of four children are targeted for approximately twenty minutes assessment every two weeks.
2. The means of assessment is through open observation, teacher interaction and questioning and through semi-structured activity.
3. An assessment action sheet (example below) is used as an *aide mémoire* and the outcomes noted as a record of the assessment. Implications for action provide the basis for future work with each child.
4. A copy of the assessment action sheet is placed into each child's portfolio offering a running record of the received curriculum to discuss with parents and receiving teachers.

EXAMPLE ASSESSMENT ACTION SHEET

Target group   Date

Suki, Dawn, Kwame, Adam (all in final term in nursery).

Curriculum activity

Following an interest in birthdays, group is wrapping up parcels for teddy's birthday.

Resources

A range of printed wrapping paper (keep a selection collected from parents), some with a repetitive pattern.
Cardboard boxes of different sizes.
Adhesive, strips of masking tape.

Assessment focus

Approach to activity e.g. concentration, decision-making.
Motor skills in handling materials.
Level of spatial awareness in covering a surface.
Understanding and use of spatial language.
Recognition of pattern, ability to read a pattern and predict its continuation (using one and two attributes).

Means of assessment

Provision of materials and initial observations of children's unaided activity.
Discussion and questioning whilst providing necessary assistance.

Learning outcomes – implications for action

- **Dawn**: selected a box quickly and persisted for 3 minutes before requiring help with wrapping. Persistently cut paper too small to cover box and confused 'top' and 'bottom', more interested in wrapping paper designs. Interpreted a pattern of rows of teddy bears (red and blue jackets) and correctly predicted its continuation.

- *Action*: work on understandings of positional language in movement and block building; consolidate pattern making with one attribute using a range of materials.
- **Kwame**: initial enthusiasm gave way to anger when another child had already selected the paper he wanted. He was persuaded to continue and proved very adept at covering all sides of his box. Kwame pointed out that not all sides of his box were the same size 'the sides which are shorter are the ends of the box'. Good understanding of a range of positional language.
Compared patterns on wrapping paper. Correctly read and predicted continuation of pattern with two attributes.
- *Action*: Kwame to describe how he covered his parcel at small group time (further check on use of positional language). Suggest that he makes his own patterned wrapping paper. (Photographs of parcel and example of home made wrapping paper may be kept in portfolio as evidence of attainment in Maths Attainment targets 1 and 3 level 1).
- **Suki**: preferred to cut up wrapping paper and stick pieces on sides of box. Absorbed in this way for 12 minutes and stated that she had covered two sides of her box. Careful attention to covering all spaces. Understanding of 'edge, side, next to'. Suki asked to continue task tomorrow. 'There is not much time left today and I want to look at a book'.
- *Action*: Check understanding of positional language when sharing books with Suki.
Develop Suki's revealed understandings of time units.
- **Adam**: Uncertain of which box to select and how to commence. 'You do it for me'. With encouragement he selected some wrapping paper and said that he would wrap a 'treasure box' for teddy. Carefully covered box with glue, then asked for more help. Adam was persuaded to cut his paper and covered his box. Constant reassurance required but he demonstrated good understandings of positional language and estimation skills. Delighted with the outcome, he showed his parcel to the nursery nurse.
- *Action*: suggest that Adam joins a parcel group tomorrow to demonstrate the activity to them. Requires lots of opportunities to develop his confidence and ability to work independently.

APPENDIX IV

DETERMINING PRIORITIES
FOR REVIEW

Please indicate (by ticking in the appropriate column)

- whether you think each aspect in the nursery is an area of strength, weakness or satisfactory;
- whether you feel these aspects would be desirable to review (i.e. gather further information and consider as a priority for inclusion in your school development plan).

Aspect of the nursery	Strength	Satisfactory	Weakness	Would benefit from review (Yes) (No)
Cross-curriculum issues				
Children as individuals				
Exploration and play				
Matching tasks				
Meeting multi-ethnic needs				
Provision for learning difficulties				
Encouraging self-sufficiency				
Areas of experience				
Language and literacy				
Mathematical				
Scientific				

Aspect of the nursery	Strength	Satisfactory	Weakness	Would benefit from review (Yes) (No)
Technological				
Aesthetic and creative				
Human, social and personal				
Links with the family				
Initial links with families				
Maintaining communication				
Pastoral support for families				
Informing and involving parents in curriculum				
Planning and organization				
Curriculum planning				
Environment				
Furniture and fittings				
Selection and purchase of equipment				
Daily routines				
Teaching and learning				
Educational display				
Assessment and record-keeping				
Professional development of staff				
Conversance with research and current trends				
Updating on materials and methodologies				
Teamwork				
Awareness of other agencies				
Training of students				
Links with community and governors				

SUBJECT INDEX

rights 28
services and support for 20
sharing information with 19–23,
  24, 25, 29–30
  see also family, home, monitoring
    records
personal development
  childrens' 108–11
  teachers' 202
planning
  the curriculum 134–8
  the environment 138–43
  resources 140–1, 143–4
  the programme 144–8
  teaching and learning 148–53,
    153–7
play
  complex 64
  for four year olds 121
  resources for 63–4
  role play 63
  spontaneous 60–1, 67
  structured 60–1, 67
playgroups xv, 6, 33
  liaison with nurseries 56
professional development
  areas to consider 194–7
  identification of need 193–4, 203
  school based 197–9
  through courses 194–200, 205–6
  through visits 200–1, 204–5
  see also appraisal, inservice
    development
programmes
  for four year olds 120–1, 122

questioning
  teacher's role in 71–2

records
  as transfer documents 170, 172
  on children 28
  shared with parents 170, 172–3
  teacher's planning 135–8, 149–50
representation 102–5
  through play 60
research
  action 195–6, 203
  studies xiii
review 218–19

science 97–9
self-esteem 47–8, 76, 80–1, 76
self help 76–9, 82
sensory stimulation 62
sexual abuse 4, 14
sounds
  children making 104
special needs 74, 9, 51, 123–9
  see also admission, assessment
staff
  communication with 188–9,
    203–4
  initial training of 178–81, 182–4
  unity 184–8
  see also professional development,
    teacher, teachers
support agencies
  links with 33–4, 35–6, 125, 129
symbols
  representing through 87, 103–4

talk
  adult's role in promoting 67–8,
    69, 71–2
  in the home 64–6
  learning through 61–2
  provision for 64–6
  with peers 69, 72
teacher
  as observer 148–9, 153–4, 167
  as planner 149–50, 154–5
  as scaffolder xiii, 150–3, 155–7
  education 178–81
  newly qualified 188–93
  role of 13, 146
  shortage 12
  see also professional development,
    staff, talk
teachers
  as people 202
  perceptions 38
technology 99–102
transition
  to the nursery 52–4, 55–7

unemployment 3

women
  changing role of 3

AUTHOR INDEX